P9-ECQ-390

17.46

A Not Unreasonable Claim

A Not Unreasonable Claim

Women and Reform in Canada, 1880s - 1920s

Edited by Linda Kealey

The Women's Press

CAMROSE LUTHERAN COLLEGE
LIBRARY

Canadian Cataloguing in Publication Data

A Not Unreasonable Claim
ISBN 0-88961-052-5 bd.   ISBN 0-88961-049-5 pa.

1. Women — Canada — History. 2. Canada — Social conditions — 1867-1918. *
I. Kealey, Linda, 1947-
HQ1453.N68   301.41'2'0971   C79-094454-5

281176

Copyright © 1979 by Linda Kealey

Nellie McClung quotation from *In Times Like These*
(Toronto, University of Toronto Press, 1972)

Cover illustration from *The Montreal Herald,* November 26, 1913

Lithographed by union labour at
The Hunter Rose Company
Toronto, Ontario, Canada

Printed and bound in Canada
Published by the Women's Educational Press
Toronto, Ontario, Canada

Believing that the woman's claim to a common humanity is not an unreasonable one ...

— Nellie McClung, *In Times Like These*

Table of Contents

Preface

The idea for this book originated at a meeting of the Canadian Women's Educational Press in Spring 1976. One of the essays printed here was submitted to the Press for consideration and the possibility of a collection of original articles around the theme of social reform was suggested.

Ten years ago, a collection such as this could not have appeared because research interest in the history of women in Canada was very small. Since then, new initiatives in social history and a resurgence of the feminist movement have encouraged work in these areas. Unlike *Women at Work: Ontario, 1850-1930,** which was largely written by women within the Press itself, this book is the product of academic historians, employed for the most part at Canadian colleges and universities. In some senses it is a further exploration of questions raised in *Women at Work*. It also reflects the growth and vibrancy of current historical scholarship on women.

A glance at the table of contents reveals, however, that more research has yet to be undertaken. We still do not know enough about areas related to the subject matter of this book. Family life, demographic changes, child-rearing patterns and birth control remain relatively unknown areas. In addition, we still lack information on the less well-studied regions of Canada. Students of Maritime history, for example, have only begun to tackle the historical questions relating to women of that region.

The gaps in our knowledge of the history of women in Canada extend even to those areas sometimes considered by social historians to be stale and overworked. In many cases the institutional and organizational histories are inadequate; in other cases they do not even exist. The task then, is many-faceted. Feminist historians must not only make the history of women available and understandable, but must attempt to influence the way Canadian history is written in the future.

This book is the product not only of the authors and the editor, but also of the assistance of the Ontario Arts Council. The Canadian Women's Educational Press provided support for the project from its inception. Gregory Kealey contributed valuable critical commentary on the manuscript. Wayne Roberts offered many helpful suggestions to the editor; both he and Deborah Gorham read an early draft of the introduction. My thanks to all.

* eds. Janice Acton, Penny Goldsmith and Bonnie Shepard (Toronto: Canadian Women's Educational Press, 1974).

Contributors

CAROL BACCHI — is currently living and teaching in Australia. She has taught courses in women's history and her research has focussed on the Canadian women's suffrage movement.

SUZANN BUCKLEY — teaches history at the State University of New York at Plattsburgh. She has published articles on health care and imperial relations.

DEBORAH GORHAM — teaches history at Carleton University. She has published other articles on the suffrage movement in Canada and Britain, and on the history of the family and of sexuality.

LINDA KEALEY — is a PHD candidate at the University of Toronto; her research interests include the history of crime as well as women's history.

MARIE LAVIGNE — teaches history and works for the Quebec government in the area of cultural policy.

WENDY MITCHINSON — teaches history as an assistant professor at the University of Windsor and is working on a study of medical practitioners' attitudes towards women.

JOY PARR — teaches history at the University of British Columbia. Her research interests are in family history and quantitative methods. She is preparing a manuscript on British child immigrants in Canada.

YOLANDE PINARD — does freelance research for radio and television in Montreal and teaches history.

BARBARA ROBERTS — is working on a doctoral thesis for the University of Ottawa, on the Canadian Friends Service Committee. She also works as a consultant for the National Museum of Man and the National Film Board.

WAYNE ROBERTS — teaches history at McMaster University. He is the author of several articles on women's history that stem from his doctoral dissertation on the Toronto working class.

JENNIFER STODDART — has taught women's history courses in Montreal and studied women's history at the Univérsité de Paris VII. She is now in law school and teaches history part-time.

VERONICA STRONG-BOAG — teaches history at Concordia University and has published extensively on the history of the women's movement in Canada, including her doctoral thesis on the National Council of Women of Canada.

Introduction

Linda Kealey

*I want to know why it is that I, a well-brought-up lady-like ... girl, am so utterly helpless and dependent. I have not been taught anything that is of the slightest earthly use to anybody in the whole world. Of course I can sing correctly; but have no special power or compass of voice.... As a pianist I am a brilliant success, and yet a humbug as regards the science of music.... I can **sew** — fancywork; but I could not cut out and 'build' a dress, even if I was never to have another.... I feel lost a little myself too — lost, useless and mean — to think that I can only look pretty — that is as pretty as I can, you know; I eat up, dress up, and spend the 'proceeds' — that's a business word isn't it? — of the labours of others without being a bit the happier for it.*[1]

This anonymous lament appeared in the *Canadian Monthly* of 1880. While its author cannot be considered a 'new woman' since the term had not yet come into contemporary usage, her sentiments echo a frequently voiced complaint against the strictures of woman's sphere. A primarily middle-class women's revolt against the uselessness of a dependent existence emerged in late Victorian Canada just as public attention was focussing on a series of social problems which seemed to threaten the smooth path of 'progress'. The much talked of 'new woman' appeared in Canadian fiction in the 1890s, ready to use her talents in the redemption of mankind. In this case, fiction reflected a growing reality as the experimentation of the 'new woman' with dress reform, bicycle riding, spiritualism and women's rights became transformed into a concern with the reform movement and the duties of citizenship.

This profound restlessness of middle-class women proceeded in part from changes in their material existence; more women remained single, and the fertility rate for married women declined. Middle-class women increasingly began to find employment in the expanding public service sector and became caught up in the professions of medicine, teaching, nursing and later, journalism and social work. As these women entered the labour market they in turn helped to shape the new professions which utilized skills of educated middle-class women. The family was not abandoned, however, despite fears about its decline. Those women who took up careers and those who became involved in reform did so most often in the name of women and children. A disparate group of middle-class women created a mission for themselves which called forth their unique capabilities as women and especially as mothers. In the process, they became involved in a wide range of social and political activity heretofore reserved for men.

[The period 1880-1920 witnessed tremendous growth in national women's organizations. Some of them were denominational missionary societies; others were avowedly non denominational groups like the Woman's Christian Temperance Union and the National Council of Women. Still others, like the Woman's Art Association of Canada and the Dominion Woman's Enfranchisement Association, united for clearly secular goals. Not every organization formed by women started with reform in mind, but a substantial number in the course of their evolution found themselves actively drawn into some aspect of reform. Women who had previously played limited roles in ladies' auxiliaries expanded the realm of what was considered proper for women, to include in their purview the fields of temperance, child welfare, urban reform, city government, public health, child and female labour and suffrage]

Women shared these concerns with men and sometimes worked with them in church and voluntary groups, but often they preferred to form their own organizations. Family ties helped to bind together the reform effort; husbands were often involved in similar reform causes. In some cases mothers passed on an interest in the reform cause to their daughters. Close friendship ties, especially among women, may have played a significant role in drawing women together.

Reform work differed substantially from the charitable activities that women participated in as part of their church work. Relief or almsgiving to needy individuals on an *ad hoc* basis was criticized, particularly after mid-century. The difficulty of deciding who constituted the 'deserving' as opposed to the 'undeserving' poor was alleviated by the adoption of 'scientific philanthropy'. In the process of performing the detective work necessary to ferret out fraudulent claims, charity workers were faced with the contradictions inherent in industrial capitalist society; unemployment, disease, insufficient wages and overcrowded housing rather than individual failure began to be seen as causes for poverty. Once the institutional and social character of distress was recognized and an argument for social justice raised, philanthropists became reformers.

The reform movement in North America was a loose collection of groups and individuals drawn mainly from the Anglo-Saxon professional and business groups that made up the middle class. Predominantly an urban-based movement, reform did find allies in farm and labour organizations on some issues. Labour organizations deplored the use of child and female labour and supported remedial legislation and the granting of the female franchise, although the latter caused some differences of opinion. Humanitarianism was not, however, the primary factor in their support; labour feared the effect of low wage competition. With few exceptions, they were unwilling to unionize female workers whose primary functions, they believed, ought to have been in the home. Farm organizations also supported the franchise with the hope that farm interests would be strengthened. Within this reform circle then, there were many shifting alliances and overlapping concerns.

Three important features characterized the reform movement which became known as 'progressive' reform in the early twentieth century. First, the movement was North American in character. On the social and economic level the concerns were similar in Canada and the United States; in the realm of politics, the political formations and solutions were quite different. Specific circumstances in prewar United States led to the formation of the Progressive party under the reform banner, for example. Canada did not establish a reform party in this period. The vast exchange of speakers across the border is only one example, however, of the North American character of the movement. Secondly, involvement in one group often meant involvement in other reform interests. Temperance often provided the first experience of political action which led women into the suffrage movement and many reformers belonged to several organizations at the same time. Finally, the epithet 'progressive' more accurately described the reformers' shared definition of the problems than their program of reform. In reality, the movement was divided by national group, regional disparity and political and social outlook. While reformers might have agreed that women workers were exploited, for example, their proposed solutions would range from the call for a government investigation to support for the unionization of women workers. A very few advocated socialism as the solution to unequal treatment in the workplace. Nevertheless, despite their failure to agree on the best path to follow, reformers shared a general sense of what were the social, economic and political ills of the country.

Women, as well as men, were disturbed by a series of transformations in Canadian society. The abuses of industrial capitalism, the congestion and disorder of the cities, the influx of new immigrant groups and declining fertility among the Anglo-Saxon elements of the population worried middle-class reform groups, who envisioned wholesale social degeneration. No less disturbing were the rise of strong farm and labour organizations and the growth of French-Canadian nationalism and Western populism.

✓ [The impending battle between 'Capital' and 'Labour' appeared especially ominous. By 1880 the economic transformation to an industrial capitalist system was well under way, spurred on by the National Policy. The expansion of business and industry brought into existence the large corporation, the monopoly and the trust as the characteristic forms of business organization. The size of industrial factories and their work force grew; artisans were transformed into industrial proletarians working for a wage and labouring under dangerous and unhealthy conditions. Women and children were drawn into the work force as cheap labour. In urban centres like Toronto in the late nineteenth century, women and children comprised one-third of the total labour force. In response to these conditions, labour organizations, especially among the skilled trades, fought against the incursions of mechanization, the high cost of housing and seasonal unemployment, as well as for wages.]

By the turn of the century and into the twentieth century, however, a period of intensified conflict began in which a more militant labour movement waged battle on the picket lines. Criticism of exploitation remained, but the solutions suggested were far less democratic. Reformers were apprehensive of class conflict and distrusted the growing labour movement; where nineteenth century reformers could envision a cooperative commonwealth, their twentieth century descendants turned to scientific management, social control and industrial relations. William Lyon Mackenzie King's *Industry and Humanity* (Toronto: Allen, 1918) perhaps best exemplifies this trend.

Reformers were not only concerned about the development of industrial capitalism, but also about the increasing urbanization that took place between 1880 and 1920. Canada's urban population rose from 1.1 million (25 per cent of the total population) to 4.3 million (50 per cent) by the end of the period. The principal urban areas of the Dominion where reform efforts found fertile ground were Montreal, Toronto and Winnipeg. In 1881 these three cities had populations of 155,000, 96,000 and 8,000 respectively; by 1911 they had grown to 500,000, 424,000 and 150,000. Rural migrants and European immigrants flocked to the cities, searching for employment. Montreal's 'City Below the Hill', Toronto's 'Ward' and Winnipeg's North End became the focus for working-class and immigrant life and the centre for social investigation. For social reformers and city officials, the city became the 'laboratory' wherein they could observe and record alien cultural configurations and the social problems that caused them great anxiety.[2]

The influx of immigrants into Canada, combined with the declining fertility rates among white Anglo-Saxon Protestants, fed fears of social degeneration. Reformers and 'imperialists' alike looked to the strengthening of the British component in Canada as a means of preventing the weakening of the nation. Reformers like Helen MacMurchy took up the cause of infant and maternal mortality. As part of their program they lobbied the government to spend more money on infant and maternal care and less on immigration schemes. MacMurchy and others, like Emily Murphy, also recommended sterilization of the 'feeble-minded'. These racist reform efforts rested on the belief that the fate of the Canadian nation depended on the health and success of the Anglo-Saxon component.

In Canada, the intellectuals and propagandists known as 'imperialists' shared with reformers a confidence in the superiority of the Anglo-Saxons. Their writings and speeches urged very close relations with Britain as a means of assuring the triumph of the British way of life in Canada. The question of race was central to the future of the Empire; indeed, the imperialists believed that Anglo-Saxons had a racial mission to perform in 'civilizing' and Christianizing other races. In this respect, the imperialists shared common ground with the Protestant churches which felt duty-bound to provide for the educational, spiritual and material needs of the predominantly non-Protestant immigrants. They shared common assumptions about the inferiority of southern and eastern European immigrants as compared with the hardier northern races. Religion and race reinforced each other; the hardier northerners tended to be Protestant while the inferior southerners belonged to the Catholic faith.[3]

Reformers most often were associated with this active Christianity known as the 'social gospel'. Primarily Methodists or Presbyterians, social gospellers abandoned specific theological concerns for the social problems of the streets. Their efforts to make the church relevant involved them in most of the social reform causes of the day. Attempts to change the conditions of immigrants or the labouring poor were not restricted to preachers of the social gospel; unlike the evangelicals engaged in various sorts of moral rescue work, however, social gospellers stressed a fundamental change of social conditions. In contrast, the revivalist evangelists blamed the individual for his failings. They believed that although institutions might erect obstacles to individual action, institutions were not the root of the problem. On the other hand, social gospellers retained a Darwinian belief in the importance of the environment in affecting behaviour.[4]

In the West, newly settled regions also had their share of problems. As the railway moved westward, settlement followed. The government sought to attract immigrant farmers and their families to the rich prairie land. As the West filled up with settlers, conflicts arose over the railway and the tariff. Farmers began to form cooperative movements to fight against the high freight rates, the shortage of rail cars at harvest time, the low prices for agricultural products, growing monopolies and the protective tariff. Farm women organized women's associations like the Women's Grain Growers' Association and the United Farm Women of Alberta to aid in the fight to change the economic system which oppressed the farmer. Prairie radicalism rooted in British socialist politics, US populism and the social gospel parallelled the growth of labour agitation in the cities.

The settlement of the West and the process of industrialization also alarmed Quebeckers. French-Canadian nationalists expressed the fear of being overwhelmed by largely English-speaking immigrants in the West and the need for French control of the process of industrial development. The industrial transformation of Quebec by non-French Canadians spurred the growth of nationalist organizations like 'La Ligue Nationaliste Canadienne', formed in 1903 with Henri Bourassa as its chief spokesman. Concerned with foreign domination, the trusts and the need to find some path between the 'calamities of communism and corporate domination', Bourassa and the *nationalistes* supported Catholic unions, higher wages, sanitary improvements and other progressive reforms. The notable exception to the nationalist and Catholic upsurge was support for reforms improving the status of women, and especially for the franchise. Bourassa himself was one of the most vociferous critics of the 'new woman'.[5]

The 'woman question' presented yet another area of concern to the reform movement. Women were especially welcome in reform for their 'womanly' qualities of nurturing, selflessness, and their skill in household management. Nevertheless, their presence in large numbers raised thorny problems about their 'proper role'. Participation in the public realm through reform groups and the new professions forced women to look beyond the domestic world; for some it meant that support for women's rights and an identification with feminism became integral to their role in reform. Not all reformers subscribed to a feminist position, but the overlap in membership between the two movements meant that reformers had to grapple with the problem.

'Feminism' itself became a widely used term only in the 1890s. As it is used here, feminism refers to a perspective which recognizes the right of women not only to an increased public role, but also to define themselves autonomously. In historical writing, until recently, feminism has been solely linked to the suffrage campaign and the women involved in groups organized to win the vote. In the late 1960s a resurgence of interest in the history of women produced considerable modifications in terminology. Historians Aileen Kraditor and William O'Neill distinguish between two generations of feminists in the United States. Feminism based on the natural rights argument differs from what they both call 'social feminism'. The former group argued for equal rights as a part of the legacy of the eighteenth century revolutions; the latter abandoned social criticism of the family and separate sexual spheres for a concern with social reform issues and justified women's involvement in the public sphere on the basis of their supposed special characteristics. Despite these useful distinctions, Kraditor and O'Neill place the suffrage movement at the centre of women's history and in so doing, identify feminism with public, organized campaigns.[6]

Somewhat later, the term 'domestic feminism' was popularized by Daniel Scott Smith in a study of family limitation and sexual control in Victorian America. Distinguishing his approach from that of Kraditor and O'Neill, Smith argues that demographic and literary evidence suggests there was greater autonomy for women inside than outside the family in the late nineteenth century. Yet because very few women of the time participated in the public sphere, the dichotomy drawn between public and private appears inappropriate. Criticism of the movement for failing to assault the ideology of the family implies, in Smith's view, an insensitivity to the changing nature of the family. He suggests that domestic feminism evolved side by side with 'public feminism' and that the two merged, in the early twentieth century, in the suffrage movement. While Smith's evidence for domestic autonomy is not convincing, his approach at least broadens the conception of women's history beyond the Kraditor-O'Neill model and suggests a less restrictive definition of feminism.[7]

In this collection the term 'maternal feminism' is used predominantly. Building from the term 'social feminist' and incorporating the important role played by domestic ideology, 'maternal feminism' refers to the conviction that woman's special role as mother gives her the duty and the right to participate in the public sphere. It is not her position as wife that qualifies her for the task of reform, but the special nurturing qualities which are common to all women, married or not. In some senses maternal feminism de-emphasizes or subordinates personal autonomy in favour of a (relatively) wider social role.

Support for the importance of female nurturing qualities came from the newly developed social sciences. The sociology of Herbert Spencer and the biology of Patrick Geddes stressed biological assumptions of female passivity and inferiority. The notion of separate male and female temperaments gained a 'scientific' basis and these biological assumptions justified a specialized role for women. It was asserted that women possessed unique biological qualities which suited them for the work of repairing the damage wrought by economic and social change. The 'intuitive social power of the female temperament' made women more sensitive to human needs, especially those of the weak and dependent. Some women in the reform movement extended and developed this view to claim that women not only possessed aptitudes and abilities in matters relating directly to family and home, but also in those relating to the larger political sphere. Some believed that only woman's intervention could salvage the wreckage of society. Women were touted as the social group capable of initiating change, while at the same time their biological rationale doomed them to a restrictive social role based on home and family. Any element of radical criticism in their social thought disappeared under the very weight of 'maternal feminism'.[8]

On the one hand the maternal feminist position challenged the private/female and public/male dichotomy that characterized much of nineteenth century middle-class life. These women understood their own isolation in the private sphere and even acknowledged the severe domestic and family socialization problems of members of the working class. Their commitment to reform, suffrage (and sometimes feminism) partially reflected this realization but stopped short of actual rejection of their middle-class values. On the other hand, despite this insight they advocated a transferral of private/female 'virtues' into the public/male sphere. A shifting of priorities and techniques could remedy flaws in the system. Many of these flaws were seen as problems of 'contamination' and took the form of a concern with disease, pure milk, 'white slavery' and 'feeble-mindedness'. Early in 1883, Lillie Devereaux Blake of New York spoke to the Toronto Woman's Suffrage Club and suggested a special role for women:

What is the idea men have of cleaning streets? They sweep the dust into piles for the wind to blow away. They take away what is left in an open cart and it blows out. We ought not to blame the men, though, for it's a woman's work to care for such things. Women ought to have charge of the roads.

Women, of course, were not content with having 'charge of the roads'; they had their sights set on higher levels of political authority. But even in the 1880s the terms of the debate had been formulated in such a way as to guarantee the triumph of a conservative maternal feminism.[9]

Feminism based on the natural rights argument quickly disappeared in Canada under the onslaught of maternal feminism. The earlier women's rights movement in the United States under the leadership of Elizabeth Cady Stanton and Susan B. Anthony had developed in the late 1840s out of their experience in previous reform efforts, especially abolition. These roots may explain the early emphasis on the natural rights argument, which was based on a perceived parallel with the oppressed slave. The Quaker background of many of these women, as well as the sweep of the Second Great Awakening in the United States certainly challenged them to think about their position in the churches. As early as the 1830s, Sarah Grimke, a Southern abolitionist, echoed the sentiments of a small group of female antislavery supporters when she declared:

> I ask no favor for my sex. I surrender not our claim to equality. All I ask our brethern is that they will take their heels from our necks and permit us to stand upright on that ground which God designed us to occupy.[10]

By the late nineteenth century, the first generation of feminists in the United States had been replaced by a younger generation who lacked the formative experience of the early pre-Civil War campaigns for reform. In Canada, the first generation of feminists appeared in the 1870s and 1880s when some of the changes in women's employment patterns were already underway. Many of them became involved in the struggle to open new areas of work to women. Teaching, for example, employed as many women as men by the 1870s, and within a decade, women began to outnumber men. Nursing, like teaching became an entirely female occupation which sought to attract middle-class women by upgrading the work to professional status. By the turn of the century civil service and clerical work were also beginning to employ women. Entirely new professions developed to utilize women's 'special capabilities'. Social work, which developed somewhat earlier in the US, combined the talents of 'social mothers' with the felt need for more scientific and systematic study of social problems. Beginning in the late nineteenth century women were encouraged to undertake the study of domestic science to prepare themselves for the scientific management of the household. These trends in education and employment for women followed roughly similar lines in the US and Canada. Whether at home or in the workplace, women were encouraged to develop roles which suited their unique capabilities and ultimate roles as mothers. The second generation of feminists and reformers by and large did not challenge these roles, but worked within these limitations and found significant strength within them. They did, however, encounter stiff resistance to their demands, especially to the suffrage which they saw as critical to the triumph of reform in the twentieth century.

In both the United States and Canada women social reformers came to view the issue of suffrage as key to their goals. Having created national organizations and utilized the tools of reform – investigations, petitions, plebiscites – women repeatedly faced the problem of their own lack of power. This realization and their acceptance of the 'special attributes' of women converged in the campaign for the vote. The faith of bourgeois liberals in the democratic process and the struggle for male suffrage invited the challenge put forward by these women, who saw themselves as protectors of home and family. As 'social housekeepers' of the city, province and nation, they insisted that they deserved the same rights and privileges as men. By 1872, British Columbian women house holders, single or married, were entitled to vote in city elections. The municipal franchise was won in Ontario in 1883, but only for widows and spinsters with the requisite property qualifications. Other provinces such as Quebec permitted single female voters as early as 1876 in Quebec City and by 1892 in Montreal. Manitoba granted single and married women the municipal franchise in 1887. The provincial franchise, however, was much longer in coming. Manitoba was the first province to grant this in 1916. The other provinces followed suit within the next few years with the exception of Quebec, which held out until 1940. Separate federal enfranchisement acts were passed by the Dominion government in 1917 and 1918.[11]

Was the focus on the suffrage and the rationale developed to obtain it an inevitable and conservative path? Were there alternative paths these middle-class women might have chosen? Until recently, historians have tended either to praise or condemn the suffrage movement from the perspective of their own times. Kraditor and O'Neill, for example, measure the 'radical' nature of the movement by the willingness of these women to criticize the family structure and domestic life. In 1975, Ellen DuBois, an American historian, offered a revisionist view of nineteenth century feminism which challenges these assumptions. She argues that the early part of the movement can be considered radical and that these women deliberately bypassed the family to appeal directly for the rights of citizenship. In the Canadian context where the appeal to equal rights was so short-lived, what can we conclude?[12]

Many of the essays of this collection, in varying degrees and from various political and historical perspectives, attempt to deal with the choices made by the women's rights movement in Canada. Several of the articles discuss the paths that were not followed and why; they underline how little attention has been paid to those involved in radical movements and to the working class in general. Wayne Roberts' lead article raises the question of the alternatives to maternal feminism and finally connects the development of the new professions for women to the triumph of maternal feminist ideology in the progressive period. His article evaluates the labour and socialist movements and the response of working-class women to suffrage. Veronica Strong-Boag and Suzann Buckley, in their articles on the medical and nursing professions, also explore the limits imposed by professionalism on the role of women in reform. Carol Bacchi's article examines the tenuous alliances forged between farm and labour organizations and the suffrage movement, that eventually collapsed over the primacy of sex or class questions to reform activity.

These articles point the way to more research. A thorough examination of the labour movement's attitude to women workers and the suffrage question is needed, for example. Why did some unions, like the International Typographical Union, decide to unionize women while others refused? Did the Canadian labour movement in the post-World War I period push protective legislation rather than unionization for women workers, as labour did in the US? These and other questions must be dealt with before we can understand the class and sex dynamic of this period in Canadian history.

Deborah Gorham's article on Flora MacDonald Denison, whose views were often in opposition to those of the rest of the maternal feminist group, raises the likelihood that there were others associated with the reform and women's movements whose opinions and actions belied more radical sympathies. Denison's contempt for temperance and organized religion, her social background, her spiritualism and interest in socialism distinguish her from her contemporaries. But what of other little known Canadian feminists like Alice Chown, who left a semi-fictional account of her struggle to find 'liberty' and independence at the age of forty? *The Stairway* records her interest in the theory and practice of 'free love', magnetic healing, dress reform, the plight of working women, socialism and the suffrage question. Her identification with the needs and problems of working women prompted her to join the picket line in the 1912 Eaton's strike and later in 1913 to go to New York for the purpose of aiding the ladies' garment workers' strike. Were Denison and Chown merely eccentrics or were they part of a radical tradition not yet uncovered?[13]

While there seem to have been very few feminists like Denison or Chown, there were certainly many of the maternal feminist type. Their predominance in numerical terms and the absence of a strong labour or socialist movement committed to the cause of female equality assured their success.

Although we cannot accept this period as merely another step forward in the quest for constitutional liberty for women, neither can we dismiss it as an unmitigated failure. The voluntary organizations supported or organized by reformers and feminists provided piecemeal social services and propaganda tools in the context of an emerging social welfare state. While their motivations were not always philanthropic, and in fact often arose from the fear of social disintegration and class conflict, the reformers provided the beginnings of a critique of Canadian society that never really evolved. The acceptance of progressive ideals of government regulation, business efficiency and class harmony helped to shape and direct the reformers' approach.

Several of the articles in the collection draw out the connection between maternal feminism and the notion of Christian stewardship. Unlike Denison, most reformers and feminists accepted organized religion and worked in church or non denominational religious organizations. The temperance women discussed by Wendy Mitchinson modeled the Woman's Christian Temperance Union (WCTU) on the Protestant church and justified their political activities in terms of their role as guardians of the home. From here it was but a short step to a view of women as 'social housekeepers' responsible for tidying up and humanizing the industrial capitalist system. The medical missionaries studied by Strong-Boag were fortified by a strong belief in their racial, cultural and religious superiority to the peoples of India and China. Barbara Roberts' article on the emigration of female domestic servants also demonstrates that the cultural and social imperialism of the British, Protestant way of life was the most important support for the maternal feminist reformers who constructed the emigration networks. In contrast, Joy Parr views the choice of child emigration work not as social reform, but as moral rescue work derived from the evangelical beliefs of its sponsors. Christian stewardship in this case operated on the principle that children needed personal and experiential conversion to correct the moral failings inherent in their upbringing.

In Quebec, religion played a very different role. The article by Marie Lavigne, Yoland Pinard and Jennifer Stoddart traces the development of the Fédération Nationale Saint-Jean-Baptiste, the first laywomen's feminist and reform organization. The Catholic church in Quebec, fearing the effects of reform and associating such activity with revolution, kept close control over reform organizations like the FNSJB, especially after 1920. In effect, the church quashed even the suffrage movement.

Maternal feminism, then, was the result of the blending of several traditions. As an ideology and rationale for women's participation in the public sphere it arose from a middle-class milieu in which women had come to question what they saw as the frivolity of upper-class social life and the viciousness and misery of working-class existence. Drawing initially on the support of the churches, women became involved in reform. Many were inspired by the social gospel attempt to make religion relevant to the mass of working people and immigrants. Nevertheless, neither the churches nor the reformers managed to shed racist attitudes toward non-Anglo-Saxons. The social and natural sciences of the day supported the notions of British superiority as well as of the nurturing qualities of women. These nurturing qualities were an important aspect of the professions in which middle-class women were employed. The shaping of these new areas (like social work, nursing and librarianship) according to maternal feminist norms reinforced the power of maternal feminism in the larger reform and suffrage movement.

In this context the focus on the suffrage campaign becomes more understandable. What they expected to win with the attainment of suffrage was the power to achieve reforms in family, property and labour laws which affected women and children. While the suffragists may have been short-sighted about the power of the franchise, they were nevertheless demanding a right, the attainment of which others perceived as deeply threatening. The formation of anti-enfranchisement leagues among the upper class attested to the very powerful fear of social upheaval that the suffragists and reformers presented. Outspoken anti-suffragists harped on the threat of female enfranchisement to the stability of home and family. Supporters of woman's suffrage responded with the maternal feminist argument.

The revolt against a dependent existence, the concern with the excesses of capitalism and the search for citizenship did not, in the final analysis, produce a 'feminist' revolution. Even the attainment of suffrage was not wholly a victory of the feminists' making. The intervention of the First World War and the conscription crisis overcame the resistance of the lawmakers. Ironically, and despite their supposed maternal and pacifist qualities, women won the federal franchise, in the short term, because politicians knew they would assure the support needed for conscription.

The much talked of 'new woman', who promised to alter substantially the shape of women's lives, became identified with the professional woman, whose career aspirations conformed to maternal feminist expectations. Feminism became associated with professional solutions devised by women, who, whether mothers or not, used a biological rationale as the shaky foundation of their authority. Feminism in the 1960s and 1970s began much in the same way as it did in the nineteenth century. Initial association with radical values and a questioning of the entire structure of women's lives in capitalist society was submerged by the emergence of a professional solution. Like the old feminist movement, much of the new has failed to address the question of class within the context of the sex question. That is not to say that the feminist movement remains in the same place that it occupied sixty years ago, because maternal feminism no longer provides an option for contemporary women. As an ideology, it was firmly rooted in the context of turn-of-the-century Canadian society.

'Rocking the Cradle for the World': The New Woman and Maternal Feminism, Toronto 1877-1914

Wayne Roberts

The 'new woman' of the turn of the century astonished, amused and frightened most Canadians in the period before the First World War. As the purveyor of dress reform, women's rights and a promised new life style, the 'new woman' seemed to challenge all the traditional notions of proper behaviour and legitimate goals for women. The essence of the 'new woman', however, was a revolt against uselessness, which became, in the course of time, tied to the reform and suffrage movements. She combined a distaste for the frivolity of upper-class social life with a sense of impending doom among the middle class. The notion of a female 'mission' transformed the old concept of dependent womanhood and expanded it beyond the domestic realm.

As Wayne Roberts' article demonstrates, however, the potential of the 'new woman' was never realized. The nineteenth-century democratic radicalism from which she arose was replaced by a twentieth-century philosophy of progressivism; in the process, women reformers narrowed their vision from an interest in labour, spiritualism, suffrage and citizenship to a professionally circumscribed role, based on an extension of 'maternal' abilities. Roberts asks the very important questions of how and why this came about. He concludes that the lack of participation of working women and the weakness of the labour and socialist movements combined with the growth of the 'helping' professions to ensure the triumph of 'maternal feminism'.

This article suggests a conceptual framework for understanding the dominant ideology of maternal feminism and in many respects introduces the issues discussed by the other authors in this collection.

The 'new woman' rode into Canadian history on a bicycle. 'Talk about the landing of the Pilgrim Fathers on Plymouth Rock!', one witness of the bicycle craze sweeping Toronto in the 1890s enthused. 'Believe me, that the ... first woman's bicycle was the real event of this or previous ages.' Indeed, the seemingly innocent craze for cycling did have a provocative, if not epochal quality.[1]

Historian of sport S.F. Wise recently characterized the cheaply mass-produced bicycle, which made the sport accessible to both 'patrician and peasant', as a 'minor transportation revolution; it was also, in a sporting sense, a social one.' Some feared a sexual revolution as well; certainly the bicycle's challenge to physical and social restrictions on the movement of women unnerved custodians of the traditional standards of Canadian cloistered womanhood. The egalitarianism associated with the bicycle was so pronounced that the rambunctious 'sisters, sweethearts and wives of the young chaps about town, the clerks, the mechanics and such like' broke from convention and took to the roads without waiting for upper-class women to initiate the trend.

The essential costume for women cyclists, pant-like 'bloomers', scandalized education trustees who charged that women teachers thus attired resembled prostitutes. Unchaperoned riders were 'exposed at the road houses to the most dangerous temptations', warned evangelical Methodists. Fantasies of blazing saddles flashed before the editor of the *Dominion Medical Monthly*, who condemned the fad as the latest outlet of carnal passion. 'Bicycle riding produces in the female a distinct orgasm,' he wrote. Already, he continued, Toronto's scorching thoroughfares made the streets of Sodom and Gomorrah appear 'as pure as Salvation Army shelters'. Pioneer suffragist Augusta Stowe-Gullen did not choose her props lightly when she ventured onto Toronto streets in this period, complete with cap, bloomers and bicycle.[2]

Brashness, irreverence and independence were among the notable qualities of the new woman of the turn of the century. Sarah Jeanette Duncan captured some of these features in her novel of 1892, *A Social Departure*. Smirkingly dedicating her novel to the proverbial 'Mrs. Grundy', Duncan sends her heroines on an unchaperoned world tour, candidly conceding that 'instruction' is secondary to enjoyment. In the course of their travels, the women develop an interest in social reform. 'Life amounts to very little in this age if one cannot institute a reform of some sort and we were glad of the opportunity to identify ourselves with the spirit of the times,' they announced. 'We were thankful too that we had thought of a reform before they were all used up.' The new woman was both spirited and public-spirited.[3]

Coexisting with these vibrant expressions of the new woman's developing personality was a seemingly mismatched passion for social purity. The image of the woman 'with a spiritual scrubbing brush in her right hand and moral uplift in her left eye' who aimed 'to make this old Earth into a Spotless Town' also came to be a trademark of the new woman's entrance into public life and reform. The interplay between these two facets of the new woman's personality is neatly depicted in Lily Dougall's 1895 novel, *Madonna Of A Day*, reputedly the first Canadian novel to deal with the new woman. The book opens with a horrified missionary, aghast at the sight of a young woman who is traipsing through the train station, and in plain view of everyone, smoking a cigarette. Along the way she dallies with strangers, many of them workmen. 'I know who you are,' the missionary sputters as he approaches her. 'You are a new woman!' The young woman defiantly agrees. She is, she insists, 'simply an average specimen of the class of women that are often called "fast" '. Without a hint of repentance, however, she maintains that, 'I am just as sound in heart and morals as if I spent my life moping by a sitting fire.'⁴

The irreverent vitality of the young heroine is soon tested. In an extraordinary turn of events, she is thrown from her snug train cabin into a mountain gorge, there to be accosted by a gruesome gang of outlaws. Just as these ruffians are about to impose their lustful designs on her, a previously incorrigible dwarf risks his life and helps her escape. The heroine is overcome by the self-sacrifice her womanhood has called forth from the unlikely hero. She concludes that other wild men such as he 'could be turned into any sort of beautiful thing that one chose, if there were women to do it and the women were angels'. The realization transforms her into a madonna, 'chill with a sense of responsibility, which she feared was a shadow from which she could never escape'. Solemnly she swears that 'never again could she see a man degraded from man's estate without knowing that women might have held him up, nay rather exalted him, had woman been pure enough to do the work that was given them to do.'

Madonna Of A Day is a reformer's 'Taming of the Shrew'. The novel telescopes a prolonged historical process, whereby the vigour and experimentation identified with the new woman was absorbed into campaigns for uplift reform.

Other novels of the 1890s shed some light on the origins of this moralistic feminism, which historians have defined as 'social' or 'maternal' feminism, in contrast with the feminism identified with women's liberation from all sexual stereotypes and discrimination. A fictional Mrs. Tim is unable to control the negligence of a club-joining husband who regularly comes home reeking of tobacco and liquor. In retaliation, she pursues a fling with twenty clubs, including the WWA (Weeping Wives Association), the WSSC (Women's Social Science Club), the SSS (Society for the Suppression of Smokers) and the WWC (Whirling Wheels Club). During one of the couple's heated domestic disputes, Mrs. Tim explains her perspective on women's crusade for equal pay, equal standards and equal suffrage. Women voters would remake man-made laws which served property rather than human rights; they would eliminate political corruption and punish drunken wife-beaters. Similarly, *Clipped Wings*, a fictional indictment of the liquor traffic that stresses women's mission to enoble society, portrays the new woman as the 'earnest browed woman, who stands on public platforms to advocate all kinds of moral reforms'. Such a woman is not content with subordination. Far from it, she 'proposed not only to rock the cradle for the world, but to rock the world for the cradle'.[5]

The conversion of all these heroines to the call of social service demonstrates the magnetism of the new standards being set for women during the turn-of-the-century period. Women were renouncing the frivolity, passivity, subordination and privatized familial role prescribed for them. Yet they did not renounce their motherly functions; on the contrary, they extended the realms of motherly responsibility.

Although women's identification with a mothering role often provided a starting point for reform concerns, and although it undermined the 'petticoat burning' image initially associated with the new woman, it did not preordain women's acceptance of subordination within the family or state. The emphasis which suffragists placed on motherhood was sometimes a muted way of enhancing the autonomy of women. Laura McCully, for instance, a 'militant' who was the first Torontonian to take to the soapbox as a means of agitating for suffrage views, believed that the 'calling of women is the rearing of the young of the race'. This did not lead McCully to idealize the subordination of women. On the contrary, she concluded that, by 'reason of her motherhood, she ceases to be at best only the beautiful frail toy of man, and becomes second only to God in the work of creation'.[6]

Suffrage statements appealing to housewives typically stressed the range of political decisions which could end the isolation of households in order to 'drive home' the need for political equality and self control.

> As long as you make the laws for us, as long as you tax us, as long as you give our babies infected milk and contaminated water ... we must ask the reasons why? And we will continue to do so until you realize that we are

determined to have our full share of direct influence and responsibility in all these matters!... The vote is ... a means of self-protection, the means of controlling the government of oneself.... Our constitution is not based on the principle of one class receiving protection from another class, but on each class having civil rights, which enable it to protect itself.

In fact, we might even suggest that the women's movement pioneered the modern concept of an active citizenry. When suffrage delegates confronted Ontario Premier Whitney in 1909, they not only disputed his opposition to female suffrage, they challenged his view of a passive consumer relation between government and populace. Whitney argued that the vote was a privilege, a device which allowed legislators to test the public mind. For women reformers, voting was not only a right, it was a duty.[7]

Even the prim moralism associated with 'maternal feminism' subverted traditional patriarchal norms governing women's access to certain kinds of knowledge. In creating concern about such issues as prostitution and venereal disease, women reformers banished the Victorian taboo which had enforced sexual purity through ignorance. In their concern for public sanitation in the workrooms and kitchens of public life, they surpassed the purely decorative cleanliness of Victorian matrons, who were notorious for keeping their parlours spotless while neglecting the rest of their home, where visitors never trod. These kinds of concerns testified to the innovative, not traditional, impulses of the new woman.[8]

Thus, the maternal self-definition of most feminists of that time did not in itself preclude a commitment to social equality, nor did it account for the limited reform fixations eventually associated with the new woman. Nevertheless, by the time the suffrage movement neared success, the major expressions of the new woman's political demands were characterized by notions of woman's place and social reform which were antithetical to basic notions of equality and independence.

The moralistic and maternal tangent of the new woman's reform thinking became aligned with conservative notions of social order in conjunction with another social process: the conversion of the lives of upper-class matrons from ones of ostentatious idleness to ones as overseers of a social spring cleaning. As a fictional representative of this trend, consider Modena, the aristocratic heroine of *My Lady of the Snows*. Paranoia punctuates Modena's *noblesse oblige* as she anguishes over the 'cruel contrasts of civilization'. Convinced that authority 'is more precious than liberty' and that the 'Noblesse have the right to govern', she is justifiably upset when everywhere she sees:

Rocking the Cradle for the World:

Mammon and Fashion, Pomp and Pageantry, Idleness and Indulgence, Monopolists and Injustice against Poverty and Illiteracy and Socialism. Wealth playing with cold charity. Philanthropy ... unconsciously sowing the seed of bitter discontent and distilleries!

Modena embraces the spirit of national betterment through social reform, conscious that 'our wealth is only a trust' and 'duty is our weapon against envy.' She is not a convert to feminism but to upper-class remedial action. People with ideas akin to hers were careful to distill only the most conservative ideas out of the otherwise ambiguous and contradictory views associated with the new woman.[9]

This article documents the rise of a conservative brand of women's social activism and explains its triumph, particularly within the suffrage movement, over earlier reform conceptions of women's place in politics and society. Conservative 'feminism' severely undercut and negated the initial impulses of suffragists. In organizational terms, this process can be viewed by tracing the evolution of the Canadian Suffrage Association (CSA), and its conflicts with and eventual defeat by, the National Council of Women of Canada (NCWC).

I.

The early suffrage movement in Canada sought women's emancipation from social and intellectual oppression. In fact, the forerunner of Canadian suffrage organization, the discreetly-named Women's Literary Club, established by Emily Stowe in 1877, was primarily a consciousness-raising group. Members were reluctant to focus on one issue, such as suffrage, fearing that 'continuous and concentrated effort upon any one course of thought or pursuit of object' would tend to 'cramp and narrow the views, to enfeeble the minds and power of the intellect'. The group preferred discussions on 'every subject that pertains to women's higher education, including her moral and physical welfare'.[10]

Although the Canadian Women's Suffrage Association, formed some years later, focussed on a single legislative reform, members continued to see suffrage from the perspective of a general commitment to individual rights, development and reason. Leading a delegation to the Premier of Ontario in 1889, Emily Stowe argued that as 'educated citizens, as moral and loving women [we] desire to be placed in a position to impress directly our thought upon our nation and times'. She insisted that the 'invidious distinction of sex is an arbitrary and artificial one, having no foundation in reason or common sense'. Motherhood should leave a woman 'as free to choose her vocation as her brother, man, tethered by no conventionalities, enslaved by no chains either of her own or man's forging'.[11]

This identification of suffrage with women's access to all human rights persisted throughout the 1890s. During a mock parliament sponsored by suffrage supporters in 1896, for instance, women legislators promised to give the question of male suffrage 'serious consideration', even as they passed laws prohibiting men from entering professions which by nature belonged to women, preventing men from wearing knickerbockers while bicycling and defending the practice of half pay for equal work. In a more serious vein, an 1898 resolution specifically repudiated the notion of a woman's sphere limited to the family, and insisted that 'woman's sphere like that of man's, embraces the whole realm of mind.'[12]

This orientation toward women's place in society was countered after 1893 by the rise of the National Council of Women of Canada, led by Lady Ishbel Aberdeen, wife of the Governor General. Aberdeen came to Canada already experienced in reform work, having edited *Onward and Upward*, a magazine which, she carefully pointed out, 'explains what we aim at — the opposite of Backward and Downward'. Social unrest in England during the 1880s led her to realize the urgency of reform activity. 'The people will feel their power: what then?' she had worried.

> The upper classes are defiantly determined to keep all they can.... Many of the best people withhold from what they feel is the contamination of politics. Yet in them lies the hope for the country, if they will only come forward as a duty, mixing with the working men, fighting their battles, leading them in the right way.[13]

The NCWC was a place where women could apprentice in this leadership. The absence of inherited wealth in Canada placed added obligations on women, since so few men could spare any time away from business. 'Our grand woman's mission' of 'mothering' was what Canada needed, she told the Council's first annual meeting. Thus inspired, delegates pledged to 'best conserve the highest good of the family and state' by uniting 'to further the application of the Golden Rule to society, custom and law'. They sponsored 'women's work in connection with social reform', philanthropic service among the aged, sick, inebriate and insane. Although Aberdeen fostered philanthropic notions of women's work and mothering, she was explicit about subordinating women's activity to a definite reform strategy. Women were advised to keep away from such issues as the sweating system, which exploited women garment workers. She urged instead that the Toronto Council launch its activities in collaboration with the Associated Charities, which 'would bring in more societies than by taking up the sweating system, for the latter would arouse the wrath of some trades people'.[14]

The Toronto chapter of the NCWC grew rapidly, from 200 members in 1893 to 5,000 in 1911, representing, in the words of Council president Huestis, 'the best portion of our sex in this city'. They campaigned vigorously for institutionalization of the 'feebleminded' in order to protect society from disease and 'degeneracy'. They declared war on immoral literature, spitting and the white slave trade. They were largely responsible for the passage of pure water and pure milk bylaws. Yet they remained aloof from issues pertaining to women's rights. Suffrage resolutions sponsored by the CSA were handily defeated by NCWC conventions in 1898, 1906 and 1907.[15]

The distinct priorities of CSA and NCWC activists were also revealed in connection with issues such as eduction. CSA founder Emily Stowe supported domestic education as a means of elevating the home and promoting efficiency that would encourage higher aspirations and freedom among women. CSA leader Flora MacDonald Denison saw vocational training as a weapon to combat social snobbery. By contrast, NCWC activist Lillian Massey thought her university-level domestic education course would make 'home the centre of moral progress and intellectual growth. When the majority of homes are ideal, many of the present social and economic evils will disappear.' One of her instructors saw vocational training as the answer to a world too 'full of talkers and smatterers'. She stressed that 'there were a good many girls who would not make much headway in the world if they had to work with their brains. Their brains were in their hands and this artwork would help them express themselves through their fingers.'[16]

Yet the NCWC did not have to reconsider its views when it began to accept women's suffrage. Leading Council figures came to support woman suffrage not as a measure of democracy or women's rights, but as an enabling tool for pet social reforms. Mrs. Huestis, Council specialist in matters of public cleanliness, came to see the vote as the 'handle of the iron' to put the heat on slow-moving politicians. It was 'not as a matter of the suffrage alone, but of all matters of public good endorsed by the National Council', she explained. Indeed, she took care to point out that suffrage was 'the last plank on our platform. We put the reforms first.' Other social service women underwent a similar shift of mind. Mrs. Torrington, for years a Toronto Council president, had long worked 'to secure better housing conditions, to have the feebleminded cared for and segregated, so that the imbecile population would not eternally be multiplying'. If women had the suffrage, she considered, 'these reforms could be won easier and with more dignity.' Prominent NCWC figures were associated, in 1912, with a suffrage group which stressed suffrage as a means to remedy other, more pressing issues. The group's founding statement expressed great sympathy for overworked husbands. [17]

The NCWC's eventual endorsement of suffrage was part of a general reform trend to divorce suffrage from the question of women's human rights. They linked suffrage with women's supposedly inbred capacities for self-denial and purity. Particularly in the period after 1908, when middle-class reformers were trying to tame the chaos of immigrant slums and unrest, women's suffrage was seen as a means of empowering the purest and most self-sacrificing sector of the public. 'Canada is politically out of joint,' the *World* said in a classic statement of this kind in 1909, and new forces were required to redress its balance.

> There is a large constituency of unenfranchised who have not been tainted by the objectionable methods of the past, whose moral sense is keener and purer ... whose whole interest be in the direction of raising the standard of living, morally, intellectually and physically.... They can be and will be the salvation of the Dominion....
>
> Because the *World* believes this, it holds the hour has now come to call the women of Canada to redress the political, electoral and social evils from which the country suffers.

With friends like this, the movement for women's suffrage lost its connection with women's rights and needs. [18]

This middle-class reform surge was powerful enough to affect the resolve even of pioneer suffragists. Augusta Stowe-Gullen, who tried to act as a liaison with the new recruits to suffrage, lost much of her early candour and radicalism. In 1905 she scorned the exclusive right of propertied spinsters and widows to vote, charging they were 'least likely to be keenly interested in the protection of home and nation'. In her youth Stowe-Gullen had treated these concessions as beneath contempt, joking that they provided an unhealthy temptation for wives to murder their husbands. Stowe-Gullen also began to master anti-immigrant innuendo. Pointing to the naturalized Poles and Italians voting in Canada, she felt that 'surely, women could vote as intelligently as these classes.' [19]

Nevertheless, the different orientations toward suffrage eventually resulted in a split within the suffrage movement. Although both CSA and NCWC forces espoused unity, their separate organizations were a fact. For example, there were two delegations to Queen's Park in 1912. The CSA coordinated its delegation to support the annual suffrage bill of Independent Labour MPP, Alan Studholme. On the other hand, a handpicked NCWC delegation was led by the conservative, Controller McCarthy, who regretted that women who controlled five million dollars worth of property were denied the vote; they were an invaluable aid to the community, he said. There were also two Pankhurst tours. Emmeline wooed the Canadian Club by defining herself as a business woman speaking on a business topic. The more radical Sylvia spoke at a public hall and denied the slander that British suffragists had broken windows with stones; for the sake of efficiency, she explained, they used hammers. She also spoke with labour leaders to a garment strike meeting. Despite collaboration during a victorious 1913 referendum campaign for municipal enfranchisement of tax-paying women, NCWC women dominated most public presentations and Flora MacDonald Denison grumbled that the traditional demand for full enfranchisement had been dropped.[20]

In 1914, the split took place when NCWC women and their allies attempted to take over the CSA, were expelled and went on to form the Equal Franchise League. By that time, however, the CSA had essentially accepted the conservative argument for suffrage. 'The women of the world are not asking for the ballot as a right or privilege but because the social and political conditions of the day make it obligatory,' CSA president Denison stated in her comment on the split. Denison was too unreliable a partisan of this view to be acceptable to the NCWC, but essentially she had capitulated. World War I completed the demise of an independent outlook for the CSA. Together with NCWC women, the CSA leaders became captivated by the war spirit and presented suffrage as a wartime measure.[21]

The record, then, is clear enough. The new woman and the women's rights suffragists were both overpowered by the forces of conservative women's social service. The task of the rest of this article is to attempt to explain why.

II.

The suffrage movement was no mere parlour rebellion, nor was woman suffrage a 'motherhood' issue. On the contrary, suffrage projected a field of possibilities which challenged woman's subordination within the patriarchal family. The fact that the suffrage movement strayed from its early democratic ideals of women's rights cannot be explained mechanically, as a reflection of the intrinsic limitations built into the suffrage question itself.

The prospects of women's enfranchisement undercut many of the restrictive norms embedded in the social and political system of Victorian Canada. On a personal level, the widening of female realms upset traditional sex stereotyping of male-female interaction. The *Globe* despaired on behalf of anxious lovers: how could they wax 'sentimental over a lady whose conversation deals chiefly with the railway subsidies and amendments to the school law'? Politically, coming on the heels of the mass enfranchisement of males, universal female suffrage would dramatically sever the last tie between citizenship rights and property. It was one thing to have granted the municipal vote to spinsters and widows; they could be allowed the rights belonging to property owners. But when suffragists visited the Ontario cabinet shortly after universal male suffrage was proclaimed in the 1880s, Liberal cabinet minister John Dryden denounced their request as 'one of the most revolutionary measures ever submitted to the legislature'. Twenty years later, Conservative Premier Whitney was surrounded by suffrage leaders in one of Ontario's largest and most remarkable demonstrations; they presented him with a suffrage petition containing 100,000 signatures. The unsettled Whitney agonized: 'It is a social and political revolution you wish to bring about.' 'Hear, Hear,' the remorseless crowd chanted.[22]

Although we should not treat hysterical reactions to woman suffrage lightly, if only because they suggest what contemporaries saw as the subversive potential of the movement, these fears were unfounded, considering the ultimately conservative bias of women's suffrage thought. It is tempting to refer to the upper-class tenor that came to define the movement as the explanation, rather than the problem to be explained, of the eventual course of the movement. However, this view is fundamentally incorrect.

Even the aristocratic pretensions of the National Council of Women, formed in 1893-94, was more a figment of the leaders' imagination than a fragment of Britain's social system. It was really a case of the bland leading the bland. Their conventions bristled with ceremonies lacking only in content.

> The president, Lady Thompson, read a cablegram from Lady Aberdeen. 'Affectionate greetings; ever altior.' Lady Taylor moved, Lady Tilly seconded, that the president, secretary and Lady Tilly be a committee to draft a reply to Lady Aberdeen's telegram. This was carried by a standing vote.

When some Toronto delegates proposed an end to the time-consuming teas and unbusinesslike procedures, they were roundly defeated. As for finances, in the days before the tax-deductible charitable donation, the Council's elite sponsors evidently considered that their names would be more valued than their money. 'It ought not to be so,' complained leading Council activist Emily Cummings in her letter of resignation, but despite 'the growing wealth of the country ... the earnest-minded women are still too far outnumbered by those to whom fashion and display are the one essential of life and money is not readily forthcoming at any time for organizing purposes.'[23]

The manners and isolation of Toronto's social elite did not normally lead to reform involvement. Lady Flora Eaton's fascination on seeing the perfectly costumed Lady Melvin Jones at the Woodbine racetrack suggests the social enthusiasms that engrossed this class. 'Such were her poise, background, wealth, and uncompromising standards,' Lady Eaton thrilled, 'that I never once heard her addressed or referred to by her first name.'

The truly upper-class women lent patronage to the formation of a women's Anti-Enfranchisement League. Founded at Margaret Eaton Hall, the group brought together Mrs. H.D. Warren, whose husband was a rubber company president, Bell Telephone and Bank of Commerce director and Board of Trade and professional sports afficianado; Lady Melvin Jones, wife of the senator, manufacturer and director of the Bank of Commerce; Mrs. Laird, wife of the eminent banker and financier; and others.[24]

By contrast, the social service women who stamped maternal feminism on the suffrage movement appear relatively humble. Mrs. Torrington, wife of the Toronto orchestra conductor; Mrs. Huestis, adopted daughter of the Gooderhams and wife of a religious publisher; Miss MacMurchy, daughter of a high school principal; and Mrs. Hamilton, gentlelady farmer and wife of a CPR executive, stand out as upwardly bound middle-class women. Even they were latecomers to suffrage and had to overcome an established leadership composed of a grouping of doctors, teachers and journalists.*

How, then, do we explain the anomalies of the suffrage movement? How do we explain its evolution from a movement inspired by ideals of

---

* Where possible, in this article and throughout the book, a woman's first name is given. However, it was common for many women at the turn of the century to refer to themselves by their husband's name, and often this is the only record available. On the whole, the suffragists used their own first names and sometimes even retained their birth names.

self-fulfillment and equality to a movement characterized by stultifying definitions of motherhood? How did it come to uphold an upper-class concept of social order and a maternal definition of women's calling?

III.

The key to understanding the evolution of the suffrage movement in Toronto can be found in the distorted and contradictory growth patterns which governed women's entry into the new professions. The growth of women's participation in the professional sector in the late nineteenth century was one sign of the extension of women's horizons that resulted from a whole new gamut of opportunities for employment. Marked expansion in the manufacturing and service sectors of the economy alleviated houseworkers' confinement in the self-sufficient domestic economy. New kinds of jobs breached the patriarchal barriers which previously had restricted women's scope to 'outside' work as servants, governesses, teachers and seamstresses. One-time teacher, dressmaker and newspaper columnist Flora MacDonald Denison relished her own social and economic independence and celebrated the prospects for working women. They were not like 'the paper society women on the one hand, the prostitute class on the other', both of whom were dependent on men for their money. For Denison, the experience of work would erase age-old prejudices and even lay the foundations for liberation: 'As property and money form the great basis of value, woman's influence will be felt just in proportion as she controls property and money.'[25]

Professional women engaged as doctors, journalists, nurses, teachers and social workers were a particularly forceful component of the trend toward wider opportunities for women. Quite apart from the greater literacy, leisure and public credibility they enjoyed relative to their non-professional sisters, they were well situated to play a leadership role. The kinds of jobs open to women, weighted as they were toward the service sector, guaranteed professionals a certain numerical ratio, concentration and social importance.[26]

The struggle for professional education in the mid-1880s rang in the first round of the women's rights movement in Canada. The movement of aspiring women professionals threatened the upside-down cake symmetry of Victorian male-female stereotypes. Middle-class women were assigned to home life where they would provide refuge for husbands exhausted by the fiercely competitive business world. While so-called 'higher education' could fit women for this task, co-education could not. It would only afflict them with the 'domestic misery of girls produced by over-education'. The *Queen's College Journal* wanted women to remain

'Mistresses of (He)arts' (not Arts), and found university degrees inappropriate. The 'delicate grace and beauty' of women had to be protected from 'the rude influences, the bitterness and strife' of the muscular world outside.[27]

Daniel Wilson, the University of Toronto president forced to implement co-education in 1884, fretted that professional training for women would undermine the universities' role as bulwarks of civilization. As 'fit counterparts' to Canada's vigorous manhood, Wilson hoped that women could provide the equivalent to a 'leisure class' whose refinement would lift the community 'above the dead level of mere greed of gain'. Women who endangered these prospects were classified as 'mischievous radical innovators', on a par with the 'native-ists' who lampooned Wilson and his 'Oxford Quartet' for their aping of British customs.[28]

In the first burst of challenge to these orthodoxies, hopeful women professionals issued a far-reaching challenge to all sex-typed behaviour. Sarah Curzon, a partisan of the movement (who is renowned for developing a cult around Laura Secord, a feminist-nationalist heroine), opened her comedy, 'The Sweet Girl Graduate', with heroine Kate indignant at her rejection from university.

> The sun-lit heights of steep Parnassus
> Reach past the clouds and we below must stay;
> Not that our alpen-stocks are weak, or that
> Our breath comes short, but that, forsooth, we wear
> The Petticoat. Out on such trash![29]

Kate resorts to a male disguise and graduates with honours as Tom Christopher. At the celebration of her MA, where she finally unveils her secret before a shocked crowd, she wears a maiden-hair corsage, 'which I mean to adopt for my crest with "If she will, she will" as motto'. She is sceptical of all convention:

> It reminds me of the saying that the nearer to church, the farther from heaven, since it is evidently the nearer to the centre of civilization the farther from a University degree so far as we unfortunate women are concerned. But never mind! I've proved that Canadian girls are equal in mental power with Canadian boys.[30]

Dr. Augusta Stowe-Gullen, the first woman to graduate from a Canadian medical school and a leading suffragist, was a product of this generation. In an 1890 article, she argued that all women should be 'self-supporting and independent'. This 'self-dependence strengthens and ennobles character', but it was also an 'imperative necessity' — there were simply too many women for all to be married off. Stowe-Gullen heaped scorn on the self-styled protectors of Canadian womanhood and enjoined them to 'expend their superabundance of sympathy upon the physical wrecks from a far larger portion of humanity' — overworked housewives. 'We hear no eloquent outcry for their protection or defence from the "over-pressure",' she said. But, if women choose 'skilled and well-paid labour, then many voices and pens are busy to warn.' With a characteristic flourish, she projected the boundless future.

> In the process of evolution, old things — old time prejudices and superstitions — ... will disappear as the darkness before the dawning day ...; thus shall we move onward until we have reached that full — that millenial day.[31]

The life of Helen McGill, descendant of a powerful Ontario family and Trinity College's first woman graduate, was as remarkable as Curzon's fiction. After educating herself privately to prepare for university entrance, McGill graduated *cum laude*. Rebelling against her parents, she took on a number of daring assignments as a freelance reporter, including one to the Canadian West. There she met a cowboy rancher and guide, whom she married after a courtship of one week. She later lived with him in California, putting him through medical school while she worked as a journalist developing investigative and reform interests. Following the death of her husband in 1901, she married a Toronto-educated lawyer and moved to Vancouver. There she became active in efforts to remove abuses in marriage, family and child-related laws, efforts which were crowned in 1917 when she was appointed Judge of the Juvenile Court of Vancouver.[32]

Helen McGill's personal evolution from an unconventional university student and cowgirl to an acceptable professional concerned with children was part of a general shift in the evolution of women professionals after the 1880s. Women's provocative initiation into the professions was quickly accommodated. British reformer Karl Pearson commented on the challenge most astutely when he announced in 1894 that 'to reconcile maternal activity with the new possibilities of self-development open to women is *par excellence* the woman's problem of the future.' The challenge would not be solved by equal opportunity, according to Pearson, but 'solely by the recognition of maternity as an essential social activity'.[33]

A glimpse of this strategic blueprint for co-option had already been grasped by a male Canadian writer who favoured co-education for women. Writing in the staid *Week* and primarily concerned with unmarried women, J.M. Loes proposed in 1884 that 'the world would have fewer miserable women in it if a field of usefulness could be found for every woman.' If women couldn't find their mission in home life, 'they should find other interests, with well-defined duties.' Calming the fears of colleagues who predicted an onslaught of masculine women, he argued that:

> [B]usy people are the happiest. Give occupation to the woman with no duties, and we shall have fewer busy-bodies and happier women. Never fear that throwing open the gates of learning will deluge the world with advocates of 'female rights'.[34]

In the 1890s, a cascade of reports on vagrants, drunks, criminals and homeless children documented the underside of industrial capitalism. As an alarmed middle class became aware of this new dimension of the social costs of industry, the public discussion on women's role was urgently renewed. The frivolity of drawing-room wives could not be encouraged in this ominous atmosphere. Instead, efforts to master the chaos of urban society required the free time of women whose virtues were suddenly redefined in keeping with the spartan tasks expected of them.

Lady Aberdeen instructed the founding convention of the National Council of Women on its 'grand woman's mission' which she defined as 'in one word, mothering'.

> The woman who aspires to make home a place for rest after work and for strengthening before labor, a center of holy associations and inspiring memories has need herself to be in touch with every side of our manifold life. She must realize that no walls can shelter her dear ones from the temptations, sorrows and discouragements of life. She must learn that if the poor around her doors are not cared for, the orphans not housed, the erring not reclaimed, because she was too much engrossed in her own house to lend a helping hand, the results of her self-absorption may be in the future to provide pitfalls for her own children whom she so desires to cherish. The high ideal of a pure and holy family life is the chief strength of all nations.[35]

B.F. Austin's 1890 anthology *Woman, Her Character, Culture and Calling* heralded the new sensibility. Himself the principal of a girls' school established to prepare women for higher education, Austin forcefully repudiated the woman 'who has run the gauntlet of the "ologies" and the "accomplishments" '. Women must forsake the narrow circle of home and parlour and lend a hand to struggling humanity.[36]

This new view placed women's role as guardians of the race above their previous role as guardians of refined culture. Reverend A. Carman's contribution to Austin's book exhorted women students to command 'discipline ... ceaseless vigilance and diligent oversight' in childrearing. For Carman, the model of self-sacrificing women provided the cornerstone of social cohesion. 'Their attraction, their restraining and binding energy gone, and all is gone. Humanity is a horde; government is robbery; empire, pillage and slaughter,' he grieved.[37]

A third contributor to Austin's book, Mrs. Dr. Parker, boldly announced that 'the educated womanhood of Canada is henceforth in the Providence of God, to be a power and a force in the nation-building.' Seeing the home as a 'miniature state', Mrs. Parker highlighted the primacy of women in early socializing. It was at home, for instance, that the mother must teach and enforce 'the law of meum and tuum, that foundation law of government, the protection of each one in his or her right to property'. She extended this role in the home to the 'womanizing of society', that is, social reconstruction on the basis of sexual political equality.[38]

Women's role in the professions was caught in the undertow of this new sexual dialectic. Women who felt restless with the limitations of home life needed an independent career, the Toronto *Star* conceded. 'It is the business of each woman to find that service to humanity which will call into play all the best energies of her nature.' The woman of today can be found in important positions everywhere, the *Canadian Home Journal* declared, 'with their tender care and brave hearts ... and wherever they go they carry with them an influence that purifies and refines.' Women's road to subordinate positions in the professions was paved with such high intentions.[39]

IV.

This change in the strategic concept of women's place carefully orchestrated women's entry into the professions in the period of progressivism. Women professionals were systematically shunted into specialized job ghettoes which reaffirmed their subordination rather than autonomy in the world of work. Dependent professionalism produced a distorted culture which was a stunted version of feminism.

UNIVERSITY WOMEN

Specialization for a truncated professional existence began in earnest at the university, which tolerated a student body of one-third women in the prewar period. There, women acquitted themselves honourably before setting out to work in professions like medicine, law, nursing, librarianship, social work and language teaching.[40]

Distance from the conventions of work and parents provided an atmosphere for suffrage support. The university harboured a credible portion of feminist activism, graduating such figures as the amazingly precocious Laura McCully, the first Toronto woman to take to the soapbox on behalf of suffrage; Evelyn McCulloch, who reportedly 'perfected her suffragettely graces during four years residence' at the University of Toronto before taking part in the seventy-four-mile suffrage march from New York to Albany; and the recently rediscovered radical feminist novelist, Edith Summers Kelley. University women unsettled Toronto gallants by refusing their offer of streetcar seats — the sterner sex was advised to look for suffrage buttons before making the offer.[41]

Within a certain framework, women undergraduates were quite insistent on their rights. They rallied immediately to protest a 1909 University Senate report favouring separate education for women. Apart from fears that women were crowding men out of fields such as modern languages, the report was based on the expectation that 'it is still true that the vast majority of women do not earn their own living and have little interest in fitting themselves to compete with men for the prizes in the various callings.' Since motherhood 'is the lot of most women ... the chief problem of women's education is to fit her for this sphere.' Women in University College and the Alumnae rejected the proposal, charging it would lead to inferior library facilities and professors. One newspaper reported that 230 of the 238 women it surveyed had signed a petition against the proposal.[42]

Women students also had to fight for their rights within the student body. In 1913, for instance, a Victoria Women's Literary Society conference protested an objectionable ruling of the all-male student council and came out in favour of a separate women's student council to manage their own affairs.[43]

However, the forces containing rebellious sentiments were powerful. The ivory tower concept of the university's place was not far removed from Victorian conceptions of woman's place. University College Principal Maurice Hutton saw the university 'in the background ... of the world's life ... as women, in wholesome societies, stand in the background of men's business life'.

And as the hearts of the world's workers turn back to their women-kind when the work of the day is over, for guidance and assistance all the more forceful because it is indirect, and for fresh inspiration of hope, gentleness and charity, so after each period of strenuous action, will the heart of the world turn back to the 'gentle mother,' the university.

The values of conspicuous consumption and parasitic idleness were still accredited in the university milieu and committed students to refined culture of the most mundane quality. Although the Women's Literary Society at one time had sponsored readings from the feminist novelist, George Eliot, by 1910, it defined itself as 'far from the seething cauldron of party politics and strife-begetting constitutions'. Members preferred the 'true end of such institutions — a true and broad culture', by which they meant the wit and wisdom of travelogues at tea.[44]

Reform advocacy in the university was steeped in middle-class paternalism and carefully adapted to sex-typed expectations. The University Women's Club became interested in social work with working girls 'in order to enable them to find work and to give them a sense of the sympathy of their more fortunate sisters'. One advocate of settlement work in the poorer areas of the city saw it as especially important for university women.

For the first time, perhaps, her mind and her sympathies are busied with human beings who can give her nothing akin to what she gives out to them. Settlement work becomes the link between her formative years and her coming career of usefulness. It reveals perhaps the first glimpse of what she may achieve through the gifts of her womanhood.

Leading Toronto settlement organizer Dr. Ware noted that women volunteered for settlement services out of all proportion to men. This was because 'there are so many fields of social work for girls and so few for men. Any girl student can teach sewing, cooking and the art of having a good time in a wise and safe way,' but men could only teach English, politics, gymnastics and baseball.[45]

The rage for domestic education converted one University of Toronto woman, who used to think it should be taught only in mission schools for the poor. She came to favour a more far-reaching approach, because 'homemaking is and always will be the profession *par excellence* of women.' She flavoured this judgment with a score of maternal feminist prejudices:

That ignorance of the principles of really good cooking and sanitary living is very general, especially among the labouring class, no one ... will dispute with me.... The strength of the forces of universal good cooking and cleanliness, pitted against the combination of disease, intemperance and crime, has yet to be tried. The importance of good cooking and cleanliness in the development of a 'socially fit' race is incalculable.[46]

MEDICINE

Women's reform and professional aspirations were more pointedly manipulated in actual workaday life. Women doctors, brimming with bitterness from the experience of male medical chauvinism and directly familiar with pressing social health problems, contributed per capita far beyond their numbers to suffrage and allied reform movements. At the same time, the terms of their practice maintained a stifling concept of womanhood and work. Suffrage leader Dr. Augusta Stowe-Gullen, with her vacillating presentation of the suffrage cause, and Dr. Helen Macmurchy, with her crusade to protect home and family through the incarceration of the overbreeding 'feebleminded', were both testimony to the schizoid legacy of the profession.

Early women medical students were subjected to embarrassing ordeals in the course of their training, as male students and faculty worked out their anxieties over the co-educational study of anatomy with lewd sketches and vulgar demonstrations. In one instance, a lecturer became so intolerable that a female student 'asked him to desist from that sort of persecution or she would tell his wife exactly what he had said. His lectures were more bearable after that.' Many medical women hoped that separate women's medical schools would eliminate this discomfort.[47]

However, the creation of separate but unequal training facilities for women marked an essential and strategic defeat for women medical students. At Queen's, co-education was forcibly terminated when male students delivered an ultimatum threatening to desert the school *en masse*. In Toronto, the first dean of the Women's College Hospital was a male who opposed co-educational medical schools.[48]

The Women's College Hospital appealed to a female clientele reticent about seeing a male doctor. It also offered specialized charitable services not available in regular hospitals. So instead of opposing hospital regulations that prohibited women from practicing, the women worked in separate facilities, which hearkened back to a tradition that promoted women's volunteerism as a safe, non-competitive outlet for women's extra-familial energy.[49]

The teaching side of Women's College Hospital cultivated an image which capitalized on women's allegedly selfless, modest and familial characteristics. The college was advertised as a place where women could prepare for examinations without the embarrassing presence of male classmates. Specialties in anatomy and diseases of women and children were offered as skills in which women were particularly adept. Such skills admirably outfitted the full twenty per cent of their graduates who entered into mission work. As late as 1905 Women's College Hospital representatives favoured the existence of a separate college, even though male doctors had come to recognize the separation as irrational.[50]

Whatever learning advantages and teaching possibilities women gained from studying in their own institution, the segregationist strategy of Women's College Hospital ultimately involved capitulation to mystifying notions of womanhood. Moreover, the college was financially dependent on patronage. As residents of a women's hospital, they were especially vulnerable to patrons who preferred womanly self-sacrifice and service to professional independence. The Board was made up of a galaxy of National Council of Women social service activists, decorated by the honourary patronship of Lady Aberdeen. Woman's Christian Temperance Union leader Mrs. Rutherford was active on the board of directors and provided the hospital with its motto: 'the union of those who love on behalf of those who suffer.'

NURSING

Professional nursing developed in the late nineteenth century in conjunction with a new division of labour in medical care. Previously, the occupation was dominated in Canada by husky women workers who scrubbed floors, washed dishes, kept fires and healed patients with equal skill. Frequently illiterate, these women were forced to live in wretched conditions in the hospital for an allowance of nine dollars a month, potatoes and regular instalments of beer. The work of Florence Nightingale and other advances in England convinced Canada's *Christian Guardian*, looking for employments 'for women of a higher grade of intelligence than the ordinary domestic servant', that 'the recovery of patients depends upon much more than upon the prescriptions of the physician. This is work that requires intelligence, firmness of purpose, and kindness of heart. It is the employment for which the natural tenderness of women especially fits them.' In 1881, the Toronto General Hospital established a school for nurses.[51]

Male doctors seemed to find this avenue of professional advancement for women more to their tastes. 'The most objectionable type of medical men who apparently hated the idea of women practicing medicine were eager for them to be nurses,' Dr. Elizabeth Shortt recalled. A medical establishment, initially resistant to Aberdeen's scheme for a Victorian Order of Nurses, had their fears allayed by one of her field workers. These nurses 'are trained to know their proper sphere. They know too much to interfere with the physicians,' the 1897 Ontario Medical Association was relieved to hear.[52]

The nursing profession was also part of the new ethos of women's service. *Massey's Magazine* discovered the solution to women who despaired of being mere butterflies, 'to whom flattery and admiration is the breath of life'. The high and noble longing 'to do her best for self and others, uplifting her standard – purity, chivalry and noble living' could be expressed in the 'womanly woman's work and love' of nursing. The developing genre of nurse-romances harped on similar themes. In *Dr. Bruno's Wife*, heroine Natalie is hospitalized following her collapse from hunger and distress. Their family fortune spent, her mother had starved to death rather than lose status by working. By the time of Natalie's recovery, she is pledged to marry her doctor and pattern her life after her nurse. 'I would have worked long ago if Mama had allowed me,' she confesses. 'I know now it is sinful to be idle in a world where there is so much work to do.... I will be no longer a worthless drone in the world's busy hive. I would like to become a nurse.'

The ideology developed for nursing was short on rights and long on responsibilities. It was permeated with philanthropy; indeed, the line between work and philanthropy was dangerously thin. The Nursing At Home Mission, devoted to the desperately poor and the teaching of cleanliness, was widely praised as a charitable organization. The Victorian Order of Nurses condescended to a nominal charge only as a token of their Canadianized respect for the pride of their clients. One nurse condemned this 'dangerous innovation' of charitable volunteerism. She insisted that 'even nurses have vested rights.'[53]

In keeping with the philanthropic thrust, self-sacrifice became a central code-word for nurses. The 'womanly woman' became the essence of nursing. 'We are women first and nurses afterward,' one valedictorian stressed. 'We are trained lifesavers, but above all, we are to be women of character.'[54]

Nursing was strongly influenced by reform. Those working out of the city health department issued calls for 'preventative work'. Some nurses operated out of social settlement houses and pleaded for industrial health and justice. Social paranoia and religious piety prevented them from drawing radical conclusions, however. One nurse, who criticized a destitute patient's landlord for charging so much for a hovel quickly recovered to add:

> However much of the dark side of life is seen in the work, there are yet many bright spots.... Who can estimate the far-reaching influence of kind words and deeds done in the name of the Master?[55]

Although one mission nurse thought 'sin is the cruelest thing in the world,' she was greatly distressed by social problems in the immigrant 'Ward'. She called for a housing and playground program to stem the tide of the slum, and warned Toronto to do its duty or 'the slum with all its vice will be upon us.'[56]

Nurses did not develop these ideas as a reflection of upper-class backgrounds or out of any sense of protecting their own interests. The ideas grew out of the process of professionalization. A majority of nurses lived in nurses' residences and were constantly under the thumb of their mentors. Their journal was initiated by the harsh genetic guardian of Canada's racial stock, Dr. Helen MacMurchy; their club centre donated by children's hospital founder and philanthropist, J.R. Robertson of the *Telegram*; the patronage for their guilds and organizations supplied by their teachers, employers and hospital directors. Nurses' professionalization was very much identified with the new woman's entry into the world of reform, but it had very little to do with women's independence or rights.[57]

JOURNALISM

Along with medicine, journalism contributed many prominent spokespersons for the new woman. The National Council of Women's domestic education specialist, Emily Cummings, wrote for the *Globe* in the 1890s; the Council's press secretary, Miriam Brown, wrote a column for the *News* in 1907-1908; suffrage leader, Flora MacDonald Denison, wrote wide-ranging columns in *Saturday Night* and *Sunday World*. These and other women journalists replaced men, who had formerly edited women's pages and expanded the permissible scope of women writers to literature, reform and general philosophy. Yet their place within the profession was still anchored to a particular format, most obvious in the case of women's pages.

The *Mail and Empire*'s Kit Coleman was Canada's first woman journalist and won world recognition as the first woman war correspondent. A warm, vibrant and sensitive writer, her popular column, 'Woman's Kingdom' won her wide acclaim, including the 1904 presidency of the Women's Press Club.[58]

Coleman applauded the trend toward jobs which released women from total reliance on marriage for livelihood and fulfillment. Women 'live in the open world and are no longer mere hot house plants', she cheered, encouraging those who had 'elected to live as rational human beings instead of remaining drudges or men's toys'. She tolerated no snobbery toward working women, reminding one 'plumed hat' that 'the dressmaker works for her living and the society woman works twice as hard for notoriety.' She also expressed compassion for overworked housewives. She commented on one woman's suicide:

> A hunger comes for rest or change and there can be none, for bread and butter have to be made, and women must work though the heart be breaking. To go away, somewhere, anywhere; to get away from the grind, grind, grind of the days and the years! Even drowning is alluring.[59]

Yet, Coleman vehemently denied being an 'equal righter'. She placed too high a premium on womanly tenderness. Equal rights, in her opinion, 'overshot the mark in the vain effort to equalize the sexes: the chief charm of which is they can never be equalized. They are each the beautiful complement of the other. Until nature changes her laws and God alters his creation, it will always be thus.' At other times, she encouraged women to stay in their secure home situations and not to be 'new women'. She was resigned to 'two codes of morality — a stringent one for the women, a loose one for the men, but what use is it to sit and rail at these things? It seems hopeless to think about reform.'[60]

Coleman advised women to manipulate the advantage of their sphere. She saw no need for nagging when no man could refuse a woman 'if she only puts the proper blinkers on her mule ... making him believe he is doing the driving'. Even suffrage seemed unnecessary. 'A pretty gown will always be more vital to a woman than the vote,' she suggested. Flora MacDonald Denison accurately noted that Coleman was 'brilliant, erratic, often brave in deed but too politic to be true to the light she really had'.[61]

Marjory MacMurchy, several times president of the Women's Press Club, was a prima donna in the new field of social journalism. Known as the 'apostle of the working girl', she wrote many features urging women workers to become well trained. One of her manuals for working women was prefaced with the 'necessary' objective 'to bring about in the life of a girl a satisfactory connection between paid employment and home-making and to show the home employments in their rightful places as occupations of the first importance'. Her style of reform advocacy paid homage to maternal virtue — women made excellent social reporters because of their womanly dedication to reform, she maintained. Because civic and national reforms were just extended variations on housekeeping, women could play a central role, she believed. She eventually took up a career of 'first importance' by marrying one of her editors, Sir John Willison.[62]

Madge Merton, wife of *Star* editor J.E. Atkinson and a popular *Star* writer herself, was earnestly pious and opposed the introduction of comics into the *Star*. 'My dear, we are not running a Sunday school paper,' pleaded Atkinson, thinking he had clinched the argument. 'I rather wish you were,' she replied stonily.[63]

Although Merton acquired a reputation as a crusading woman journalist, especially because of her work for the *Star* Fresh Air Fund, she specialized in reform homilies that stressed cleanliness, careful budgeting and housekeeping. 'There is one thing women ought to try to do in politics and that is ... keep the peace,' she urged. She held fast to a strict separation of male and female spheres.

> One fact is certain and underlies the whole matter. The man eternally remains the man, and the woman, the woman; and that education is most profoundly wise which recognizes the difference and trains a girl thoroughly for her own work and her own place in life.

Merton's column, credited with initiating the revolution in women's journalism, proudly sported the logo 'for women, by a woman'. But her writing did not testify to the power of the new journalism to lift women out of their assigned realm.[64]

In general, the early hopes of women professionals were unfulfilled. The very name 'helping profession' betrayed the occupational limitations open to women. Women were not integrated into professions as autonomous individuals or as independent members of the working class. Their professional existence was designed to extend the characteristics of familial subordination to the public arena, reinforce the ideology of separate spheres and secure them in a network of confining structures and obligations. Women professionals became hostages to the new ideology as they adapted to survive. In the process, their rights became conditional on special attributes — self-denial rather than self-advancement, helping others rather than themselves and service rather than leadership. It was this contradictory preparation for public life that accounted for their ambiguous support of political equality and which so ill-suited them for leadership in a movement which had once aimed for the emancipation of women.

v.

The adaptation of professional women to the demands of their sphere in the expanding public sector was a decisive precondition for the triumph of conservative, maternal feminism. Could other constituencies have successfully presented a more radical and democratic perspective on women's rights?

Working women, widely regarded as suffrage supporters, were the most logical group to provide an alternative to the ambiguities of maternal feminists. Women in menial jobs had never been placed on a pedestal. They had never been included in middle-class norms which protected women from the harsh and cruel world. They had also been spared an upbringing designed to instill austere and policing virtues into the 'guardians of the race'. Therefore, they appreciated a little 'feminine' fun and frivolity in their lives and heartily resented the behavioral demands of solemn matrons. Indeed, one factory woman reversed the standard stereotype and cited the story of the New York shirtwaist girl who 'feared the ignorant vote of the Fifth Avenue women'.[65]

They saw the vote primarily as a protective device. 'It is not the vote which is vital,' an office worker explained, 'it is the legislation.' Shortly after the popular and dramatic strike of telephone operators against Bell in 1907, union president Miss Gibson promised a suffrage meeting that 'if women are granted the suffrage, they will be able to vote for taking over the telephone system by municipal authorities.' Condemning the wage differential between male and female teachers ($500 per year for women and $1,100 for men) a woman teacher concluded that, 'undoubtedly were a woman a political unit, there would be no such discrimination.'[66]

One 'working woman', who believed she represented the opinion of her co-workers, replied to two women opponents of suffrage. She wrote as a 'representative of the average woman of the masses ... as opposed to the classes as represented by the aforesaid vestal matrons'. She personally favoured the pro-suffrage efforts of Hamilton's lone Labour MPP, Allan Studholme, and wished there were more labour representatives for him to work with. However, she apologized, 'as a busy women earning my living by the sweat of my brow, I have less time than the vestal matrons ... to lavish on newspaper effusions.'[67]

Time, of course, was the real problem limiting working women's participation in the suffrage movement. Time was a precious commodity for

Toronto's overworked, unorganized and politically inexperienced female workers. Moreover, the youthfulness of Toronto's female work force made age restrictions on voting as exclusive as sex discrimination. Thus, working women's support and understanding of suffrage rarely crystallized in organized form. The one attempt to form a working girls' suffrage club in 1912 appeared to have only short-lived success.[68]

VI.

Intervention by the larger labour movement might have compensated for the lack of working women's direct involvement with suffrage. The Toronto Labor Council was an early supporter of woman suffrage and continued to endorse it by overwhelming margins. Labour MPP Studholme persistently and courageously brought the measure up in the provincial legislature. The Independent Labor Party pledged in 1911 that a Labor government would immediately acclaim the political rights of women. They hoped that women's 'natural altruism' would lead them to support labour.[69]

In 1913, suffrage organizers carried their 'Votes for Women' banner in an honorary position in the huge Labour Day parade and were warmly received. In the face of mounting pressure for a qualified extension of suffrage to propertied women, the popular labour paper, *The Industrial Banner* joined the more democratic suffrage leaders in supporting unqualified suffrage. The *Banner* campaigned actively for the 1914 municipal referendum on extended suffrage, while pointing out it represented at best 'partial justice'. Confident that labour had 'fought the battle of womanhood and childhood down from the earliest days of its development, and what is more, it stands right today on every moral question,' they believed in enfranchising 'every working girl in Toronto who toils for an honest livelihood'.[70]

However, in the midst of the prewar reform upsurge, the labour movement was involved in a complicated ricochet romance with progressives. The labour movement opposed many progressive measures that they believed adversely affected male labour. Labour leaders vehemently denounced the National Council campaign for manual training in the schools as a threat to organized labour. They also suspected the motives behind other projects pertaining to housing, town planning and public morality. But in cases where labour interests were removed or where interests coincided, labour leaders frequently adopted middle-class reform rhetoric.

The labour movement's longstanding prejudices about womanhood and an auxiliary role for women made them peculiarly susceptible to the 'soft' side of maternal feminism. Labour spokesmen could, for instance, envision women voters as keepers of the morality of the city:

> Mothers are by nature and training possessed of just the knowledge to enable them to help in the city.... Men have already more than they can attend to in politics: why not give the married woman a chance to help in municipal politics.[71]

The *Banner's* 'Votes for Women' column by the one-time daily journalist, 'LAC', reflected this unevenness. LAC was a vigorous suffrage advocate who occasionally chided the Canadian Suffrage Association for its lack of aggressiveness. She stressed the necessity of universal suffrage for working women to advance their economic interests and win equal pay for equal work. LAC's column also incorporated many concerns of maternally-inclined social service women. She endorsed liquor prohibition and encouraged repressive measures to control the 'feeble-minded'. She adopted another progressive control weapon, obligatory premarital health certificates, in the hope that this would check the high death rate of women newlyweds caused by unhealthy work conditions, overbreeding, marital rape and the diseased conditions of some of the men. She did not consider legislative antidotes such as strict work regulations, sex education and birth control clinics.[72]

The official labour movement's approach to suffrage and allied women's causes was a barometer of both longstanding presumptions about women and recent adaptation to reform pressures of the time. Women, along with immigrants, were labour's 'loss leaders' in the attempt to sell labour legislation to the government with the aid of middle-class reformers. Labour did stress the reform and democratic thrust of suffrage, but its uneven and limited understanding of women's needs made a mass-based alternative to the leadership of aggressive and consistent maternal feminists impossible.

VII.

The main body of organized socialists in the first decade of the century suffered no such lapses into progressive reformism. Indeed, socialist intervention in the suffrage movement was hindered by the essentially abstentionist position of the Socialist Party of Canada (SPC). Denouncing all individual reforms as deceptive manoeuvres of 'respectable wage-skinners' (capitalists), they were fierce partisans of the 'impossibilist' or 'one-plank platform'. In other words, the only demand relevant for them was the abolition of capitalism. Exclusively women's issues did not merit particular attention in the overall revolutionary struggle.

The woman question and women comrades helped to break down the SPC's rejection of all reforms. The editor of the SPC's *Western Clarion* provoked a lively debate in 1908 when he refused a request for a woman's column. He not only opposed 'catering' to any interest group; he added insult to ignorance by charging that most women in the movement were there only because of a man. Toronto's B.O. Robinson responded sharply: 'Women with the spirit of revolt aroused in them can never be encouraged to join such an obvious MAN's movement.' Toronto activist Edith Wrigley asked if the editor wanted to 'cater' only to the men with a vote and the price of a subscription and retorted that:

> I have come in contact with women full of the spirit of revolt and very often it is not because 'some man is a socialist' but because of some man she is working for.... She is 'sex-conscious' as well as 'class conscious' and recognizes the SP as the only existing force in society that will help her attain her freedom.

Another woman calmly insisted that she did not wish to be catered to in the manner of fashion papers. She just wanted 'some common sense and logical revolution ... to include the working woman's field'.[73]

The subsequent Socialist Party convention adopted a pro-suffrage position as one of its few immediate demands. It was supported not as a palliative, but as a means to win power for the workers. Following this convention, B.O. Robinson led a Toronto Socialist Women's Study Club, whose members pledged to study the evolution of woman's place from a materialist perspective.[74]

Despite sectarian blinders, the Socialist Party of Canada was the first party to grant women full membership rights. Women often played prominent roles within the SPC. Margaret Haile, a socialist recently emigrated from the US, was the first woman parliamentary candidate in Canada. A special campaign meeting on behalf of her 1902 provincial campaign featured endorsation from suffragist Augusta Stowe-Gullen. Women occupied leading posts in other groups as well. May Darwin was president of the Canadian Socialist League. Mrs. Bellemarre was a major organizer of the Social Democratic local. Mrs. Crockett ran as a socialist candidate for the Board of Education in 1913. Backed by the Independent Labor Party and Labor Council, she mustered almost 2,000 votes in her first campaign.[75]

Outside of the SPC, every current of the socialist movement was a forceful advocate of the suffrage. The pioneer socialist paper, *Citizen and Country*, with which Augusta Stowe-Gullen was identified in the late 1890s, and the turn-of-the-century People's Party supported suffrage. *Cotton's Weekly*, a major propaganda organ of the socialist movement after 1909, stood for the absolute equality of the sexes, the right of women to vote, abolition of all prejudicial laws, equal pay for equal work and exclusion of women from industries harmful to their health and therefore to the health of future generations. Although *Cotton's Weekly* frequently couched its appeals to women in motherly rhetoric, its analysis stressed the relation between women's low status and their economic dependency. It was from this perspective that the SPC's rival Social Democratic Party explained the importance of suffrage:

> To remove the bonds that hold the working woman in double slavery, to combat the crying evils that today make woman's work a curse instead of a blessing, to give women political freedom as a means of winning economic freedom, it is for this that the Social Democratic Party demands votes for women.[76]

Socialist women made some contribution to the suffrage movement in its period of enthusiastic expansion after 1909. Helen Cunningham, a university graduate with degrees in optics and music, broke from the Canadian Suffrage Association's plans for a 1909 deputation to Queen's Park. The deputation method was too mild and conservative for Cunningham. With her Women's Political Club, she bragged that 'we are going to divide the MP's among us and make their lives miserable, night and day.... We will do anything to make them concede our request.' The Women's Political Club met weekly to practice oratory and lobbying, and spiced their literature with appeals to 'militance'. Reportedly, members went about with a copy of Henry George's single tax propaganda and even read it at their meals. (George was a famous advocate of the public ownership of land and commanded a large following among the working class.) Cunningham also organized a 200-strong junior militant club as well as a socialist women's group.[77]

In general, however, socialist intervention in the suffrage movement was negligible. With the absence of an organized working women's presence, they could not parallel their accomplishments in the male trade union movement. Augusta Stowe-Gullen and Flora MacDonald Denison kept them at arm's length, despite certain shared views and allegiances. The role of socialists in the suffrage movement was also very dependent on their general isolation. Quite apart from the fact that some of their activity around suffrage was strategically ineffective, socialists were not in a position to alter the relation of forces in the suffrage movement.

Quite apart from the occupational hazards which influenced the development of maternal feminism, the lack of a consciously anti-capitalist perspective subjected the suffrage movement to certain basic imperatives of capitalism, which, in turn, maternal feminism expressed. The denial of women's rationality, self-interest and autonomy was bound up with the sexual economics of the capitalist production cycle. The family, with its unpaid housewife, was and still is an essential institution which privatizes the many costs incidental to sustaining present and future generations of workers. Subjecting the function of unpaid household labour to liberal standards of market rationality, self-interest and autonomy would challenge its very fundamentals. Liberalism has therefore always suffered a blind spot in its inability to apply its ostensibly 'universal' values to women. Instead, feudal notions of inherited station and obligation have prevailed.[78]

Far from challenging the terms of this relationship, maternal feminism highlighted additional obligations for women in the family. Just as factory production of household goods was diminishing women's productive functions in the home, women's social role in the home was invested with new importance. In the late nineteenth century, as social institutions became less conscientiously moralistic, wives became mothers. A lengthier process of education was increasingly seen as training in morally neutral skills. This kind of development, together with the moral anonymity of an industrial city where work and community were forcefully separated, put a premium on privately-derived restraints and anxieties. Heightened responsibilities for mothers were a prerequisite in this modern, streamlined industrial order. Maternal feminists interpreted their new responsibilities as part of a package deal leading to extended social responsibilities and rights.

Despite the strivings of women in the turn-of-the-century period, they were unable to overcome the occupational and social injunctions of the era. Maternal feminism expressed the adaptation of women's strivings to these overpowering pressures. It is this adaptation which led to the contradictory nature of maternal feminist aspirations and which accounts for the ultimately disappointing and limited ideological and political gains made by the first self-conscious generation of women's activists in Canadian history.

CHAPTER TWO

Flora MacDonald Denison: Canadian Feminist

Deborah Gorham

———————————•◦•———————————

One of the most fascinating women in the Toronto suffrage and reform scene was Flora MacDonald Denison, writer, dressmaker and leader of the national suffrage organization. Denison stood apart from the early women doctors involved in suffrage as well as from the later generation of suffragists who were the wives of the business and commercial middle class because of her unorthodox beliefs and her lower middle-class status as a dressmaker married to an unsuccessful salesman. Denison's democratic vision and 'ethical-social critique of capitalist society' along with her interest in spiritualism and her rejection of orthodox Christianity gave her a broad conception of social change which manifested itself in an interest in socialism near the end of her life. While she never accepted a strictly Marxist approach to social inequality, her faith in democracy, her castigation of 'caste' and her respect for personal autonomy gave her feminism a tenor different from the predominant notions of the reformers. This is not to say that Denison did not use or partially accept the maternal feminist arguments; however, she did not succumb to the dominant view that the woman's vote represented a vote for purity, nor did she envision woman's contribution as merely social housekeeping.*

This study of Denison provides a glimpse of the radical side of suffrage and reform and demonstrates the potential of the women's movement for a thoroughgoing critique of domesticity, marriage and work. US feminist, Charlotte Perkins Gilman wrote several books, which influenced Denison, in which she advocated a complete rearrangement of domestic life to free women from the burden of housekeeping. This biographical study suggests that with more research, other women, less famous, but perhaps as unorthodox, may be discovered who shared some or all of the radical critique.

———————————•◦•———————————

* See Wayne Roberts, 'Six New Women: A Guide to the Mental Map of Women Reformers in Toronto,' *Atlantis*, Vol. 3, No. 1 (Fall 1977), pp.145-64.

The fact that women were important participants in social reform movements during the decades immediately preceding World War I is significant both for the history of Canadian social reform and for the history of Canadian women. Like their counterparts among male social reformers, a large number of the women who involved themselves in reform activities were inspired by the socially concerned Christianity of the 'social gospel' movement: above all, most Canadian women reformers wished to strengthen the Canadian family and maintain the moral purity of family and community life. Most of these women were themselves convinced that men and women had different natures, and therefore had different tasks to perform. Yet women all over the country were, often without conscious intention, expanding and therefore altering their own roles as women through their participation in such activities as the temperance movement, urban reform and cultural development. From a desire to create better homes and families, women were led to assert their own political rights and thus, gradually, the role of the Canadian wife and mother was extended from the private sphere to the public. Ultimately even that most daring of nineteenth-century women's rights demands, the vote, could be made in Canada from an ideological position that did not challenge the bourgeois notion of womanhood.

Much, but not all, of Canadian women's activism fits this picture of conservative social reform. But in the period before World War I, some women, like some men, had a more radical vision than that implied by social gospel reformism; and some women had more radical views about the position of women than those implied by the demands of conservative 'maternal' or 'social feminism'. A few of these more radical figures achieved positions of importance in reform movements. Flora Macdonald Denison, who was for several years a prominent figure in the leadership of the Canadian suffrage movement, was one such woman, a woman whose life history is worthy of analysis not least because she provides a contrast to such well-known Canadian women activists as Nellie McClung and Emily Murphy. Denison, unlike McClung and Murphy, had little sympathy for the temperance movement, and even less for organized Christianity. About the church, for example, she made many statements like this one, delivered in a suffrage speech:

> The Church with its doctrine of the total depravity of the human race founded upon its assertion of the inherent wickedness of woman has built up a false morality, a mock modesty, a sneaking hypocrisy. It has murdered innocence.... The teaching of the Church is at the bottom of women's slavery.

At the time, such attacks on Christianity were both unwelcome and unusual. How did a woman who made such statements, who supported divorce, birth control and even attacked the sanctity of the nuclear family, become leader of Canada's national suffrage organization, a position she held from 1911 to 1914? What were the influences on her development and what effect did she have on the women's movement in Canada?[1]

At first sight, Denison's early circumstances appear to have furnished unlikely soil for the nourishment of a nineteenth-century radical feminist. Flora MacDonald Merrill was born in 1867 and grew up in the small Ontario towns of Belleville and Picton. Picton, in her youth, was a prosperous, complacent, attractive town, the sort of place that is proud of its solid citizens rather than of its rebels. Flora, moreover, was born into a family whose roots went back to the early period of the town's history. Her grandfather had been a pillar of the community, and his son, Judge Edwards Merrill, who was Flora's uncle, followed in his father's footsteps. For a girl born into such a milieu, the transition from girlhood to an adulthood shaped by the dominant culture of the community might well have been easy, tranquil and inevitable. The position of women in a community like Picton was well defined. As wives and mothers they were expected to provide both a spiritual and a material focus for their homes. At the same time, they were encouraged to accept a limited definition of their lives, a definition that emphasized their secondary position in relationship to men. As Denison wrote some years after she had left the town, in Picton:

> [G]irls took their position from what their fathers were, women took their
> position from what their husbands were. As long as they had a brother or a
> husband to support them they were respectable. They did not lose caste
> and when old enough captured a husband on whom they were dependent.[2]

Flora escaped the usual fate of Picton womanhood largely because of her father's business misfortunes. Although her uncle Edwards became a judge, her father was both less wise and more adventuresome than his elder brother. Trained as a teacher, George Merrill became dissatisfied with life as master of the Picton grammar school, and in the early 1860s, embarked on a mining venture. He took his family with him into the wilderness to prospect, and it was there that Flora, the sixth of a family of eight children, was born. The mine proved to be a financial disaster from which George Merrill never fully recovered. He and his family moved to Belleville, but he was not able to find steady employment and began to drink heavily. In the light of these circumstances, the years of Flora Merrill's childhood and early youth must have been difficult. After attending school in Belleville, she went to live in Picton with an aunt and uncle, where she attended the Collegiate Institute. She left school at fifteen, and like many other young women from impoverished but genteel backgrounds, she took up teaching. But she soon abandoned rural schoolteaching and went to Toronto, where she trained at a commercial school and worked for an insurance company. The Merrill family had relatives who had settled near Detroit, Michigan, and in the late 1880s she left Toronto and moved to Detroit, where it appears that she did office work.

The first twenty years of Flora's life are important, because in the circumstances of her childhood and youth we can see patterns that help to explain the choices she made as an adult. Although her immediate family was close and the family members supportive of one another, they were beset with financial and personal misfortune. Moreover, as a family group they had suffered a loss in status relative to the other branches of the Merrill family. In the context of the social structure of the period, they had become marginal individuals with weakened connections to the established middle class. For Flora, this marginal status may have been a benefit. Like her father, she had a sense of adventure, and the fact that her position as a young woman was not firmly defined may have made it relatively easy for her to leave her family and make an independent life for herself.

To what extent were the beliefs of Denison's later years foreshadowed in her girlhood? It is difficult to answer this question, because nothing that she wrote before she was twenty-five survives. However, certain aspects of her later beliefs seem to have had their origins in her childhood. Her unorthodox ideas about religion, for instance, probably arose from her family's attitude towards the supernatural. Although from the outside they appeared to be conforming Protestants, several members of the family also believed in parapsychology. As Flora described it in the autobiographical novel she later wrote, they were forced to conceal their psychic gifts for fear of arousing suspicion and hostility. The eldest daughter Mary, who died in 1880, supposedly had extraordinary psychic powers and Flora admired her intensely. The sense that her range of experience was unusual apparently made Flora sensitive to alternatives to orthodoxy even as a girl, and the pattern of religious belief that she adhered to throughout her life was established before she left Picton. It combined a rejection of orthodox Christianity for being small-minded and stifling, with an openness to mysticism. Later in her life this openness led her to embrace groups like the Free Thought movement of the American poet Ella Wheeler Wilcox, and Theosophy, which was the religious movement that she found most congenial.

Even though she did not become an outspoken advocate of women's rights until after 1903, like many girls, she resented with an instinctive feminism the treatment meted out to her. Recalling her childhood feelings about churchgoing in Picton, she wrote that she 'must have been born a rebel, because she resented the Church and its doctrines most because women were given such a miserable position within its sacred portals'.[3]

Flora's actions also indicate that she conceived her dislike of small towns and her romantic love of cities as a girl. In 1910, she wrote of Toronto in glowing terms, describing it as a place where the 'mental atmosphere is kept clear and crisp by the spirit of investigation and controversy, where one is not ostracised because he doubts many of the old fossilized beliefs ...' And she may well have had her own youthful experience in mind when she castigated the mentality of a small town in the following comment:

> They do not seem to know that in the big centres women are using their time, energy and brains and money to make conditions better for the daughters that will probably one day drift to the cities.[4]

Denison's own first years of independence in the city were not easy, and at one point, soon after she had moved to Michigan, she was so unhappy that she considered suicide. But life improved for her and it was in Detroit that she began her career as a journalist. It was also in Detroit that she met her husband, Howard Denison, who must remain a shadowy figure in this account, because little is known about him. The reasons why Flora chose to marry Denison are unclear; probably the marriage was the result of a sudden (although shortlived) romantic attachment. The couple were married in Detroit in August 1892. The previous February, when Howard had been courting her, he had written the following verse in the autograph book that she had kept since her girlhood in Picton:

May our hopes grow bright with promise
Emblems of the years to come
When we round our hearthstone rally
And the toils of day are done
In these happy peaceful hours

Flora MacDonald Denison:

May our lives more closely blend
And loving union bind us until life's journey ends.[5]

Flora and Howard may have entertained such conventional sentiments about marriage in 1892, but any such illusions must have been rapidly dispelled. Although they may have been fairly happy together during the early years of their marriage, they do not appear to have ever been very compatible and they later separated. Flora, who became such an outspoken advocate of independence for women, was spared any ill-judged flirtation with dependency. Howard Denison was not reliable, and he was especially unreliable about money. In consequence, Flora, unlike most middle-class wives, was always financially self-supporting. Howard does not appear to have been a major figure in any aspect of her life after the first year of their marriage. His great contribution to Flora's happiness was to father their son Merrill, who was born in 1893 in Detroit. Merrill, who grew up to be a successful writer, was Flora's only child. Even when he was still a young man, he was as much a friend as a son, and in her later years he became the most important person in her life.

Soon after Merrill's birth, the Denison family moved back to Toronto. Here Flora Denison began working as a dressmaker, the occupation that from that time forward was her major source of paid employment. After a brief time as a small dressmaker, she was hired in 1898 by the Robert Simpson Company as a 'modiste' and given the responsibility of managing their custom dress department. She remained at Simpson's until 1905, when she set up in business for herself, as 'Mrs. Denison — Costumer'.

Her choice of occupation was of crucial significance in the formation of Denison's political ideology. The needle trades were a fundamental part of the economy of early twentieth-century Canadian cities. In Toronto, in the first decade of the century, the clothing industry overshadowed all other industrial activity. It played a major role in women's employment, and in terms of numbers, women dominated the trade. But although more women than men worked in the trade, women were clustered in the most poorly paid jobs and suffered the most exploitative working conditions. Conditions were worse in small shops than they were in factories, and the most vulnerable workers of all were outworkers, who tended to be female.[6]

The fact that Denison made her living from an industry that had such significance in the history of women's employment forced her to think about the economic structure of society and about women's place in that structure. Denison was acutely aware of conditions in the needle trades; after all, she saw them at first hand in her work for Simpson's. At the same time that she went to work for Simpson's, she began contributing to *Saturday Night* and the plight of the sweated needlewoman was a theme that she wrote about frequently. In a column written for *Saturday Night* in 1898 she asked, 'Have I a right to two coats while a more deserving brother has none? Have I a right, even as mistress of a Government House, to 500 gowns while my sister has not enough to cover her nakedness, she having done more in her life to produce wealth than I?' In another column, her comments took the form of a poem, which she entitled 'The Woman With the Needle':

> Pale blue lips — a ghastly picture
> Stitching she to dress a world
> That, perchance, does not dress her
> Nor indeed but barely feeds her,
> Hardly gives her bread enough
> To keep soul and flesh together
> This 'The Woman with the Needle'[7]

Although she was sensitive to the plight of the sweated needlewoman, Denison was faced with a basic ambiguity in her approach to injustice in the needle trades, since she was after all a participant in that injustice. She began as a highly skilled worker in the trade. Later, as a manager for Simpson's, she was to some extent an agent of the exploitative conditions she abhorred. Finally, she was the owner of a small shop. Much of the labour for Denison's was done by Denison herself and her sisters and nieces, but some outside labour was employed, and although she may have treated her workers well, she did not pay them unusually high wages. During her years as a successful dressmaker, Denison was in fact caught between the need to support her family and certain social causes, and the awareness that the business she worked in existed only because of an exploitative economic structure.[8]

The particular area of the clothing trade in which Denison worked mirrored the injustices of the social structure with unusual poignancy. Both during the period she worked for Simpson's and when she worked for herself, Denison made clothes for Toronto's wealthy. The following newspaper story gives some idea of the sort of 'creation' for which she became well known:

Denison, the clever modiste of the Robert Simpson Co. made a number of the swell dresses worn at the Yacht Club Ball. One donned by a leading society lady was of black moiré with billows of white accordion pleated chiffon, overstrung with cut jet about the shoulders, a necklace of diamonds and pearls giving an elegant effect.

A dress of this sort is not primarily designed to serve as clothing in the usual sense of providing warmth, comfort or even adornment. It was, rather, a way of advertising the social status of the wearer. While Denison may have enjoyed the aesthetic challenge and craftsmanship involved in producing such garments, she found it increasingly difficult to reconcile her work with her political beliefs. She hated snobbery and objected to symbols that separated one class from another. She believed it was wrong, for instance, for employers to ask domestic servants to wear a distinctive uniform. Her occupation thus came into conflict with her ideas about class structure. It also came into direct conflict with her feminist convictions. Turn-of-the-century female dress was uncomfortable and unhealthy; heavy skirts impeded the wearer's movement and tight lacing could damage the internal organs. Although Denison was not much concerned with dress reform in the 1890s, perhaps as her own health began to be damaged by unwise clothing, it later became an issue of major importance for her. 'Women,' she said in a speech on dress reform, 'have been deformed by tight corsets, high heels and pointed toes, and could the long list of female ailments tell of their origin, they would lay the blame on the altar of dame fashion.' The cure for harmful fashions was sex equality: 'The economically free and self-supporting woman is the most hopeful earnest of a saner dress for women.'[9]

If a middle-class standard of life had offered no attractions to Denison, she might have abandoned her dressmaking business and attempted to support herself in a way that would have involved fewer compromises with her beliefs. She liked comfortable surroundings and, much as she disapproved of it, she was not immune to conspicuous spending. Her inability to reject the symbols of middle-class status can be partly explained by the fact that the snobbery of Toronto society that she objected to so much was directed at times against herself. As a working woman who was the wife of a travelling salesman, she was never genuinely acceptable to the ladies who dominated middle-class social reform activities in the city, and the snubs she received were wounding to her.

In view of the contradictions inherent in her own situation, it was not surprising that the social philosophy Denison developed avoided the question of the inevitability of economic exploitation under capitalism. The most fundamental element in her ideology was a naive belief in democracy. Denison believed intensely in the dignity and importance of labour, but she also believed that all labour was equal in value. The democratic conviction that led her to insist that the servant was equal to her mistress also led her to regard the labour of the factory owner, if honourably performed, as identical in quality to that of his workers. Although Denison was attracted to socialism, even after the First World War, during her most radical period, she never accepted the analysis of capitalism which by definition views the capitalist employer's relationship to his workers as exploitative. Exploitation, in Denison's view, came about because people failed to perceive their true spiritual comradeship with one another, and instead, set up what she called barriers of 'caste'. The notion of 'caste' as a metaphor for inegalitarianism recurred in Denison's writings throughout her life. By caste, she meant social exclusiveness and snobbery. Caste created the gulf between servant and master, but in an ideal society, everyone would work and people would develop mutual respect for each other's work. They would see each other as comrades and companions, and would recognize the unique importance of each individual. As she said in a speech made at a meeting of Toronto's Progressive Thought Club in 1907, 'I despise the spirit that makes people apologize because they have to work.... Workers are necessary, but servants and slaves are a disgrace.'[10]

The most important source for Denison's democratic philosophy was the work of the American poet Walt Whitman. As a child from a Scottish background, she had been raised on the democratic poetry of Robert Burns, but as a young adult she discovered Whitman, whom she found even more inspiring. Denison's interest in Whitman involved much more than an appreciation of his work as a poet. For many people in the early twentieth century, Whitman was a folk hero, the central figure of a mystical, quasi-religious movement. The Whitmanite movement, which burgeoned after the poet's death, spread from the United States to Latin America, France and Russia, and it had adherents in Canada, including Denison. After 1916, she was instrumental in establishing the Whitmanite Fellowship of Canada, but even before this period, Whitman had a great influence on her. Her Whitmanite beliefs influenced her views on religion, on nature and on the women's movement, as well as on democracy.[11]

The most important period in Denison's life began in the early 1900s, when she was already in her mid thirties. In this period she left Simpson's to set up in business for herself, and became actively involved in the women's movement. An interest in feminism can be found in her early writings, and in her own life she embodied the principles she was later to articulate, but it was her meeting with Emily Howard Stowe, the pioneer Toronto suffragist, that caused her instinctive feminism to flower into an open commitment. Denison met Dr. Stowe not long before Stowe's death in 1903. Dr. Stowe not only introduced Denison to the women's movement, but also befriended and encouraged her. Denison found a central cause around which to focus the sense of injustice she felt both on her own behalf and on behalf of others she perceived as less fortunate. As she said a few years later: 'To the question of an interested admirer ''are you a socialist, a Christian, a spiritualist, a freethinker, an Ibsenite'' I would simply reply ''I am a suffragist.'' '[12]

Denison very quickly became an important figure in the Toronto suffrage movement. By 1906, she was secretary of the Dominion Women's Enfranchisement Association, and in the same year she went to Copenhagen as the official Canadian delegate to the Third World Conference of the International Suffrage Alliance. Denison had never been to Europe before, and the experience of meeting the leading suffrage activists from all over the world and participating in the conference increased both her own self-confidence and her awareness of the strength of the suffrage cause. The sense of euphoria that she gained from the conference is vividly evoked by the pencilled note she scribbled to herself on her copy of the conference program: 'Henrick Ibsen said — women will solve the problem of humanity.'[13]

Denison came away from the International Alliance meeting with a deepened understanding of the suffrage movement. Her experiences strengthened her conviction that Canadian women activists need not feel isolated. As she put it in a 1912 speech, 'The present day movement for women's suffrage is neither local, nor intermittent but international in scope.' Denison also changed her mind about the militant tactics that were being employed in England by the Women's Social and Political Union. When asked to comment on these tactics before her trip, she had told a *Toronto News* reporter that she thought the demonstrations in Parliament Square were 'unwomanly'. But after hearing Dora Montefiori, the WSPU 'unofficial' delegate in Copenhagen, Denison became an immediate convert to the cause of militancy. She said on her return:

Having met Miss Montefiori ... I am inclined to think that the press has woefully exaggerated the behaviour of the women who are not lunatics or fanatics, but earnest women anxious and willing to sacrifice themselves that the race may be benefitted and moved nearer to an ideal civilization of cooperative brotherhood and sisterhood. [14]

In a Canadian Suffrage Association pamphlet entitled 'Women's Suffrage in Canada', Denison explained that Emily Howard Stowe was the founder of the movement in Canada, but that after the first few years of activity, 'interest lapsed and it was only kept alive by the devotion of Dr. Stowe-Gullen,' Emily Howard Stowe's daughter. It was revived, she said, in 1906 'by Flora MacDonald Denison going as a delegate for Canada to the International Suffrage Alliance in Copenhagen'. Denison was not exaggerating the importance of the role she played in the suffrage movement in Toronto in the period from 1906-1914. This was the most energetic period in her life and the suffrage movement benefited from her enthusiasm in several ways. [15]

Although she was active in the leadership structure of the suffrage movement, her greatest contribution to the cause was as a journalist. Before 1906, Denison wrote for a variety of publications, including the *Detroit Free Press* and *Saturday Night,* and she published her autobiographical novel, *Mary Melville,* in 1900. But not until 1906, when she began writing for the *Toronto Sunday World,* did journalism become Denison's most important contribution to the reform causes to which she was committed. The *World* was a 'people's' newspaper with a large circulation. The paper's reporting style was informal and breezy; it used innovative techniques in its layout that the more respectable dailies avoided; and its commitment to social reform was usually expressed through the kind of muckraking journalism that relies heavily on personalized vignettes, rather than on an analytic exploration of social issues. Denison became an irregular contributor to the *World* in 1906. In September 1909, the newspaper's editor agreed to make her column into a regular weekly feature. For some years the column was entitled 'Under the Pines', and was in theory devoted to the women's movement, although Denison's wide conception of the movement meant that she also discussed other social issues. In 1911, she changed the title of the column to 'The Open Road Towards Democracy', after Walt Whitman, so that she could easily discuss a wider variety of issues. After 1913 her contributions again became irregular and usually appeared under the heading 'Stray Leaves from a Suffragette's Notebook'. Through her column, she provided her readers with two different kinds of reporting. Not only did she publish detailed reports of local, provincial and national activities of the women's movement, she also exposed her readers to wide-ranging discussions of issues related to the ideology of feminism. [16]

In keeping with her conviction that Canadian women were part of an international movement and that, therefore, they could benefit from contact with activists from outside the country, Denison was instrumental in bringing several well-known suffrage speakers from the United States and Britain to Toronto. She played a major part in bringing the American leader Anna Howard Shaw to Toronto to the International Council of Women meeting in 1909, and it was solely because of her interest and enthusiasm for the English militants that Emmeline Pankhurst came to Toronto during her American tour of 1909. In 1909, Denison's enthusiasm for Pankhurst and the Women's Social and Political Union was at its height. Pankhurst was her heroine, 'the liberator of her sex', and she perceived the women of the WSPU as being totally selfless and as especially admirable because they spoke for working-class as well as middle-class women.[17]

In addition to these efforts to publicize the women's movement, Denison made substantial financial contributions to suffrage activism in Toronto during the years 1906-13. She and her family lived in a large, centrally located house, and for several years it served not only as home and business premises for the family, but also as the headquarters for the Canadian Suffrage Association. In addition, in 1910 Denison also paid the rent on a separate headquarters on Yonge Street, complete with a vegetarian suffrage restaurant. She also paid her own way when she represented Canada overseas in 1906 and again in 1913, and it appears to have been her money that was advanced when suffrage speakers came to Toronto.[18]

Denison's energy, enthusiasm and material assistance help to explain why she so quickly became a major suffrage activist. Up until 1910, the leading suffrage workers in Toronto were a group of women doctors, of whom Augusta Stowe-Gullen was the most important. They were a somewhat insular group, and by 1905, new ideas and new energy must have been welcome. Denison found herself accepted by them, even though as a small businesswoman with a husband of questionable social status, she was not really of the same class as the lady doctors. She maintained good relationships with most of them and fairly close friendships with a few. Margaret Gordon was a good friend, and so was Augusta Stowe-Gullen, although Dr. Gullen appears to have been somewhat jealous of Denison's success as a speaker. In any case, Denison was much more acceptable to the doctors than she was to the women who became adherents of the suffrage cause after 1910, many of whom, ironically enough, were drawn into the movement because of a new vigor for which she herself was largely responsible.[19]

CAMROSE LUTHERAN COLLEGE
LIBRARY

In prewar Toronto, most women's activism was more directly related to conservative social reform than it was to a commitment to equal rights for women. The temperance movement had been a well-spring for women's activism since the 1870s and it continued to be important in the new century. In Toronto, as in other large cities, concerned citizens became involved with urban reform in the early twentieth century. Much urban reform energy went into the development of private charities and limited public welfare policies that were designed to alleviate the distress of industrial capitalism. Many women participated in such activities, sponsoring refuges and creches, or working for better public health policies. The majority of these women reformers accepted the belief that women ought to be primarily mothers and custodians of the family. For them, conversion to women's suffrage came only when they were convinced that the vote was necessary to achieve the social ends for which they were working. Their support for women's partici-pation in politics did not involve a fundamental challenge to society's dominant ideology. On the other hand, Denison, although she vigor-ously supported many of the same social reform measures and some-times even used 'social feminist' arguments, worked for the vote because it was a symbol of woman's personhood.

Denison was one of the few Canadian women activists who described herself as a feminist. The fact that the word 'feminist' gained widespread usage in the 1890s is of significance to the intellectual history of the women's movement. By the 1890s, the women's movement in England and in the United States had attracted so many adherents that its intellec-tual position was becoming increasingly amorphous. On the one hand, there were women activists like the American Elizabeth Cady Stanton, who not only supported the expansion of women's political rights but worked for other, more fundamental changes. On the other hand, there were women activists like the English novelist Mrs. Humphrey Ward, who were anti-suffragists. It seems likely that the word 'feminist' emerged at this time because of the need to identify those individuals who supported not merely an increased public role for women, but also a woman's right to define herself as autonomous, to regard herself, as Simone de Beauvoir later put it, as 'self' rather than 'other'. As the same split between radicals and conservatives began to become apparent in Canada in the 1900s, a few of the more radical women began to identify themselves as feminists. Denison was one of them.

In the period before the vote was achieved, Toronto women activists, both the conservative majority and the feminist minority, found that they could sometimes work together. The organization that provided the locus for the uneasy alliance between the disparate groups was the National Council of Women of Canada (NCWC). The Council's founder, Lady Ishbel Aberdeen, had a vision of an organization that would unite women of widely differing viewpoints. As she said in a message to the International Council meeting, held in Toronto in 1909, the International Council of Women was respected

> because its National Councils have, as a whole, steadily endeavored to be truly representative, and to include women from all classes and creeds and sections of society. We have ever to remember that to be truly national ... we must be able to unite the most conservative women of each country together with the most progressive, not forgetting the great body of middle average opinion. [20]

In the period before the First World War, the attempt to draw together the progressive and the conservative elements under the aegis of the National Council appears to have been at least partially successful. The suffrage women wished not only to have a place in the Council, but to convert the Council to support for the vote. Many of the suffrage women were genuinely committed to the National Council of Women. Others, like Denison, became active in it because of their suffrage involvement. The tensions between the progressive and the conservative women in fact centred around the suffrage issue. The National Council's endorsement of suffrage in 1910 did not come about without a struggle. There were many women who were opposed to it on principle, and it appears that few of the most active Local Council women in the Toronto area in the period before 1910 were active suffragists. [21]

It was the new suffrage interest of the Local Council women after 1910, combined with Denison's open hostility to the Council, that brought about her removal from her leadership position in the Toronto suffrage movement. Denison had for many years been critical of the Council's conservatism. As she said in a 1909 column, it 'endorses measures only after it is quite sure it is the popular thing for it to do'. When, as president of the Canadian Suffrage Association, she became an *ex officio* member of the Council executive, she sat as an avowed outsider. During the first year of her participation, she was a quiet but persistent critic of some policies, but in 1912, her differences with the majority of the executive became acute over the issue of the treatment of sex offenders. [22]

'White slavery' and child prostitution were major issues in Britain, the United States and in Canada in the period from 1910 to World War I. The National Council of Women took the issue up, and their concern reached a climax in their 'women's platform' of 1912. In this statement, the Council not only demanded that the age of consent be raised to eighteen, it also recommended stringent penalties for procurers and brothel keepers, including a mandatory sentence of flogging for all male procurers. Although Denison herself saw the 'white slave traffic' as a problem, she believed that the underlying causes of prostitution were economic. 'Reform must be sought first of all by reforming the bad surroundings due mainly to bad economic conditions which sweep young people into vice wholesale ...,' she wrote in 1910. She realized that it was not procurers who were the problem, but rather that the whole social system was responsible for the existence of prostitution. Moreover, she disapproved of violence as a form of punishment. Therefore, in 1912, she spoke out vigorously against the flogging recommendation both within the National Council executive and in the press.[23]

Denison's courage was admirable, but her opposition to majority Council opinion only served to widen the rift between herself and women like Mrs. Huestis, the leader of the Toronto Local Council, and Mrs. Boulton, the vice president of the Women's Canadian Club, both of whom were representative of the new, more conservative group of suffrage supporters. The leaders of this new wave of suffrage activism in Toronto included Sonia Leathes and L.A. Hamilton. Although the evidence is limited, there is some indication that they and their followers found Denison unsuitable as a leader because of her social status. In Denison's papers there is an ugly anonymous letter of 1914 addressed to 'Mrs. Flora Dennison, Dressmaker', which reads in part:

... you had better keep yourself quiet on the subject of the honored president of the Equal Franchise. What did you or your party ever do for the cause compared to her. The fight is right out of the dressmaking class with the help of Mrs. Leathes and good ladies such as Mrs. Meridith and Mrs. Boulton and for them suffrage in Toronto would be among the first people. Keep to your own class ...[24]

The 'Equal Franchise' referred to in the letter was the rival organization, the 'Equal Franchise League', which the dissident women established in 1912. This split was very painful to Denison, but during 1912 and 1913 her old friends in the suffrage movement supported her and she retained her presidency of the Canadian Suffrage Association. 1913 was the climax of her suffrage career; in that year, she went to a suffrage rally in Washington, D.C. as the leader of the Canadian delegation and later, she attended the International Suffrage Alliance conference held in

Budapest. On her way back from Budapest, she spent some time in England and renewed and strengthened her ties with the Women's Social and Political Union. This time she joined the wspu and spoke from the platform at a large Caxton Hall meeting.[25]

Denison's support for the wspu during the period of its most overt violence was too much even for her supporters in the Canadian Suffrage Association and she resigned as leader in 1914. The Association made her a handsome tribute on the occasion of her resignation, and she maintained personal contact with both Margaret Gordon and Augusta Stowe-Gullen, but her close ties with the suffrage movement in Toronto were broken for good after 1914.

Flora MacDonald Denison, although powerful, was always to some extent an outsider as an active suffragist. She was an outsider partly because of her social position, but the ideology she espoused also made her unwelcome to many conservative Toronto reformers. Denison was not an original thinker and the writing of popular pieces for a 'people's' journal encouraged her to blunt and simplify her thoughts rather than to refine and develop them. In spite of these limitations, she remained remarkably receptive to new and unusual ideas. Among the writers who influenced her feminism were the German Socialist August Bebel; the novelist Olive Schreiner, whose book *Women and Labour* had such a widespread influence in Britain and the United States; the free love advocate and socialist Edward Carpenter; and the American feminist sociologist Charlotte Perkins Gilman. Their work helped her to develop her own thoughts, and by 1909 she had worked out a fairly coherent feminist ideology.

Denison avoided making economic exploitation a central issue in her definition of the problem of class differences. However, she maintained that women's emancipation could only be achieved through their economic independence. She had arrived at this conclusion long before she had read any of the writers who influenced her, and it was a fundamental belief she retained throughout her life:

> Women's sphere should only be limited by her capabilities and I believe there is no sex in the human brain. Women are at last in the commercial arena and each day becoming more independent. Their final salvation will be achieved when they become the financial equals of men.[26]

The most important influence on the development of Denison's feminism was Charlotte Perkins Gilman, whose books *Women and Economics* (1898) and *The Home* (1903) remain today among the most thoroughgoing critiques ever written of the family under industrial capitalism. Gilman attacked the ideological superstructure associated with the idea of the home at the turn of the century, insisted that women had to be economically independent of men, and developed plans for communal living arrangements and the professionalization of domestic work as a solution to the problems of child care and housework. Denison was a regular reader of Gilman's magazine *The Forerunner* and she and Gilman were personal friends. Through Gilman's writings, Denison was able to develop her own interpretation of women's economic dependency and of the negative features and contradictions that were part of the structure of the family.[27]

Denison's attack on conventional family structure began with an assessment of the psychological damage for which the romanticization of the home was often responsible. As she wrote in 1909, many women were imprisoned in the home:

> Now we all know there is a great deal of maudlin sentiment written about the home, for we see on all sides, women whose lives are dull and monotonous if not tragic, just on account of this wonderful talk of the sacredness of the home. The only sacred spot is the place where human beings are so circumstanced that they can live up to their own ideals to the end of attaining happiness, and too long have the four walls of a kitchen crushed the lives of the mothers of the race kept there with the idea that her duty was in the home.[28]

In Denison's view, not only was the home confining, it also placed women in a damaging and contradictory position as workers. Encouraged by her reading of Gilman and Schreiner, she was able to articulate her belief that industrialization and the privatized home had deprived women of many of their previous functions. In addition, society often prevented women from doing new kinds of work by restricting them to occupations defined as 'feminine':

> Labour is not defined by gender and washing dishes is no more feminine than the sending of a marconigram is masculine. When the industries such as weaving and knitting and spinning were all done in the home this argument of women's sphere being in the home had more in its favor than it has today ...[29]

Unlike some writers, (including Gilman and Schreiner) Denison rejected the definition of the dependent woman as a parasite on the male wage earner. Although she did not put it in these words, she perceived that even though women's labour in the home might be defined as outside the market economy, and even though women's labour was much more restricted than it had been in the past, the work done in the home did have value. She expressed this view in her ironic comments on a speech made by a male speaker at the 1909 American Federation of Labor convention, which was held in Toronto:

> ... The very chivalrous speaker said 'we want to do away with not only child labor but we want to take women out of the industrial world and put her back in the home where she rightfully belongs.' This sounds real nice — but one might imagine by this that women in homes were not in the industrial world ... the home is an industrial institution, only most of the managers of homes have no eight-hour labor laws nor a scale of wages. The homemakers have been the workers with too often neither freedom, hours or wages.[30]

'Before there can be democracy in a nation while that nation consists of individual homes there must be democracy in the home,' wrote Denison, whose strongest objection to the middle-class home that employed servants was that it contained in microcosm all of the evils of the class structure of the larger society. Within the home, women were led to act out roles that both exemplified and reinforced class differences. The servant girl, like the wife, worked at a job where her hours and wages were unregulated. Moreover, her work was particularly odious, Denison believed, because she was forced to give deference: 'Badges of servitude, back doors, meals on kitchen tables, do not inspire girls with the idea of any dignity being attached to their position.' The home thus became the bulwark of the 'caste' system. The solution that Denison advocated first was to 'democratize' the home. By 1913, however, she was suggesting a much more radical redefinition of the home. Following Gilman, she asserted that housekeeping and child care should be taken over by trained specialists: 'Wifehood does not spell cook, not does mother love spell trained nurse.... Doing human work is what develops human character and human work is specialized activity in some social function ...' Denison was especially concerned that women should not be afraid to relinquish cooking: 'The one industry we seem to hang on to with a deathlike grip is the meal getting. Now meal getting ... is no more necessary to a home than the making of clothes.... I contend that meal getting should be and is in fact becoming a social industry.'[31]

The mythology surrounding the home presupposed that all women have men on whom they can be dependent. Denison repeatedly reminded her readers that this was not the case. The women who were worst off were those mothers who had to be out in a labour force that did not recognize their right to be there and that therefore provided them with little or no support or protection. Denison believed it was preferable for mothers of very young children to care for them themselves, and she advocated paying poor mothers a wage so that they would be free to do so. In spite of this belief, she herself was employed throughout her life, even when her son was very young. Denison's housekeeping problems were eased because she enjoyed the benefits of a communal household. For several years, she and her husband shared a home with an elder sister and her husband and family, thus approximating on a small scale the sort of shared living arrangement that Charlotte Perkins Gilman advocated.

Even though Denison was a working mother at a time when it was most unusual for a middle-class mother to be employed, she shared many of the attitudes of her period on the subject of motherhood. Both in theory and from her own experience, motherhood appeared to her to be fundamentally different from fatherhood. Her relationship with her son Merrill was intense and Denison's biggest private concern was that he should prepare himself for a fulfilling adulthood. She made great sacrifices for his welfare. In 1914, when she had been forced to resign as president of the Canadian Suffrage Association and when she was very short of money, she moved to the small town of Napanee and worked as a dressmaker so that she could earn enough money to send Merrill to the University of Pennsylvania to study architecture.

During the years he was at Pennsylvania and later when, much to her regret, he served in the Ambulance Corps and then in the US Army during the First World War, she wrote to him almost daily. In long letters, she not only expressed her concern for his welfare, but also shared with him all her thoughts, hopes and difficulties. In return, she received a gratifying amount of love and loyalty from Merrill, who answered his mother in letters that were equally as long and frank, and almost as frequent.[32]

Their correspondence reveals that even though Denison could at times express conventional Victorian ideas about motherhood, she achieved a level of frankness and intimacy with her son that would not have been possible had she subscribed to the prevailing view, so essential to the hierarchical, partriarchical family structure, that children owe their parents deference. Denison believed that parents should respect children's personal rights, she objected to the use of harshness in child rearing and she supported educational innovators like Froebel, who stressed the need for active, practical teaching in place of rote learning.[33]

In keeping with her progressive ideas about childhood and family structure, Denison also had remarkably advanced views about divorce and birth control. On divorce, she took the position that individual happiness is a more important and more moral goal than stability. She used a review of H.G. Well's novel, *The Passionate Friends*, as an opportunity to express her feelings about marriage and free love: 'Because youth inadvertently chooses the wrong mate, Mrs. Grundy, or the church or the state should not clamp and rivet them together to the eternal destruction of both. There is more immorality in unhappiness than appears on the surface ...'[34]

Denison commented less frequently on birth control than on divorce, but she supported it, although she usually emphasized its economic benefits rather than the increased personal freedom it gave women. In a 1909 article about the problem of neglected children, she chided those churches which attacked birth control as 'race suicide'. 'Better look after the children that are here,' she said, 'than to fuss too much about the ones that will never exist.' It took courage to make even such cautious statements as this one in a period when birth control was usually attacked as immoral. Denison's ideas about sexuality itself were influenced by her Whitmanite spiritualism. In her view, sex was not only necessary for both men and women, it was an exalted function, 'the keynote to all the harmonious rhythms of life. All life is permeated with the dual-sex male and female principle.... It is of utmost importance that women should recognize the great benefit to her in a proper complement in sex life.'[35]

Denison's feelings about women's problems with work, self-identity and love were very clearly expressed in an unpublished novel she worked on over a number of years. The novel reflects all of her strengths and weaknesses as a writer and thinker. Although it is crudely written and sentimental (the title *L'l Sue* is particularly unfortunate), the central character is a genuine 'new woman' with strong feminist convictions. In constructing the plot of *L'l Sue*, she employed a device common in nineteenth and early twentieth-century fiction. Sue is an orphan, whose mother is forced to give birth to her in a home for unwed mothers. The young orphan girl is placed as a servant in an upper middle-class Toronto household. She grows up, and in classic 'penny dreadful' style, the young son of the household falls in love with her, much to the disgust of his parents.

So far, so bad. But from this point onward, the novel diverges from the usual pattern. Sue resists her lover's blandishments, not because she is pure and virtuous, but because she values her independence. She leaves the household, trains as a secretary and eventually rejects his offer of marriage. She writes him a letter, telling him that she wants to earn her own living, which would not be possible if she were his wife, and expresses her fear that as a middle-class wife, 'I might become dulled with luxury, my ideals might topple, and following the line of least resistance, might drift into becoming the thing I now despise.' Sue tells her lover that she has been reading Edward Carpenter's *Love's Coming of Age* and suggests that he read it too. 'Our love has not come of age,' she says. 'We must see life and independence and achievement should be just as dear to me as to you.' At the end of the novel, Sue leaves Toronto for New York City. The closing scene finds her travelling down the Hudson River on the overnight train. She anticipates that in the morning she will find the city stretched out before her in the sunrise.

For all its sentimentality and blunted characterization, this is an avant garde novel, in the tradition of the novels with independent heroines written during this period. However, there are few 'new women' novels in which such a clear and unequivocal case is made for independence. Usually the heroine's desire for independence is defeated in the end: either she marries (like the heroine of Nellie McClung's novel *Purple Springs*), or she dies (like the heroine of Virginia Woolfe's first novel, *The Voyage Out*), or she kills herself (like the heroine in Kate Chopin's *The Awakening*). Male novelists like George Gissing and H.G. Wells often punish their heroines for seeking independence. In contrast, Denison is straightforward in the choices she has provided for Sue, whose independence should undoubtedly be seen as a reflection of her own courage and self-reliance.[36]

Denison's radical views on sex and marriage, coupled with her unorthodox ideas about religion place her in a tradition of revolt against puritan respectability that is more recognizable in an English or American context, but that was present to some degree in turn-of-the-century Canada. In England, much of this revolt against respectability appears to have been purely aesthetic or personal in nature. The work of the English artist Aubrey Beardsley, or the artistic and sexual adventuresomeness of the Bloomsbury Group can be put in this category. But some of the rebels who spoke out against the bourgeois family or bourgeois religion saw a connection between these institutions and a class structure that they believed was exploitative. Two such rebels were the English socialist Edward Carpenter and the American suffragist and 'free lover' Victoria Woodhull, both of whom were admired by Denison.

In Canada, protest of this sort was usually directed against the stifling effects of Canadian Protestantism. It manifested itself in such developments as the growth of the Theosophical movement in Toronto in the early 1900s and in the rise of groups like the Progressive Thought Club and the Rational Sunday League, of which Denison was vice president and in which Dr. Stowe-Gullen was also active. In 1908, when the Rational Sunday League protested against the attempt by sabbatarian groups to ban Sunday tobogganing, Denison actively participated in the campaign to forestall this restriction on Sunday recreation.

Denison was one of very few Canadians who took this revolt against respectability to the point of a revolt against the structure of the family and of conventional sexual morality. She was not as outspoken in public or as free in her private life as the Englishwoman Annie Besant or the American Victoria Woodhull. But it was more difficult to flout convention in Toronto than it was in New York or London, and within the limitations of her own life, Denison was attempting the same kind of revolt.

Denison's unconventionality flourished most vigorously during the last eight years of her life, which were not easy ones for her. Her break with the Toronto suffrage movement meant that the central focus of her public life was lost. In addition, after 1914, the Denison family's prosperity collapsed and she was in serious financial difficulties. Even under these circumstances, however, she reached out to new experiences and new ideas. After her unpleasant time as a seamstress in Napanee, she moved temporarily to New York State in 1916 and worked as a paid speaker and organizer for the New York State Women's Suffrage campaign, then in the final stages of the fight for state suffrage.[37]

The financial crisis in Denison's life came at the outbreak of World War I, and the war reinforced the uncertainty and apprehension in her life. She was personally repulsed by the war and came out in opposition to it very quickly. Throughout the world, the women's suffrage movement was divided over the issue. In England, Denison's old heroine Emmeline Pankhurst became an enthusiastic patriot, but other suffragists were horrified by the conflict. Denison was not only convinced that 'war is hell,' she also believed that the world could only be saved from war by the participation of women in politics. In a pamphlet entitled 'War and Women', she wrote that '... the male through centuries and centuries has been combative' whereas 'women's thought and action have always been constructive.' Her biggest private worry was that Merrill would join the war effort and her anxiety increased when he finally did so.[38]

Denison turned to the countryside for solace during this difficult period. Although she did not like small towns, she loved the wilderness. From the safe vantage point of city life, she romanticized its peace, beauty and lifegiving qualities. In 1910, with some money she and her husband had made in a lucky real estate deal, Denison bought 'Bon Echo', a beautiful Ontario highlands property. Bon Echo assumed great importance in her life after her return from New York State in 1916. Her goal was to transform it into a combination summer hotel and avant-garde spiritual community, dedicated to the memory of Walt Whitman. Meals were served from Women's Social and Political Union dinnerware, bearing the motto 'Votes for Women', and one guest remembers that Denison pressed him to contribute to Bon Echo's shaky finances.[39]

It was during this last period of her life that Denison's involvement with the Whitmanite movement and with the Theosophists overshadowed all her other public concerns. While she had always believed in the existence of a bond of comradeship among all the peoples of the earth, the war gave new urgency to this belief. Through the Whitmanites, she met a new group of people, including Horace Traubel, who was one of the most important American Socialist Whitmanites. In 1916, she started a magazine called the *Sunset of Bon Echo*, of which she managed to produce eight issues over the next few years. The *Sunset* did not have great literary merit, but it is interesting because it reflected the enthusiasm of some Canadians during this period for a social consciousness reinforced not by orthodox Christianity but by an eclectic spiritualism.[40]

In the postwar period, Denison used her membership in the Theosophical Society to become active for the first time in an organization with avowedly socialist aims. Throughout her journalistic career, she had given support and publicity to women's trade union activities and had on various occasions expressed a cautious interest in socialism. However she did not actively participate either in the trade union movement or in any socialist group until 1918, when she helped to organize the Social Reconstruction Group of the Toronto Theosophical Society. She served as its honorary president and attended the 1918 Convention that launched the Ontario section of the Canadian Labour Party as a delegate from the Social Reconstruction Group. In 1918 and 1919 the Canadian Labour Party advertised her as an official speaker and she gave some lectures for them on Whitman and on the women's movement.[41]

Had she lived longer, Denison almost certainly would have continued her involvement with these social concerns. But she was not in good health and when she contracted pneumonia early in 1921, she was not able to withstand it; she died on May 23, at the age of 54. Like another Toronto suffragist, Emily Howard Stowe, Denison left directions that she was to be cremated. In 1921, this could not be done in Toronto, and, following her last wishes, Merrill had her body transported to Buffalo, New York, where the cremation was performed.

Flora MacDonald Denison never wrote a great novel, nor did she achieve a reputation as a women's suffrage leader comparable to that of other Canadians like Nellie McClung, Emily Murphy or Emily Howard Stowe. Still, given her sex and the milieu into which she was born, it took courage, resourcefulness and resilience to create the life she made for herself.

As an early Canadian woman activist she was, no doubt, atypical. Certainly, by the time she had become leader of the Canadian Suffrage Association, women of her sort were in a minority. Conservative women had begun to dominate the movement by 1910, and even before that date, it is probable that Denison's rapid rise to a leadership position in the suffrage movement came about by default; it was probably a leadership vacuum that allowed her to become so quickly not only a major office holder but also an important influence as a publicist. Once having achieved her position, she did perform an important function: as an outspoken and articulate writer and speaker, Denison acted as a voice for that radical, genuinely feminist minority that formed a small but significant part of the early Canadian women's movement.

The Fédération Nationale Saint-Jean-Baptiste and the Women's Movement in Quebec[*]

Marie Lavigne, Yolande Pinard and Jennifer Stoddart

———————◆———————

Between 1916 and 1922, the federal government and all the provincial governments, except Quebec, extended the franchise to women. An intensification of the suffrage campaign after 1910 helped to bring the issue to a crisis in the war period. The federal franchise was granted as a war measure to aid the Borden government attempt to win approval for conscription. As part of the bargain, conscientious objectors and foreigners from enemy countries who had been naturalized since 1902 were disfranchised. Quebec women were also excluded on the grounds that they would vote against conscription and they did not receive the vote until 1940. Wartime manoeuvres cannot completely explain the particularly long battle of the Québécoises to obtain the franchise. Part of the answer to this puzzle is provided by Lavigne et al. in their article on the Fédération Nationale Saint-Jean-Baptiste (FNSJB).

Women joined the reform effort in Quebec (and especially in Montreal) to remedy the social problems associated with industrial capitalism. Despite its image as a rural province, Quebec actually experienced a level of industrialization comparable to Ontario in the late nineteenth and early twentieth centuries. The key difference lay in non-French Canadian control of industrial growth. The English-French split permeated the women's movement as well. Until the founding of the FNSJB in 1907, francophone women interested in reform and suffrage belonged to the Montreal Local Council of Women.

[*] An earlier version of this article appeared in the *Revue d'Histoire de l'Amérique Française*. See 'La Fédération Nationale Saint-Jean-Baptiste et les revendications féministes au début du siècle,' RHAF, 29, No. 3 (Dec. 1975), pp. 353-73.

FNSJB and the Women's Movement in Quebec

The history of the FNSJB *reflects the powerful conservative and nationalist forces at work in Quebec in the early twentieth century. This article examines the* FNSJB *and traces its evolution from a reform-oriented women's organization into a conservative, Catholic group, hindered at every turn by the clergy. Even the suffrage campaign was viciously attacked by the clergy, who saw it as a threat to the family. The authors also stress the extremely class-bound nature of its programs and structures; the women of the* FNSJB *favoured domestic education for the daughters of farmers and labourers and founded 'professional associations' to counter the possibility of revolutionary unionism, as well as to remind women to act within the confines of their family role. In conclusion, the authors see the decline of the Fédération after 1920 as an inevitable result of its contradiction between traditional and reform ideologies. The* FNSJB's *attempt to speak for all women, regardless of class, led to its demise.*

Feminism developed in Quebec at the end of the nineteenth century in the wake of the international women's movement. Inspired by the shared ideal of elevating women's status in society, groups whose values and actions otherwise varied as greatly as their ethnic and religious identities coalesced for a brief period in the name of feminism and in the wider cause of social reform.

In Montreal, most women's groups were associated with either the Montreal Local Council of Women (MLCW — anglophone) or, after 1907, with the Fédération Nationale Saint-Jean-Baptiste (FNSJB — francophone). For a short time, these groups achieved a remarkable unity of action in charity and reform, women's work and equal rights.

The FNSJB was the first large-scale association to bring together a significant number of Catholic lay women in the framework of the feminist movement. Although one of the important aspects of the history of Quebec women was the presence of dynamic and resilient religious communities, whose role in charity, education and hospital work had been an essential part of the social fabric for generations, feminist organizations seemed new and threatening to turn-of-the-century francophone society. Strong, outspoken women were nothing new in French Canada, provided they were shrouded in habit and veil. Parish priests encouraged women to join lay orders, confraternities and other Catholic associations. These associations, although definitely overshadowed by the work of the nuns, increasingly attracted restless and energetic upper-class women.[1]

Divided between the parlour, the parish hall and the convent, French-Canadian women, until the formation of the FNSJB, lacked a single, comprehensive association that could build on common concerns and mobilize women to confront the issues of the time.

The FNSJB attempted to direct the energies of lay women toward feminism and a cautious support of social reforms, but with only moderate success. Between 1907 and 1933, the birth, growth and decline of the FNSJB reflected the fate of feminism within French-Canadian society.

THE FNSJB: ORGANIZATION AND IDEOLOGY

Montreal women were encouraged to join the reform effort because of the need to solve the numerous social problems that arose with capitalism and rapid urban growth. Their practical experience in trying to gain reforms in public health, education, temperance and the working conditions of women and children made them question the limits imposed by their scanty education, their legal disabilities and their lack of political rights, and impelled many women to join the women's rights movement. The necessity of connecting social and political action and thus the reform movement and feminism, was becoming increasingly clear.[2] Marie Gérin-Lajoie, francophone feminist and founder of the FNSJB, made the link in her call to action, sent anonymously to newspapers.

> Ladies, do you realize how important it is for you to vote in the municipal elections.... You will complain that your son dissipates his health and fortune in the neighbourhood bar, you will be overcome with sorrow at the sight of your daughter whose virtue is gradually being eroded by immoral theatre, you will condemn the death of a child, contaminated by the filth in the streets and still you do not attempt to remedy these evils.[3]

Initially, francophones and anglophones worked together in the Montreal Local Council of Women, founded in 1893. However, the need for a Catholic and francophone organization that would better diffuse reform ideals among French-Canadian women became increasingly evident. Most of the francophone women in the MLCW were also members of the Ladies' Auxiliary of the Association Saint-Jean-Baptiste de Montréal, a French-Canadian nationalist association dedicated to the preservation of French culture. From this group, whose leading members were drawn from the higher echelons of Montreal society, came the idea of a federation independent of the MLCW that could bring together francophone women under the twin banners of Catholicism and the French language. In 1907, Caroline Béique and Marie Gérin-Lajoie founded the Fédération Nationale Saint-Jean-Baptiste. Gérin-Lajoie acted as the organization's centralizing force for over twenty years.[4]

The leaders of the FNSJB had already acquired, principally within the MLCW, solid experience in political and social action. This legacy influenced the style and direction of the Fédération in its first few years. Indeed, its very structure was the replica of the MLCW's. (The major exception was that the Bishop of Montreal appointed to the FNSJB a chaplain who ensured that all activities were carried out in accordance with church doctrine.) The FNSJB brought together in a loosely-knit association some twenty-two previously isolated women's groups, the membership of which totalled almost 12,000. It organized them into three sections: a charity section, composed of already existing charity societies; an education section, made up of professional groups like the Association of Women Journalists and the Ecoles Ménagères Provinciales (home economics schools); and an economic section, which included various professional and trade associations formed to improve the situation of working women. Each member society was homogeneous insofar as its members shared the same goals, occupation or social class. The FNSJB's activities were publicized through annual meetings, congresses, *semaines sociales* (weeks devoted to the study of chosen social problems) and, from 1913 on, through a monthly newspaper. *La Bonne Parole* reached a circulation of about 2,000 in the first few years.[5]

In the same way that the FNSJB divided its associated groups into three separate sections, it approached problems by sorting them into isolated issues, thus obscuring their common roots. This approach reflected both the bourgeois nature of the feminists' interests and their link to philanthropic and reform ideals of the era. Through the work of each section, the Fédération hoped to provide women with the moral and vocational education appropriate to their respective positions in the bourgeoisie or the working class.

The church-centred, French-Canadian nationalist ideology and antifeminist feeling created a climate ill-suited to modifications in the status of women. The formation of the FNSJB was also accompanied by a debate over 'good' and 'bad' feminism. 'Good' feminism was of course that which heeded the traditional boundaries defining women's existence. There was a consensus within the Fédération on the primacy of the homemaker and the family. The definitions of male and female roles were never questioned. This first generation of feminists believed men and women were complementary rather than equal beings and they defined the social role of women accordingly. They were content to attack the discrimination resulting from the division of men's and women's roles without questioning the full meaning of this inequality. At no time did their actions or writings reveal a search for the underlying causes of women's oppression. The fact that the Fédération adopted the nationalistic and Catholic content of the dominant ideology explains both the excessive caution of these first feminists and the contradictions in their philosophy.[6]

The FNSJB had triple roots: in social feminism, which subordinated the struggle for women's rights to wider and more urgent social reforms; in Catholic feminism, which was inspired by the church's social doctrine; and in the women's rights movement, which was linked to the liberal tradition of political reform.

The class interests of the FNSJB's members limited the content and scope of their action as women. The only solution envisaged for the problem of women's inferior status, as for all other social evils, was essentially legal and reformist. Over several decades, the Fédération gradually dissociated itself from the most controversial political and professional demands, withdrew further from the influence of the progressive reform movement and became increasingly influenced by Catholic feminism. Nonetheless, the progressive aspects of the FNSJB's ideology and its questioning of the status quo severely weakened some of the most persistent prejudices concerning women. Its action cleared the path for their political and legal emancipation.

SOCIAL REFORMS

The activities of the charity section corresponded most closely to the traditional ideal of women's social action. Yet, for the Fédération, charity took on a meaning more dynamic than that of the symbolic redistribution of the wealth from one social class to another with food hampers and old clothing. It was part of the movement for social reform. The preoccupations of the first years (1907-1920) of the Fédération's existence were characteristic of social feminism and differed significantly from those of the later years (1920-1933), which were increasingly tinged with Catholic moralizing.

The FNSJB played an important role in introducing French-Canadian women to a new way of looking at social problems. Scientific philanthropy, with its minute observation of situations, its personal supervision of remedial treatment and its insistence on the possible rehabilitation of poverty's victims, was a relatively new concept for the patronesses of charity in French Canada. The FNSJB opened up new perspectives on the practice of charity and connected these women with the reform movement and eventually with social feminism. For this reason, the social reforms demanded by the FNSJB were often identical to those made by the MLCW, at least until the 1920s. While the Fédération's main thrust was in the direction of reform in housing, child welfare, education and working conditions, purely philanthropic or charitable work continued to occupy many of its affiliated members. Indeed, it provided the necessary conservative counterweight to some of the Fédération's more radical demands.[7]

The Fédération's members, who defined women's sphere of action almost exclusively in terms of household and family problems, gave wholehearted support to any effort to aid children or preserve the home. Close links were formed with the Sainte-Justine Children's Hospital, for example. In Montreal, organizations providing pure milk attempted to reduce the rate of infant mortality in Montreal (among the highest in North America) by distributing pasteurized milk to deserving families. These efforts received the Fédération's enthusiastic support in publicity and finance campaigns. The FNSJB itself founded at least seventeen pure milk committees during the war and organized numerous lectures on public hygiene.[8]

Two committees were founded to assist mothers during and after childbirth. Maternal Assistance, set up in 1912, was designed to aid working-class women exhausted by numerous closely-spaced births. For those mothers who could afford domestic help the Committee for Mother's Helpers was set up some eighteen years later. In fact, Marie Gérin-Lajoie was convinced that one of the causes of the high rate of infant mortality was childbirth in hospitals. Her desire to keep women in their own homes prompted her to declare before the Quebec Commission on Social Insurance that the best way to help families was not by building new hospitals, but by directly assisting mothers.

> I ask you ... not to favour any movement which will pull women towards the hospital instead of keeping them at home. Even from her bed of pain, a mother can direct her household and ensure that everything is running smoothly.[9]

One of the FNSJB's major concerns in the prewar period was the campaign against liquor. Few women's organizations of the time could avoid taking a position on the question of alcohol abuse, generally seen to be the principal enemy of family and domestic peace. From the beginning, the Fédération collaborated with the MLCW in trying to limit the number of liquor outlets in the city and even drafted a bill to curtail liquor licences.

Each year the temperance committee joined with other like-minded organizations such as the Woman's Christian Temperance Union. In the 1910 Montreal municipal elections, the FNSJB appealed to the sense of solidarity of some 8,000 women voters (tax-paying owners and tenants) in order to garner votes for candidates espousing the platform of the Anti-Alcoholic League. For, like many feminists, the women of the FNSJB believed that women possessed a sense of political cohesiveness and a unique capacity for moral regeneration.

The abduction of women for prostitution, called at the time, 'the white slave trade', was another of the FNSJB's preoccupations. Although it is difficult to estimate the exact proportions of the problem in Quebec and Montreal, it seems to have captured the imagination of the well-to-do ladies of the Fédération and the MLCW. The Fédération organized a welcoming committee to supervise railroad stations where the recruitment of victims allegedly took place. It also mailed lists of respectable institutions to parish priests in the lower St. Lawrence region for the guidance of young parishioners who were job-hunting in Montreal.

Other social questions periodically claimed the Fédération's attention: the payment of prisoner's salaries to wives, medical assistance for the unemployed, the creation of child welfare courts, the need for better working-class housing, the presence of policewomen at each neighbourhood station and the fight against tuberculosis. Like other women's organizations in Canada, the FNSJB participated in the war effort and founded the francophone section of the Red Cross and the Patriotic Fund, despite French-Canadian resistance to participation in World War I.

The conservative orientation of the Fédération became increasingly evident after the beginning of the war. Criticism of 'immoral' movies and attempts to restrict the access of minors seemed to involve an increasingly large number of its members. Action focussed on posters outside theatres and on 'immoral' fashions. The FNSJB gradually followed more and more closely the steps of the clergy, who were attempting to impose a rigid code of puritanical ethics on Quebec society.[10]

The distinction between the prewar and postwar phases of the Fédération's work was not a radical one. There was, however, a major reorientation of its approach to social problems. During its first years of existence, the Fédération's social goals resembled those of other reform groups in Montreal, whatever their religious and ethnic affiliations. After the war, it had less and less in common with nondenominational feminist or reform organizations and was increasingly close to Catholic social doctrine.

The Fédération did allow lay women to study social problems more closely than before and conferred upon their work a level of organization and an aura of prestige hitherto possessed only by religious communities. The definition of works of charity was stretched to include moderate social changes (partly brought about through legislation) as solutions to specific problems. However, twenty years after the establishment of the FNSJB, its efforts in the direction of reform were once again firmly under church control. Reform largely subsided into Catholic and conservative philanthropy.

THE STRUGGLE FOR EQUAL RIGHTS

The absence of equal rights prompted feminists to consider their legal and political status as the source of their inferiority as women. Long drawn-out battles to gain the right to vote at all levels, to enter the male reserves of the professions and higher education and to abolish legal discrimination drained a great deal of feminist energy. Most of the struggles were begun under the instigation of the MLCW and continued in conjunction with the FNSJB.

At the turn of the century, although no Canadian women had the right to vote federally or provincially, widows and spinsters who paid taxes could vote in municipal elections. In Quebec, all property owners could vote for and were eligible to run for the position of school commissioner, and a few feminists tried to have a woman elected to the Protestant Board of School Commissioners. In reaction to their pressure, the provincial government simply withdrew their eligibility in 1899. The MLCW and the FNSJB challenged this restriction; women's participation seemed especially important, because 'the inspection of schools by nurses, the health of children, the education of girls are questions which chiefly concern women.'[11]

One of the most important struggles centred on municipal suffrage, especially since most of the feminists were already deeply involved in the urban reform movement. In 1902, when the Montreal municipal council tried to withdraw this right, then held by some 4,804 women tenants, Marie Gérin-Lajoie, the MLCW's legal expert, promptly drafted the Council's petition to the mayor and aldermen requesting its retention. The petition was partly responsible for the maintenance of these women's electoral rights.

French-Canadian women did not play a major role in the campaign for the vote on the federal level. In general, they supported any action taken in this direction. In 1917, when the *Wartime Elections Act* granted the vote exclusively to the relatives of soldiers, Marie Gérin-Lajoie wrote:

Women will vote because of the ties which bind them to the soldiers on the front; thus the suffrage is less a privilege conceded than a right granted to each soldier to vote several times through the intermediary of relatives.[12]

She believed that even those who opposed woman suffrage should demand its extension to all Quebec women, who would become 'a valuable help in the orientation of national policy' by demonstrating their opposition to the conscription law, which the Fédération denounced both for feminist and nationalist reasons.

On the provincial level the vote was still to be won, and meanwhile, intense campaigns were being organized to block the feminists' efforts. In order to strengthen the women's movement in Quebec, in 1921 Marie Gérin-Lajoie proposed the creation of a new committee to unite English and French supporters. However, the FNSJB's participation in the Provincial Franchise Committee was short-lived because Gérin-Lajoie was forced to bow before church pressure and resign the presidency.[13]

The extensive anti-suffrage campaign waged by conservative forces led Catholics to believe that advocating the vote for women was contrary to church doctrine. Marie Gérin-Lajoie consequently took steps in order to rally Quebec bishops to the cause. Faced with their refusal, she attended the congress of the International Union of Catholic Women's Leagues in Rome and requested explicit instructions on the point of view to take. The congress reiterated that woman suffrage was not incompatible with Catholic doctrine. Nonetheless, a resolution stipulated that episcopal approval must be obtained before taking any new initiatives in this direction. The FNSJB was consequently subordinated to the wishes of the bishop of Montreal and forced to withdraw from the suffrage movement.[14]

Access to the professions and higher education was of particular interest to feminists; however, there were divergent opinions concerning the question of compulsory education. Here the FNSJB was cautious in order to avoid antagonizing the clergy, which was vehemently opposed to any such project. In 1909, an article written for the Fédération in favour of compulsory education was censured by Montreal's Archbishop Bruchési. Its author, journalist Françoise (Robertine Barry) protested to Gérin-Lajoie:

I recognize that, for the Fédération to triumph, you need the force of the clergy, all-powerful in our country. Sacrifice your burnt offerings to them. I only hope that they will not ask you for yet greater sacrifices such as, for example, giving up woman suffrage. In the meanwhile, I pity you, because in sacrificing me you go against the sense of integrity, loyalty and justice which I have always admired in you, since, as you avowed yourself, you saw nothing reprehensible in what I wrote.[15]

Françoise's analysis of the clergy's influence on the Fédération was almost prophetic. In 1922 the struggle for suffrage was abandoned.

The Fédération's program on education included increased opportunities for higher education, the establishment of domestic science schools and the creation of study circles. Marie Gérin-Lajoie, particularly interested in the problem of higher education, was instrumental in founding Quebec's first Catholic college for girls in 1924. But efforts to have women admitted to medicine, accounting and law were unsuccessful.

However, these demands coincided with the aspirations and interests of only a minority of women. Conscious of this fact, feminists formulated much more traditional educational programs for women of social classes other than their own. The type of education suitable for the daughters of labourers and farmers would be one which would prepare them to carry out all the domestic tasks assigned to women — household science training. The FNSJB supported the Ecole Ménagère de Montréal (Montreal School for Home Economics), a project which was part of the movement to professionalize housework. In spite of the highly traditional character of this undertaking, the school attracted the hostility of several mothers. Its founder, Caroline Béique, related that even this small step brought accusations against her of straying in the wrong direction.[16]

Higher education as a means of emancipation did not seem desirable for all Quebec women. The formulation of these educational programs corresponded to the respective social roles attributed to the daughters of the bourgeoisie and the working class. The programs bore witness not only to differences between classes, but also to the opposition between the role of women according to conservative (domestic science) and reformist (higher education) ideology. Finally, the creation within the Fédération of study circles offering different programs based on the social origins of their members was intended to train an elite among French-Canadian women, chiefly through the study of Catholic social doctrine.[17]

The absence of equal legal rights was one of the fundamental ingredients of women's subordinate position at the turn of the century. In Quebec, the legal incapacity of married women was the principle on which the entire organization of the family rested. Only widows and unmarried women enjoyed full civil rights. As early as 1902, Marie Gérin-Lajoie had published her *Traité de Droit Usuel*, a popular handbook of civil and constitutional law. The book was aimed at a wide public and, in fact, according to its author, especially at women. Her legal knowledge gained her recognition as the feminists' resource person and many campaigns were undertaken at her instigation. [18]

A complete reform of the Quebec Civil Code was essential. This frequently voiced demand was not seriously considered until 1929, when the Taschereau government agreed to set up the Dorion Commission, which was charged with reviewing and revising women's civil rights. In spite of their request, women did not succeed in obtaining a seat on the Commission and were barely conceded a women's subcommittee. The FNSJB took up the defence of the legal marriage regime, community of property, which seemed to protect women best. The changes which it put forward for more than twenty years were intended, first and foremost, to minimize the effects of the legal incapacity of married women. It failed to attack the underlying principle of the superiority of the masculine head of the household, for this would have necessitated a new conception of the family.

All in all, the different areas in which the struggle for equal rights was carried out suggest a relatively high level of feminist consciousness in the FNSJB. Yet the elitist character of their projects for emancipation and their refusal to reconsider the traditional role of women severely limited the extent of their demands for change.

PROFESSIONAL ASSOCIATIONS FOR WORKING WOMEN

The creation of a section within the FNSJB dealing with women's work signified the recognition of the phenomenon of women entering the work force while at the same time it betrayed the anxiety of the bourgeoisie. Fearful of any threat to the traditional functions of the family, and careful to protect the primary role of women in childbearing and housekeeping, the bourgeoisie sought to protect women workers as future wives and mothers.

At this time, few women in Quebec belonged to unions. The working women's organizations set up within the Fédération expressed feminist and reform values and rejected the concept of class struggle. The FNSJB likened each association to an 'extended family' and proposed the following definition:

[A]n assembly of persons of the same trade or profession, who by pooling their small individual energies, wish to acquire a common force capable of operating desirable improvements in their economic situation, in order to obtain the necessary intellectual development too easily compressed by daily labour, to increase the treasure of moral life conferred on their souls by the Church and of which Catholic professional associations are the effective and recognized guardians.... Let us make haste to enroll our people before neutral, socialist or openly anti-clerical unions become too strong a force.[19]

The Fédération hoped to morally elevate working-class women to form an elite of female workers. It drew a clear distinction between such an association and a union, which it identified only with the protection of economic interests.

[T]his slightly aggressive manner is not at all compatible with the peaceful role a woman must play in the political economy, even when it involves demonstrating her own just demands. The term union did not receive general approbation and was rejected.[20]

This formula took into account the double role of the female worker 'who, being a woman, must act both within her family and her profession'.[21]

Haunted, like their contemporaries, by the fear of revolutionary unionism, the members of the Fédération hoped to absorb part of the labour movement in order to prevent socialist infiltration. All the associations within the Fédération were Catholic in character and operated under the guidance of a chaplain. Their passivity reflected their desire to avoid alarming employers with overly radical economic demands which would undermine the Fédération's prestige.[22]

In spite of their cautious stance, based on an interpretation which saw the relations between capital and labour as essentially harmonious, the creation of professional or trade associations provoked a great deal of concern in clerical and nationalist circles. In any case, the associations were clearly distinct from both political and business unionism in their ideology as well as in their tactics.

Established to improve strained relations between employers and employees, the associations grouped together workers — including factory employees, store employees, office workers, servants, teachers and even 'business women' — on the basis of religion or ethnicity. Nearly all the associations enjoyed the 'protection' of a board of female patrons, a remarkable example of the FNSJB's commitment to an ideal of social harmony. Madame Dupuis, wife of the owner of the large Montreal department store Dupuis Frères, presided over the committee of the Professional Association of Store Employees and Madame Rolland, the wife of the president of the Canadian Manufacturers' Association, assumed the leadership of a similar committee of the Professional Association of Factory Employees. Marie Gérin-Lajoie believed this to be a skilful policy since:

[I]f we have the wives of our Employers with us and on our side, we will be surer of obtaining a hearing and it will doubtless be easier to obtain certain reforms.[23]

These associations, which had many of the features of mutual aid societies, offered members not only support for their religious beliefs, but also a series of technical and homemaking courses. The courses were always organized around what was thought to be the immediate professional interests and the primary vocation of women workers. However, over the years, the associations progressively abandoned technical training in favour of a greater number of domestic science courses. Another association benefit was a sick fund, but the available aid reached only a fraction of the members.

Although their activities were generally tailored to the concept of woman as homemaker, each association did in its own way further the economic interests of its members. For example, in 1912 the Professional Association of Office Employees succeeded in obtaining the recall of a bill banning women from becoming Superior Court stenographers.

The Professional Association of Factory Employees, founded in January 1907, was the most dynamic and important offshoot of the Fédération's efforts in the area of women's work. When it affiliated with the FNSJB in May 1907, it already numbered some 471 members, chiefly drawn from the Dominion Textile plant in Hochelaga, the Tétrault shoe factory and the John P. Black clothing factory. In conformity with the FNSJB's spirit of elitism, it primarily attracted women supervisors from large companies:

We must devote ourselves to our association, we must create an association of elites — whose role is, in turn, to create other elites through education and training. Our association raises up others and places them in higher social classes. Let us not stop them nor be jealous of them, for it is they who elevate the condition of the working woman.[24]

The Professional Association of Factory Employees pressured employers to observe religious holidays, to improve the insufficient artificial lighting in the Hochelaga cotton mills and to separate men from women workers by giving each sex different sections. It also requested the hiring of female supervisors for women workers in order to shield them from the all too frequent insults and unsolicited attentions of foremen. In 1915, the Association demanded that the names of women factory inspectors be clearly posted in the workshops. One of its greatest successes was the inauguration of the popular, but short-lived, Women's Labour Day in 1908.[25]

The influence of international unionism on its members caused great apprehension among the leaders of the FNSJB, who encouraged the women to avoid recruitment. Not surprisingly, a union never emerged from the ranks of the FNSJB and in 1932 the Professional Association of Factory Employees was taken over by the Society of Catholic Workers, which was under direct clergy control.[26]

The Montreal branch of the Association of Catholic Teachers had more than fifty members at its inception. Working closely with Protestant anglophone teachers, it gained a doubling of their pensions in 1908. Unfortunately, this was its single notable victory, and in 1921, under pressure from church-appointed school commissioners, it was integrated into the women's section of the Montreal Catholic Teachers' Alliance.

If the women of the bourgeoisie were the first to take an interest in the struggle for their rights, it was certainly in part because they enjoyed more leisure than working women. Domestic help relieved them of many household tasks. What these women termed the 'domestic crisis' clearly revealed the class origins of their demands. The Household Helpers' Society listed among its aims, recruiting better domestics and improving the quality of their domestic skills. The demise of this group in 1911 was explained by the great occupational mobility of domestic servants and the consequent difficulty in recruiting them. The women in the Fédération did not for a moment question whether it was reasonable to expect servants to take courses in domestic science during their rare hours of leisure time.[27]

The Fédération also tried to respond to the needs of middle-class women, often widows, who operated small businesses. Defining itself as a commercial association to guide women in business, the Business Women's Association aspired to form a female elite, to provide a study centre on economic questions of concern to women and to develop women's moral and professional interests. But most of its efforts were concentrated on a single issue, the protection of small shopowners.

Speaking out in favour of the smaller stores, which were subject to the 'unfair' competition of the larger establishments, it obtained an exemption to the new law regulating early closing hours for stores. The Business Women's Association's demands were in direct contradiction with those of the Professional Association of Store Employees, also affiliated with the FNSJB, which lobbied to reduce the working hours of saleswomen.

The FNSJB revealed one of the major contradictions of its ideology in the brief which it presented to the Royal Commission of Inquiry into Industrial Training and Technical Education in 1911. Although the Fédération had always demanded political equality for women, it recommended more extensive protective legislation for women's work. Its members, unlike their anglophone counterparts in the MLCW, did not seem to realize that protective measures for women implicitly meant designating women's work to a marginal status and institutionalizing the already low wages of female workers. By calling for the exemption of women from arduous or dangerous jobs they thus weakened any demands for equal pay. Their attempts to hasten the application of the Women's Minimum Wage Law of 1919 (many years before male workers gained a minimum wage), stemmed from their belief that women needed special treatment. Another contradiction inherent in the Fédération's position was found in the encouragement it gave to women working in their homes. A special committee supplied unemployed women with home sewing. Although the conditions of work at home were often similar to those of the sweating system, whereby manufacturers gave piecework to women at notoriously low rates, the Fédération encouraged home sewing while denouncing the sweating system.

The decline in the activities of the various professional associations in the 1920s is explained by the support which the clergy gave to the fledgling Catholic unions. The associations might have become actual women's unions, but autonomous women's unions did not fit into the conceptions entertained by church authorities. The Fédération attempted to reconcile interests as contrary as those of manufacturers' wives and women workers, domestic servants and their mistresses, saleswomen and the 'business women' employers. The relatively feeble impact of these associations and the protectionist nature of their few timid demands can doubtless be attributed to the influence and ideology of their leaders, for the most part representatives of Montreal's bourgeoisie.

CONCLUSION

The decline of the Fédération as a focal point for feminist forces in Quebec illustrates the impossibility of long-term survival of an association simultaneously rooted in both traditional and reform ideologies. This contradiction was clear from the very beginning of the FNSJB. In order to thrive in the French-Canadian society of the time, the feminist movement had to secure support from and make alliances with those who represented the dominant ideology, namely the church, business and professional elites. These alliances led the movement to compromise, subordinating its demands for a greater autonomy for women to the effort of preserving and maintaining the family. The refusal to question the role of women within the family prefigured the failure of many demands for change. One of the paradoxes of the Fédération was that, while adhering to a conservative conception of the family, it nonetheless demanded political rights for women. Yet the political aspect of its platform, drawn from the women's rights movement, led it to contest women's prescribed role. The Fédération's eventual withdrawal from political battles confirmed the victory of Catholic feminism, the only variation acceptable to conservative forces.

The bourgeois feminist elements themselves gave rise to numerous contradictions caused by their division of society according to sex, not according to economic interests or the relations of production. These women asserted, for example, that there was a 'natural' solidarity among women. The FNSJB therefore attempted to bring together women of different class origins in the name of common 'feminine' interests, a tactic which sometimes forced it to adopt illogical or contradictory positions.

The FNSJB's loss of influence in Quebec appears to coincide with the division that emerged in the 1920s between conservative and reform interests. The years after World War I saw the rise of new women's associations which were either resolutely Catholic and conservative or nondenominational and reform-oriented. The Farm Women's Circles and the Daughters of Isabella, closely supervised by the church, moved increasingly further from the feminist and progressive groups headed by Thérèse Casgrain (League for Women's Rights) and Idola Saint-Jean (Canadian Alliance for the Women's Vote in Quebec), both of which refused the services of a chaplain. Henceforth, it was impossible to fuse these divergent paths of women's action. Little by little, the Fédération entrenched itself in Catholic conservatism, while other women's organizations, whether they were political or charitable in orientation, continued to evolve in a more liberal direction. From then on, the newer generation of women in the French-Canadian bourgeoisie increasingly chose associations other than the FNSJB, which faced the problem of an aging membership.

In spite of the history of its absorption and domination by conservative forces, the decline of prewar militant feminism that focussed on women's rights in Quebec must be placed within the perspective of the decline, during the 1920s, of the feminist and reform movements in Canada and the West in general. This first generation of women reformers prodded consciences in a society that was profoundly anti-feminist. Whatever their failings, their courage and their influence on the history of Quebec women should not be underestimated.[28]

CHAPTER FOUR

Divided Allegiances:
The Response of Farm
and Labour Women to Suffrage

Carol Bacchi

While the campaign for the suffrage succeeded earlier in the rest of Canada than in Quebec, it was far from unified. Regional differences, the urban-rural dichotomy and class differences tended to divide and fragment the movement for women's rights and the suffrage campaign. By the time of the First World War the question of militarism versus pacifism further divided Canadian women.

Carol Bacchi's paper touches on these divisions through her examination of, firstly, the suffragists' backgrounds and secondly, the relationship of the labour and farm movements to suffrage. Labour organizations such as the Women's Labour Leagues looked warily on the professionally-dominated suffragists and their state-interventionist philosophy. Farm women disagreed with suffragists on the primacy of sex oppression over economic oppression and strongly criticized eastern suffragists for their part in the founding of the Women's Party, which although it was supposedly committed to reforms all women agreed upon, was clearly allied to the urban bourgeoisie. As Bacchi suggests, these differences and divisions persisted in the postwar period, perhaps demonstrating that historians have minimized the conflict within the movement itself.

The organized farmers in the Prairie West — the Saskatchewan and Manitoba Grain Growers and the United Farmers of Alberta — and some elements of the Canadian labour movement were among the earliest and staunchest advocates of woman suffrage in Canada. Yet very few farm or labour men or women managed to penetrate the ranks of suffrage societies like the Manitoba Political Equality League and the Montreal

Suffrage Association, which remained predominantly urban and middle class. Farm and labour women preferred to work for the ballot through their own associations rather than join the suffragists, who showed little real understanding of the problems of farmers or workers.

The women managed to cooperate in several joint ventures for the specifically female goals of equal homesteading privileges and a dower law guaranteeing a married woman a one-third interest in a deceased husband's estate. But a series of confrontations between the suffragists and the farming and labour women suggest that more divided than united them.

The women and men who belonged to suffrage societies formed a part of a larger, chiefly Anglo-Saxon, Protestant, middle-class reform coalition which operated in Canada at the end of the nineteenth and the beginning of the twentieth century. The middle class stood on the defensive in this period, challenged by the power of corporate monopolies, the new strength of labour unions and the influx of eastern and southern European immigrants. Idealists within this class hoped to moderate the pace of change, to preserve the essence of the old order by accepting minor modifications and to establish themselves as the directors of a new social Utopia. The coalition drew together professionals, reform-minded businessmen and social gospel clergymen. The reform package consisted of several interrelated reforms, all intended to reinstate Protestant, middle-class values and to raise the prestige of the groups concerned. The package included temperance, applied Christianity, child welfare, purity reform, civic and education reform and woman suffrage. Woman suffrage was a part of the package due to the conviction that good, pure, Christian, middle-class womanhood would help vote in the legislation required to control a decadent society.

Many women in the suffrage societies endorsed the goals of the reform movement. In fact, most were reformers first and suffragists second. A small minority wanted the vote to advance female interests. A few feminists even challenged the middle-class family structure which kept women in subjection. However, these women were going against the tide of middle-class opinion which saw the patriarchal family as the chief bulwark against the forces of social disruption. The majority of female suffragists accepted the traditional allocation of sexual roles and desired the vote simply as the means to an end, to double the representation of both their race and their class. Many farm women and many working-class women found it impossible to work through the 'official' suffrage societies because of their obvious middle-class bias.[1]

WHO MADE UP THE SUFFRAGE ELITE?

The statistics from a study of active suffragists substantiate the generalization that the overwhelming majority of Canada's English-speaking suffragists belonged to the Anglo-Saxon, Protestant middle class. The nature of the available research material dictates the scope of a study of Canadian suffragists and limits it to an examination of the elite: the presidents, vice-presidents and most active members. The sample in this study includes 200 active Canadian suffragists, 156 women and 44 men.

Ethnically the suffrage leaders were mostly native or British-born. Among 28 male executive members, 16 were born in Canada (12 in Ontario, two in Quebec, one in Nova Scotia and one in the Northwest Territories), eight came from Britain and one from the United States. No place of birth could be ascertained for three. The high preponderance of Ontario men reflected the fact that Ontario remained the centre of suffrage activity from the very beginning of the movement in Canada. Of 114 female executive members, 41 were Canadian-born (21 in Ontario, 14 in Quebec, four in Nova Scotia, one in New Brunswick, and one in Newfoundland), nine were British, eight came from the United States and one from Iceland. For the 42 active but non-executive female members, the proportions are roughly the same. The names of most members, even of those for whom no birthplace could be discovered are Anglo-Saxon.[2]

Table I shows that the movement contained a broad-based Protestant representation. Presbyterians, Methodists and Anglicans were predominant and matched their relative numerical strength in the general Canadian population. Congregationalists were also well represented. Given the English domination of the movement in this period, the number of Roman Catholics was understandably disproportionately low.

An occupational analysis of the male suffrage members in Table II reveals a preponderance of professionals, clergy and businessmen, while the employed female suffragists were mainly professionals, doctors, authors and educators. (Both business and the ministry were impermeable to female infiltration in Canada.) A glance at the occupations of the husbands of married suffragists in Table III confirms the movement's monolithic middle-class character. Most were professional or disaffected businessmen.

Almost 60 per cent of the female suffragists held jobs, a rather exceptional number given the fact that of the total female population over age ten in 1911, only 14.3 per cent and in 1921, only 15.2 per cent were gainfully employed. The categories 'philanthropists', 'lecturers', 'agriculturalists', 'musicians' and 'artists' have been excluded from this figure because they generally implied an 'interest' rather than full-time employment. Of course, several in the category 'journalists, authors' may have worked on a part-time basis also, but the majority seem to have occupied important positions as editors of women's pages or were major novelists like Nellie McClung and Frances Fenwick Williams.

Approximately 42 per cent of the suffragists who held jobs were single. This figure reflects the need of these single women to become self-supporting. Nevertheless, the other 58 per cent, the married working suffragists, were an unusual phenomenon in a period when the idea of a married women working was generally unacceptable. Of course, several of the employed married suffragists might have been widowed or divorced and therefore forced to support themselves; unfortunately the title 'Mrs.' says nothing about the health or whereabouts of the husband.

The suffragists also included a more conventional group. Based on the assumption that those women for whom no occupation could be discovered worked at home, housewives probably constituted some 34 per cent of the leadership.

TABLE I
Religious Affiliation of the Suffrage Elite

| | Numbers | | % Distribution of Those Identified | | | |
	Male	Female	Male	Female	Total	*Canada
Methodist	6	22	21.4	30.5	28	14.9
Presbyterian	10	13	35.7	18.0	23	15.5
Baptist	3	5	10.7	7.0	8	5.3
Anglican	3	17	10.7	23.6	20	14.5
Congregational	4	1	14.2	1.4	5	.5
Unitarian	1	3	3.5	4.2	4	
Protestant		3		4.2	3	
Roman Catholic		3		4.2	3	39.3
Agnostic	1	2	3.5	2.7	3	
Quaker		2		2.7	2	
Free Church		1		1.4	1	
Unknown	16	84				
Other						10.0
Total	44	156	**100	**100	100	100.0

* Percentage breakdown based on 1911 Census.

** Figures do not add up to 100 because of rounding errors.

TABLE II
Occupations, Activities of Suffrage Leaders

| | Numbers | | Percentages | |
	Male	Female	Male	Female
Ministers	12		27.3	
Journalists, Authors	4	39	9.0	25.0
Lawyers	3	1	6.8	.6
Doctors		19		12.2
Civil Servants, MPs	7	7	15.9	4.5
Educators	7	23	15.9	14.7
Businessmen	2	4	4.5	2.6
Labour Reps	1		2.3	
Union Organizers		1		.6
Philanthropists	1	2	2.3	1.3
Lecturers		2		1.3
Agriculturists		2		1.3
Musicians		1		.6
Artists		2		1.3
Unknown	7	53	15.9	33.9
Total	44	156	*100	*100

* Figures do not add up to 100 because of rounding errors.

TABLE III
Occupations of Husbands of Married Suffragists

	Numbers	Percentages
Medicine, Physicians, Dentists	12	11.0
Lawyers	7	6.0
Educators	8	7.0
Journalists, Publishers	4	3.6
Public Servants, MPs	11	10.0
Businessmen	19	17.0
Ministers	6	5.4
Unknown	43	39.0
Total	110	100.0

The level of education attained by the majority of male and female suffragists testifies to their middle-class background. Among the 28 male leaders, 14 held university degrees, two graduated from normal school, three were educated privately and only one attended English national schools. Of the 156 female suffrage leaders for whom information on education was available, 33 held an MA or better, 17 a BA, 13 attended normal school, 12 graduated from ladies' colleges and collegiate institutes and five were educated privately.

Statistical comparisons between the suffragists and the population as a whole are difficult to make owing to the imprecise occupational categories used in the censuses. Nevertheless, one is struck by the all but complete absence of blue-collar workers, who represented 34 per cent of the labour force in 1911, and by the disproportionately high number of managers and professionals.

Moreover, while it is valuable to make generalizations, the following examples suggest the importance of exceptions. Although the majority of female suffragists were well-educated professionals, Helena Gutteridge of the BC Pioneer Political Equality League was a union organizer, a member of the Garment Workers' Union and of the Vancouver Trades and Labour Council. Although most suffragists were self-professed Protestants, Flora MacDonald Denison, President of the Canadian Suffrage Association in 1909, believed in spiritualism and was critical of the traditional churches. A member of the Canadian Woman Suffrage Society in 1883, T. Phillips Thompson, well known for his radical religious and political views, believed in Theosophy and edited a labour newspaper, the *Labour Advocate*. On one level, the movement is straightforward, both in ideology and composition; on another, it is extremely complex.

The conflicts between the suffragists and women in the labour and organized farmer movements provides additional evidence that the suffrage societies were controlled by the middle class. Moreover, the ideological and tactical disagreements between the women in these three groups indicates the weakness of the suffragists' feminist commitment and the strength of their class motivation.

LABOUR AND THE SUFFRAGE MOVEMENT

Labour was one of the earliest supporters of female enfranchisement in Canada. Certain labour newspapers, the *Winnipeg Voice*, for example, began publishing articles in favour of the measure as early as 1902, the same year a British Columbia labour conference passed a resolution supporting woman suffrage.[3]

Labour, of course, was not a monolith. Broadly speaking, Canadian labour adopted three different but often interconnected approaches to reform. The conservative element, the business unionists, were mainly skilled workers who followed the American Federation of Labor's policies under Samuel Gompers. Long-term goals were subordinated to short-term gains for skilled workers under this policy. Business unionists eschewed independent labour politics until 1906 and showed great hostility to any form of socialism. 'Labourites' promoted independent labour politics along the lines of the British Labour Party. A small but not insignificant sector in the labour movement called for the abolition of capitalist exploitation and the wage system.[4]

The suffrage issue divided the labour movement in spite of some official support. Business unionists who sided with the Conservative party came to support suffrage only at the last minute. For them, woman suffrage was a means of protecting the skilled worker's bargaining position against unskilled women workers. Unorganized and untrained women undercut men's wages and weakened the union's effectiveness. With political recognition women might improve their position in the market place and make it easier for them to win equal wages. In the mind of almost every unionist the two reforms of woman suffrage and equal pay were inseparable. In 1916, for example, the president of the Canadian Trades and Labour Congress, J.C. Watters, promised Toronto suffragist, Constance Hamilton, to support votes for women in exchange for an agreement on the principle of equal pay.[5]

Labourites supported suffrage because they believed that if working-class women had a vote, they stood a better chance of electing working-class representatives. Like the business unionists, they hoped that capitalism could be reformed from within. The sections of labour which had little confidence in political action or Parliament doubted that woman suffrage, a purely parliamentary reform, would achieve anything. In 1915, the *Winnipeg Voice*, begun as an independent labour paper, endorsed the radical view that the wage system needed to be abolished completely. Therefore, the woman's vote had limited value because it rested on the belief that the 'present system of wage labour and capital is all right if you give it a little tinkering'. Labour radicals in Canada detected the suffragists' class bias and were cautious about the movement's usefulness. The *Voice* called the Winnipeg Political Equality League 'a left wing of the Liberal Party', scorned its members for their patronizing attitude towards working women and dismissed them as 'noisy advocates' campaigning for a 'pet Hobby'.[6]

Despite these hesitations, the socialist movement was forced to take up the question and eventually came to support suffrage. Even the Socialist Party of Canada adopted suffrage after an initial phase of denouncing all individual reforms.

The suffragists generally shared the anti-labour attitudes of their class. True 'paternalists', they found it difficult to let labour do things for itself. They opposed strikes and unionization and recommended palliatives like factory legislation to remove the most blatant evils of the industrial system. Constance Hamilton, for example, rejected the idea of unions and argued that the solution to industrial unrest lay simply 'in the shortening of hours of labour'. Emily Murphy, an Alberta suffragist and later the instigator of the famous Persons' Case, believed that the 'machinations of lawyers' (her version of the outside agitator) drove workers to strike, and that most workers were quite capable of self-sacrifice and even of genuine affection for their employers. She added that strikes ought to be avoided at almost any cost because 'they punished the operator far too dearly both in the expenditure of nerve and of money.'[7] Despite their political cautiousness, suffragists courted the support of labour in order to win some powerful new allies and to increase their chances of success. Hamilton, hardly a labour enthusiast, made the deal with Watters for this reason.

At the same time the suffragists generally ignored female workers since they had neither the organizational base nor the political strength to mobilize them. On one occasion, in 1912, Alice Chown, one of Canada's few radical suffragists, tried to elicit support among her fellow Toronto suffragists for the New York ladies' garment workers' strike. She failed. The women reacted favourably only when she had some tale of hardship to tell. They refused, it seems, to support the strike, because they feared that an overt association with such an unpopular cause would jeopardize the whole suffrage campaign.[8]

Canadian suffragists, moreover, made no effort to conscript working-class women into their associations. In fact, according to Flora Mac-Donald Denison, they treated the working women who dared to attend their meetings like social pariahs, belittling them for their poor dress and ungrammatical speech.[9]

Only in the more radical political climate of British Columbia did one extraordinary woman, Helena Gutteridge, manage to acquire sufficient political prestige to surmount the class barrier and join a regular suffrage society, the Pioneer Political Equality League. Yet Gutteridge did not see eye to eye with the suffragists. She ranked enfranchisement second in importance to unionization, which she considered the working woman's only *real* defence against exploitation. Gutteridge also criticized the suffragists' stance on protective legislation. She argued that laws restricting women's hours and conditions of labour only made women less employable and drove them out of work they were well able to perform. She called the minimum wage 'an experiment' the male workers wished to try out on women. As reformers, the suffragists were primarily concerned with preserving the health of the nation. Undoubtedly, in the circumstances of early industrial society, the worker required some protection. Granting protection only to women, however, had the dubious advantage of placing them under an additional competitive burden. Only one suffragist, Carrie Derick, McGill professor and president of the Montreal Suffrage Association, seemed to understand that special protection had this negative side. [10]

The ideological differences between the suffragists and working-class women were dramatically demonstrated in the confrontation between the suffragists and the Women's Labour League. The WLL was a different type of working-class woman's society, composed, originally, of the wives and daughters of trade unionists. Based on a British model founded by Margaret Macdonald, the Labour Leagues were really an extension of the male unions. By 1910 Canada had branches in Port Arthur, Fort William, Winnipeg and Toronto. The women in the Leagues encouraged working women to form unions primarily to protect their husbands and fathers from wage undercutters. They realized that their men, and consequently themselves, would prosper only if the women were organized along lines similar to the men. The League leaders endorsed woman suffrage in order to facilitate organization among working women and to win equal pay for equal work. [11]

Although both the Leagues and the suffrage societies agreed on the need for a vote, the relationship between them was strained. One of the founders of the Winnipeg League, Ada Muir, maintained that the suffragists represented one distinct interest group, the professionals, while the Labour Leagues spoke for another, the working men and women of the nation.

Muir considered the suffragists part of a professional monopoly which was trying to take effective control of the country through the middle-class reform movement. The large numbers of professionals in the suffrage societies undoubtedly strengthened this suspicion. Muir argued that the public health, social welfare and education reform campaigns were simply attempts on the part of professionals (doctors, social workers, teachers) to make their services indispensable to the community and guarantee themselves an income. Because professionals used the state to create conditions conducive to their occupational security, by encouraging the building of more public schools, imposing public health standards and legislating morality, Muir and many other members of the working class suspected the state interventionist philosophy.[12]

The prohibition issue created additional tension. Many working-class men and women considered prohibition to be class legislation, designed to impose middle-class standards on them. The suffragists, on the other hand, usually favoured prohibition. For a time, the issue lay dormant. Then in 1918, with the First World War nearing its end and class consciousness at a new high in Canada, the Winnipeg Women's Labour League publicly endorsed the sale of light beer and wine as a deliberate affront to the prohibitionist suffragists.[13]

Finally, in the same year, the suffragists revealed their class colours by giving their support to a group of Local Council women who acted as scabs during a Winnipeg strike. In protest, the Labour League withdrew all support from the Manitoba Political Education League, the successor to the Political Equality League, thus ending the period of toleration and accommodation between the two groups.

A few suffragists tried to break free of their middle-class bonds and joined the labour movement. Although they were a minority, these women represented an important ideological subdivision within the movement. Their attitudes illustrate the way in which a philosophy endorsing increased government intervention could lead to radical politics and they also suggest the limitations of that radicalism. For, despite their best efforts, these women continued to carry middle-class concerns and biases with them.

In 1915 the District Labour Council of Toronto hired suffragist Laura Hughes to investigate conditions in local plants engaged in the manufacture of war supplies. Hughes obtained an under-cover post as a factory worker in the Joseph Simpson Knitting Company. She conducted an on-the-spot inspection and submitted her observations in a report which the District Council sent on to the Minister of Labour. Her experience converted Hughes into an outspoken labour sympathizer. She became a popular lecturer at Toronto Labour Conventions and in 1916 was elected second vice-president of the Greater Toronto Labour Party.[14]

Despite her apparent radicalism, Hughes failed to break the bond of middle-class morality. Helena Gutteridge considered her little better than a patronizing reformer and repudiated her for appealing to the 'humanity' of the employers and for recommending clubs to 'reform' working girls. She also criticized Hughes for her obsession with political solutions. Hughes promoted a political party of labour, while Gutteridge encouraged unionization and workers' political action without the intermediary of a labour party.[15]

A second Toronto suffragist, Harriet Dunlop Prenter, the president of a small group called simply the Political Equality League, also joined the labour movement. She submitted articles to the Toronto labour paper, the *Industrial Banner*, and lectured on behalf of the Labour Lecture Bureau. In 1920 she became the assistant secretary of the Toronto Independent Labour Party. Her social vision, however, did not differ significantly from that of the majority of suffragists. She endorsed a more limited notion of equality without challenging class privilege. The means, not the ends, distinguished her from the larger body of suffragists. She discarded 'uplifting' and 'committees', the traditional strategy of the female reformer, in order to cooperate with the 'intelligent efforts' of organized labour.[16]

Rose Henderson, a Montreal suffragist and probation officer, agreed with Prenter that significant change would come about only if the newly enfranchised women joined forces with labour and marched together 'to attain the emancipation of the toiling masses'. But middle-class assumptions also restricted her vision. Henderson led the campaign for mothers' pensions, which aimed ultimately at removing women from the labour force and returning them to their homes, hardly a viable alternative for most working women.[17]

Even the radical suffragists failed somehow to escape the paternalism which characterized the movement as a whole. The suffrage women belonged to a group which, like labour, stood on the defensive in this period. The suffrage program, therefore, tried to remove social ills but not their sources. For tactical reasons the suffragists were willing to court the support of important labour spokesmen. But working-class women, the people the suffragists should have been helping if their claim to speak for all women was to have any meaning, were left to fend for themselves against the prejudice of male unionists and the harsh economic realities of low wages and intolerable working conditions.

THE ORGANIZED FARM WOMEN AND THE SUFFRAGISTS

Tensions also arose between the organized farm women in the Prairies and the Western suffragists who, as in the East, tended to be urban and middle-class. As in the case of labour, class interests prevented sexual cohesion. While there are problems in considering farmers as a class, the term may be used in a modified sense in this instance since articulate farm leaders, male and female, spoke of themselves as a producing class and described their situation in class terms. The organized farm women wanted a vote for several reasons: to rectify certain injustices against women, to strengthen the Protestant, Anglo-Saxon clique to which they belonged and to increase the political awareness and representation of the agrarian sector. The urban middle-class suffragists could readily sympathize with the first two goals but the last made it difficult for the women to work together.

Developments within the West encouraged the growth of political consciousness among Canada's farming population. It may be true that the entire West felt constrained by the Eastern presence, but the farmers seemed to suffer more and more vocally. They experienced specific economic grievances which did not equally affect the cities. The farmers, for example, bought in a protected market and sold in an unprotected one. The world wheat price fluctuated outside their control, yet at home the protective tariff compelled them to buy the necessities of life and much of their farm equipment at prices only partially competitive.

Meanwhile, the Western cities began to resemble Eastern urban centres. Urban growth proceeded at a rapid rate in Western Canada, the urban segment of the population having risen, in Alberta, from 25.4 per cent in 1901 to 36.8 per cent in 1911 and in Manitoba, from 27.6 per cent to 43.4 per cent. The natural consequence — rural depopulation — seemed to undermine the agriculturalist's way of life. The culture of the city alarmed the farmer. 'Hotbeds of vice' and centres of 'alien congestion', they represented the opposite of what they thought to be their virtuous prairie farm life. Finally, the farmers began to fear the disproportionate political influence of the urban sector, particularly of the professional and entrepreneurial elite who ruled the cities. To protect their special interests and strengthen their political voice, the farmers decided to organize, forming the Territorial Grain Growers' in 1902, the Manitoba Grain Growers' in 1903, the United Farmers of Alberta in 1909. Later in the century they turned to independent political action (the Progressive party) to redress the balance in favour of the country.[18]

The growing political consciousness of the farmers encouraged them to involve their women in an attempt to mobilize their entire strength. They urged their wives and daughters to join their organizations and to form coordinate auxiliaries. Logically, they concluded that in order for rural women to help implement the farmers' program, they needed a political voice. The Saskatchewan Grain Growers' and the United Farmers of Alberta both passed resolutions in favour of woman suffrage in 1913, a few years before the organized suffrage campaign really got underway in the West. Moreover, like the urban reformers, many rural leaders conceived of good, Christian women as the 'harbingers of civilization' and wished to enlist their assistance in taming the West and controlling urban vice, principally drunkenness and prostitution.

Western farm women eagerly joined the new associations, demonstrating an untapped political consciousness and a keen desire to organize. A referendum report issued by the *Grain Growers' Guide* in 1914 confirmed that farm women were as aware as their men of the needs of the agricultural community. The *Guide* asked its readers their opinions on the major political questions of the day, which included the entire farmers' platform: direct democracy, free trade, the single tax and government ownership of public utilities. The women endorsed reform in the same high proportions as the men.[19]

The political awareness of the farm women produced a conflict of interest between them and the urban professional women in the suffrage societies. The history of the formation of the farm women's associations and the Prairie suffrage societies confirms that Western women divided sharply along urban-rural lines.

When the Saskatchewan Grain Growers decided in 1913 to inaugurate a female auxiliary, the secretary, F.W. Green, invited suffragist Francis Marion Beynon to help. She did so by publicizing the meeting through her column in the *Grain Growers' Guide*. Several other suffragists, notably Nellie McClung, Lillian Beynon Thomas and Cora Hind, attended the opening meeting. In Alberta, Miss Jean Reed, a former British suffragist and a journalist, became the first president of the Woman's Auxiliary to the United Farmers of Alberta (UFA).[20]

But once under way, the wives and daughters of farmers took over the executive positions and the suffragists retreated to their city-based societies. Violet Jackson MacNaughton, an English-born school teacher who arrived in Saskatchewan in 1909 and a year later married local farmer John MacNaughton, became the first Women's Grain Growers' (WGGA) president. In 1915 Jean Reed retired in favour of a local farmer's wife, Irene Parlby, whose father, Colonel Marryat, had been one of the main instigators behind the formation of the Alix local of the UFA, and whose husband, Walter Parlby, became its first president. The suffragists continued to comment favourably on the new farm women's organizations but they no longer joined actively in the proceedings – the auxiliaries now belonged to the farm women.

Meanwhile, the Western suffrage societies, like those in the East, were strictly an urban phenomenon, directed by professional men and women or the wives of professionals and businessmen. The Manitoba Political Equality League (PEL) was ruled by a city executive and operated out of

Winnipeg and not the surrounding countryside. Alberta never acquired a provincial suffrage body, but in 1915 two local suffrage societies emerged in the two largest urban centres, Calgary and Edmonton.[21]

Only in Saskatchewan did farm women initiate the suffrage campaign. In 1913 Premier Walter Scott received over 170 letters and 190 petitions containing 2,500 names, all from country women, again attesting to the farm women's political awareness. This unusual situation disturbed Violet MacNaughton, who felt that, unless city women became equally vociferous, the movement could hardly claim a broad national base. In an attempt to stir the city women out of their lethargy, she organized the Saskatchewan Political Equal Franchise Board (PEFB) in 1915 to coordinate the efforts of the WGGA, the Woman's Christian Temperance Union (WCTU) and the few small city societies which already existed. MacNaughton apparently underestimated the strength of the city leagues, however, for they dominated the first PEFB meeting and introduced a method of selecting representatives which guaranteed their ascendancy at future meetings. Each city franchise league received one representative for every 25 members, while the WGGA and the WCTU received a restricted total representation of two members each. Representatives from the newly formed suffrage societies in Regina, Moose Jaw, Prince Albert, Yorkton and Moosemin, all growing town communities, took over the PEFB executive, reaffirming the traditional pattern of the urban-based suffrage association.[22]

MacNaughton had anticipated that city and farm women might have difficulty cooperating and for this reason had suggested that the Board act simply as a clearing house for ideas, along the same lines as the National Council of Women of Canada (NCWC). But soon the Board completely ignored its founder and her advice and introduced a single platform for both city and country women. The program repelled MacNaughton for two reasons. First, the Board showed too great a willingness to cooperate with Eastern suffragists. MacNaughton, a good barometer of farm sentiment, distrusted all Eastern associations and refused to consider working with them. Second, MacNaughton objected to the suffragists' obvious Liberal bias. Personally she favoured the formation of an independent farmers' party. Alienated by these developments, the farm women declared that they no longer considered the Board representative of farm women's interests and in 1916 refused to endorse it. Except for the two token representatives who occasionally attended meetings, the Franchise Board now rested completely in the hands of city women.[23] The reason for the dichotomy between the suffragists and the farm women was simply that economic interests separated them. Granted, country and city women faced many common problems — the drudgery of the domestic routine and unjust property and marriage laws. But the women interpreted the causes of their problems, especially economic problems, differently. The suffragists attributed the farm women's hardships to their husbands. Francis Beynon, for example, blamed the farmers for refusing to purchase the new kitchen conveniences to lighten their wives' work load.[24]

Vocal leaders among the farm women stressed that their husbands were not at fault. According to Irene Parlby, tariffs, not men, were the villains and the real reason why farm women were overworked or grew old before their time. Tariffs raised the price of farm machinery and left little surplus income for luxuries such as household labour-saving devices.[25]

The organized farm women placed economic above sexual discrimination. They felt no more oppressed than their husbands, with whom they faced a common oppressor, the Eastern interests. They wanted a vote to help protect women against the visible inequities of the system but, more than this, to help their men recast the economic structure in favour of the agrarian interests. In Parlby's words, 'First and foremost as organized farm women we stand shoulder to shoulder with the men's organization in the demand for a reconstruction of our economic system.'[26]

The divergent attitudes of the farm women and the suffragists surfaced in their quarrel over the Homemakers' Clubs and the Women's Institutes, government-sponsored organizations designed to upgrade the farm wife's domestic capabilities. The Women's Institutes were founded in Ontario in 1898 by Adelaide Hoodless at the suggestion of G.C. Creelman, the Superintendent of the Farmers' Institutes, and soon became popular throughout Manitoba and Alberta. In Saskatchewan, the Agricultural College Department of the Saskatchewan government launched a parallel association, the Homemakers' Clubs. Both groups had the same purpose, to improve the quality of homemaking among farm women by offering them instruction in cooking, sewing, health and hygiene. Both also received financial assistance from their respective provincial governments. The Institutes received a grant of ten dollars a year to assist them in holding their meetings and had access to the Department of Education travelling libraries and to literature from the Department of Agriculture. Similarly, the Homemakers became a ward of the Saskatchewan government and received a stipend of three dollars yearly, which the government claimed gave it the right to 'supervise and govern their activity'. The governments considered it a worthwhile investment which would counter the trend towards rural depopulation and raise 'the general standard of health and morals of the people' and thereby contribute to the emergence of a powerful nation.[27]

As reformers, the suffragists were dedicated to improving the health and excellence of the race and they therefore enthusiastically promoted the new associations. They considered them the rural counterpart of the urban domestic science courses that most suffrage societies endorsed. Several suffragists assumed prominent positions in the new societies. Emily Murphy and Nellie McClung became department heads in the Institutes while Lillian Beynon Thomas organized and directed the Homemakers' Clubs.[28]

Meanwhile the organized farm women were suspicious of the new associations. They believed that the Liberal governments in Saskatchewan and Alberta feared the potential power of the organized farmers' movement and introduced these conservative women's societies to draw attention away from the WGGA and the UFWA. In the 1890s the Patrons of Industry in Ontario had accused Queen's Park of creating the Farmers' Institutes for a similar reason, to channel and quell rural discontent. Violet MacNaughton called the Homemakers' Clubs 'an appendage of the Provincial Liberal Party', designed to compete with and to help suppress the politically dangerous farm women's associations. Irene Parlby considered the Alberta Institute nothing but 'another political machine', bought and paid for by the government. The provincial Liberal parties, despite their association with the Prairie reform movement, had not quite convinced farmers or farm women that they represented their interests. It was becoming increasingly clear that nothing but an independent farmers' party could speak for farmers.[29]

The Western suffragists and the organized farm women, therefore, while united in their desire for a ballot, were divided by party and economic interests. Within an emerging Western consciousness country and city vied for political influence. The suffragists lined up with the reform-minded Liberals, the farm women with the organized farmers. The suffragists represented an urban professional and entrepreneurial elite; the farm women, a group of primary producers.

THE WOMAN'S PARTY

The organized farm women had disagreements with Eastern as well as with Western suffragists and for basically the same reason, the incompatibility of agrarian and urban middle-class values. The Woman's Party provides a good test case. In 1918 Constance Hamilton and several other Toronto suffragists from the breakaway 'national' association, the

National Equal Franchise Union, established a Woman's Party, ostensibly to continue pursuing the elusive goal of sexual equality, following the granting of the vote to women. The Woman's Party, dominated by the East, attracted little support in either the urban or rural West, but Violet MacNaughton and Irene Parlby, representing the farm element, became its most vociferous critics. They attacked three planks in the party's platform − war till victory, stronger imperial ties and opposition to labour unionization − their views on which illustrate the different priorities of the agricultural West and the business-oriented East.

The WGGA and the UFWA exhibited a greater tolerance towards Germany after the war than did the Eastern suffragists. Irene Parlby denounced the Woman's Party's pledge 'not to buy, sell, or use any articles made in Germany or by her allies', to withdraw all subject populations from Germany's jurisdiction and to reduce Germany's mineral resources. She predicted that such behaviour simply guaranteed the antagonism which would produce another war at some time in the future. Some important farm women had definite pacifist sympathies. During the war, for example, Violet MacNaughton corresponded with Laura Hughes, the head of the Toronto branch of the Women's International League for Peace and Freedom, and continued a campaign for peace into the 1920s.[30]

The WGGA and the UFWA both rejected the appeal for close imperial ties. The Woman's Party recommended that the 'natural resources, the essential industries, and the transport system of the Empire be under strictly Imperial ownership and control'. The economic implications of this plan disturbed farm women. They believed that the position of the farmer in Canada was unique, that even the federal government stood too far removed to understand his problems and that, therefore, no remote imperial body could possibly hope to grasp his needs.[31]

Although various attempts at farm-labour coalitions failed dismally during this period, the organized farm women spoke of themselves as members of a larger producing class which included labour. They described farmers and labourers as 'brothers beneath the skin'. For this reason they could not condone the Woman's Party's patronizing attitude towards labour and its general anti-union stance, which Parlby called a 'knock-out blow' to democratic principle. They defiantly suggested that, despite its claim to speak for all of Canadian womanhood, the Woman's Party represented only the Eastern ladies of wealth and leisure, the plutocracy and indirectly, Eastern vested interests.

Beyond the platform, the farm women objected to the whole idea of a woman's party, one founded on sex distinctions. In contrast, they believed that economics, not the 'antediluvian fetish of sex distinction and discrimination', moved people. Some women, they argued, believed in free trade and others believed in protection, depending on their class. According to Mary McCallum, the editor of the Woman's Page in the *Grain Growers' Guide*, women, like men, fell into their respective occupational groups: 'The women labour class [sic] became a part of the labour party as a whole; farm women had a voice in the platform of agriculture.' It was foolish, she maintained, ever to expect women as a group to unite on a national policy.[32]

On the other hand, the president of the Woman's Party, Constance Hamilton, argued that women constituted a class unto themselves and that they were quite justified in forming a party. 'If it is of advantage to agriculturalists to unite for their own special interests, then it is equally advantageous to unite women for their own special interests,' she declared. Under the heading 'Special Women's Interests', the party listed the reforms which women had fought for during the past four decades, reforms all women agreed upon: equal pay for equal work, equal marriage laws including equal conditions of divorce, equality of parental rights, raising the age of consent and equal homesteading privileges. But Hamilton failed to realize that other parts of the party's platform, particularly those dealing with national economic policy, bore a distinct class bias. Stated simply, the suffragists owed their allegiance to the urban bourgeoisie. Irene Parlby realized this. In her opinion, the category 'Special Women's Interests' simply provided a 'sugar-coating' to the bitter pill of unsound economic policy which ran throughout the whole program.[33]

Labour women also recognized the bias of the Woman's Party. The editor of the Woman's Page in the *Industrial Banner* labelled it an 'annex' to the Conservative party. She pointed out that its organizers were the same women who had defended the *Wartime Election Act,* who had worked for the re-election of Sir Robert Borden in 1917 and who asked the Trade and Commerce Minister, Sir George Foster, to become their mentor.[34]

Despite many common objectives, women in the turn-of-the-century period were unable to surmount their class divisions. In part, they were caught up in the heightened class consciousness of the era, evident in the proliferation of businessmen's associations, professional societies, labour unions and farm cooperatives. Moreover, while the suffragists claimed to speak for all women, they really represented only the urban middle classes. Farm and labour women understood this and refused to join the urban suffrage societies. Although these women managed to cooperate for several female-oriented goals, ultimately they identified with their class rather than their sex.

After enfranchisement, women followed voting patterns which were determined by their political and economic affiliations. The revolution in social values and in woman's social status which the suffragists had anticipated was never realized.

CHAPTER FIVE

Canada's Women Doctors: Feminism Constrained

Veronica Strong-Boag

Women's attempts to enter the male-dominated professions began in earnest in the period after 1850; prior to mid-century only a handful of women under unusual circumstances managed to receive medical training. Medicine, unlike other male professions, proved more susceptible to feminist argumentation because activists could point to the long history of women healers. The arguments that proved most effective, however, were based on a notion of female guardianship, particularly of the medical and moral needs of women and children. Infused with a sense of mission, the first pioneer women doctors linked the cure of physiological ills with greater access to the moral and spiritual well-being of their patients. The later generations of female doctors also concentrated on the problems of women and children but seemed to lose the initial fervour for improving the social, economic and political plight of women to a narrower allegiance to professional goals.

This paper examines the background and record of the first graduates of two women's medical colleges which were founded to provide the training denied them by the universities of Ontario. Although some historians view the training of women and men in separate spheres as a source of strength for women rather than as a damper upon their potential, the case of women doctors in Canada is instructive. Women doctors who stayed in North America gravitated to the service of women and children; others, under the banner of British imperialism, found their mission among the women and children of India and China. Common to both was a sense of high moral and middle-class womanhood and a long tradition of Anglo-Saxon superiority. While Strong-Boag finds many advantages in the separate female medical colleges, she concludes that the early promise for these women as new role models was never fulfilled. Very few challenged the female role for women doctors; most became absorbed in their professional interests.

Professional women have long been feminism's prize exhibits. Hailed as heroines, they are cherished as the well-spring of future feminist victories. Historians have largely accepted this flattering assessment when dealing with the early women's movement. Yet an examination of the background and record of doctors trained in the Kingston Women's Medical College and the Toronto Woman's Medical College between 1883 and 1905 challenges the untempered optimism of the traditional account.

The struggle for medical training in Canada was hard and courageously fought. Almost without exception the first women students pledged themselves to the assistance of their sex and the improvement of their world. Despite the prominence of several female physicians in Canada's first women's movement, however, these women did not guarantee continuing feminist advance. The triumph and disappointment of their achievement has helped to shape the course of Canadian feminism.

In the nineteenth century neither Canadian universities nor professions were wholly happy with the prospect of female recruits. Opponents of higher education for women were legion. Their prophecies painted gloomy pictures of desexed, enfeebled and arrogant female students. The co-ed, much the worse for her efforts to win a university diploma, would not take her 'proper place' in the social order. Ill-suited to her primary tasks, she threatened the sanctity of the domestic circle. In place of the 'suitable' occupation of wife and mother, 'the professions and employments of public life' would be hers, a 'consummation devoutly to be deprecated'. Rejecting such dire forecasts, women began to win entry to the nation's universities by the 1850s; by the 1880s they were installed in institutions across the country. But acceptance by the universities did not always include the right to enrol in professional faculties on the same basis as males. Medicine, law and theology had their own traditions, which were rarely generous to women. Even when female students won the formal privilege of registration, difficulties with male professional monopolies were by no means over.[1]

Like lawyers and ministers, many doctors were determined to close their ranks to female candidates. Their resistance was a complex combination of sentiment and practicality. Male antagonism originated on the one hand from the conservatives' defence of an idealized womanhood. According to this faith, women were both the Almighty's special creations and beings uniquely susceptible to a multitude of emotional and nervous disorders. Under any rigorous program of study such as medicine, female students must, almost inevitably, collapse. Success could be won only at the unacceptable cost of a coarsened sensibility. The few masculinized and repulsive survivors would forfeit 'the noblest quality a woman can possess ... modesty'. Potential female students were cautioned that it 'would be far better for women to devote their energies to that which they are so much suited ... bearing children and nursing children'. Medicine was not for women because the world itself was not for them. Men alone were capable of combatting its stresses. In order to 'fight the good fight', however, these men needed good women at home to reassure them, to purify them and to put up with them.[2]

Women doctors were not suspect on account of their sex alone. Male opposition stemmed also from a transformation in the nature of the medical profession itself. In the late nineteenth century the occupation was undergoing an intense period of professionalization, a process which required a tightening up of qualifications and restrictions on accreditation. Professional prestige and power depended on the assertion and maintenance of a readily identifiable orthodoxy in personnel and opinion. To achieve this, the curriculum and standards of medical schools were increasingly subject to the authority of such ruling bodies as the College of Physicians and Surgeons of Ontario. Deviance of any kind was suspect lest it raise doubts about hard-won professional standards. The association of some female doctors, excluded from most orthodox schools in North America, with controversial remedies such as electrotherapy, hydropathy and homeopathy linked the entire sex with just the kind of questionable practices the orthodox were attempting to eliminate. One suspects too that women's particular identification with healing cults, like Mary Baker Eddy's Christian Science, provided further justification for anti-female prejudices.[3]

The growing insistence on formal and standardized qualifications for acceptance by recognized medical schools and provincial licencing bodies was one especially effective means of excluding the deviant. Stricter requirements weeded out not only the poor, as the radical Patrons of Industry in Ontario foresaw, but also female candidates. As a group, girls were offered less rigorous and less scientific training at every educational level. The Latin requirement, for instance, was especially onerous because girls were routinely discouraged from attempting this 'university' subject. Too often the elevation of medicine to the status of a scientific and educated discipline meant a renewed emphasis on masculinity.[4]

Women not only posed a potential risk to standards and status, they also presented an economic threat in an occupation which was thought to be overcrowded. An abundance of male rivals was serious enough but female physicians were a special hazard. What if pregnant women preferred their own sex for obstetrical matters? Childbirth was often the occasion which initiated a doctor's association with a family and its illnesses. Without such contact male practices could decline precipitately. In view of medical men's hostility to the ancient trade of midwifery and their reluctance to licence midwives, it is not unlikely that medical education for women in Canada, as in Great Britain, was viewed as the Trojan horse by which midwives might enter the kingdom of 'legitimate' medicine.[5]

Even after women wrung reluctant acceptance from medical schools, opponents had not shed their sexist assumptions. Internships and residencies in Canadian hospitals were commonly denied women. Male physicians often were reluctant to consult with female colleagues. Such resistance continued far into the twentieth century, in the form of female quotas in medical faculties and discouragement at every stage of a woman's life.

Despite their frosty reception by the medical profession, Canadian women were not to be put off. By mid-century they had cause for optimism. American and British medical schools were slowly beginning to graduate women. Many of the early institutions were restricted to women, founded as they were only after established programs had refused female applicants. The Woman's Medical College of Philadelphia (1850), the New York Medical College for Women (1863) and the London School of Medicine for Women (1874) were leading examples of the separatist impulse. There were many others. Between 1850 and 1895, for instance, Americans founded 19 medical colleges for women. After mid-century, opportunities for co-educational training were also increasingly available at Western Reserve College (1850s), the University of Michigan (1869), Boston University Homeopathic College (1874) and Johns Hopkins Medical School (1893). The acknowledged ability of such pioneers as Doctors Sophie Jex Blake, Elizabeth Blackwell, Elizabeth Garrett Anderson and Mary Putnam Jacobi in Great Britain and the United States further justified the struggles of Canadian admirers.[6]

Admiration soon led to imitation. By the 1860s at the latest, Canadian women were making their way south for further education. With the notable exception of Augusta Stowe-Gullen, who completed the requirements in Toronto in 1883, all of the female physicians practicing in the Dominion before 1884 had trained with doctors or in schools outside Canada, generally in the United States or Great Britain. Among their number there were such outstanding feminists as Doctors Emily Howard Stowe (New York Medical College for Women, 1867), Jennie Kidd Trout (Women's Medical College of Philadelphia, 1875), Leonora Howard King (University of Michigan, 1876) and Amelia LeSueur Yeomans (University of Michigan, 1883).

By the late 1870s advocates of 'made-in-Canada' training were armed with the knowledge that opposition everywhere was retreating. The development of the Canadian women's movement in this decade gave further cause for good cheer. The emergence of the first branches of Young Women's Christian Association, the Woman's Christian Temperance Union and various foreign missionary societies, together with a host of more local associations, raised up new sympathizers for female initiatives. Medical education was a particular beneficiary of this more receptive environment. More easily than law or theology it could be justified as a 'natural' outlet for women's nurturing instincts. Support was all the more likely when medical pioneers like Emily Howard Stowe and Jennie Kidd Trout became leaders of groups such as the Toronto Women's Literary Society, later the Women's Suffrage Club. Organized women, imbued with a roused sense of sisterhood, formed a natural clientele for female doctors. Benefits were not one-sided. Female health professionals would give other women's efforts at reform new authority and stature. Doctors were after all 'living proof' that women could succeed in demanding occupations and testimonials to the value of liberal reforms in general.

Inspired by advances elsewhere and reassured by growing support at home, advocates of female medical education set forth their case. First, like feminists on so many other issues, they submitted women's claim to equality before the law and justice within all institutions. Few speakers failed to acknowledge the larger principle for which they fought. Repeated emphasis on practical benefits suggested, however, that it was on these grounds that they anticipated widespread support. Women's champions reminded listeners that women often urgently needed wage employment. The unmarried, the deserted and the widowed were frequently without any economic assistance whatsoever. To those who characterized medicine as essentially unwomanly, they retorted that 'this objection is not raised when a woman toils all day at chain-making or the heavy sewing machine, both more exhausting and less remunerative than professional work.' Nor for that matter had women always been considered unsuited to the doctor's task. Feminists insisted on countless occasions that in former times the 'ancient office of healer' had been women's, in their role as family nurse. Male jealousy had caused women to be driven from their natural field of labour. As Dr. Alice McGillivray, the first valedictorian at the Kingston College, concluded, 'Woman's sphere has hitherto been chiefly defined by the half of creation, not woman, and therefore by her open to criticism.' It was high time for female citizens to set the parameters of their own lives.[7]

Supporters also foresaw that female physicians would rectify shortcomings in the profession itself. So long as only male assistance was available, the female population would remain inadequately attended. As one advocate observed, 'it is well known that there are many female complaints which cannot be properly treated for the simple reason that the medical *man* does not and cannot fully understand them.' Nor was masculine ignorance the only difficulty. Modesty's rigorous code made women embarrassed and prudish patients. The widespread acceptance of a lower level of personal morality for males — the double standard — added to the unhappy predicament of timid patients. Either modesty or health seemed at stake; there was no easy way to reconcile the two. Nor were adults the only sufferers. Youngsters could also be intimidated by an aggressive male presence in the sickroom. In contrast, female assistance was familiar and unthreatening. The suspicion that male attendants were somehow inadequate recurred constantly in the pleas for women doctors. Women and children were commonly acknowledged as the special patients of the new practitioners. According to some observers at least, female treatment of adult males was also somewhat improper. Underlying these sentiments there lay, if not a basic antagonism between the sexes, at least a fundamental mistrust. Many women, like many men, believed that the male sex was particularly contaminated by urban industrial society. By comparison, women, less wedded to the business world, seemed purer and finer. With such a viewpoint it was easy for women to distrust male doctors.[8]

Since men were at best uncertain custodians of civilization's highest values, it was essential that women, particularly those of the middle class, assume active guardianship. Feminists believed that female doctors would initiate and inform women's work for their sex and their community. Their example would inspire others with similar zeal and convince the sceptical of women's essential contribution to the world outside the home.

The first women licenced to practice medicine in Canada, Jennie Kidd Trout and Emily Howard Stowe, insisted that young women be given opportunities to study in the Dominion. Their own arbitrary treatment by the Toronto School of Medicine lent these women the strength of bitter resentment. Both employed a combination of practical and egalitarian points to justify the innovation. Stowe inspired her own daughter, Augusta, to take up medicine, but she also had a wider impact through her leadership of the Toronto Women's Literary Society and later of the Dominion Women's Enfranchisement Association. In the 1880s, Trout, originally a prodigy of Stowe's, was at least as influential. It appears, however, that Trout's deep religious faith, in contrast to Stowe's mounting scepticism, made her not only somewhat more conservative but also, in a religious age, more influential. This contrast may help to explain the apparent antagonism of some women students to Stowe and perhaps even the slow growth of the Women's Suffrage Club. More research needs to be done in this area before we will know for sure.[9]

One of those who chose to come to Trout for guidance was Elizabeth Smith of Winona, Ontario. She left 'resolved to go through my profession and do in what measure I may be able the work that she has done'. Consecrated to medicine, Elizabeth successfully wrote the matriculation exams for the College of Physicians and Surgeons of Ontario which she had previously failed. Toronto newspapers soon published the following advertisement:

> Ladies wishing to study medicine in
> Canada will hear something to their
> advantage by communicating with Box
> 31, Winona, Ontario, P.O.

With the exception of a few cranks, the replies were encouraging. Particularly heart-lifting was praise from a father whose 14-year-old daughter intended to take up medicine as soon as she was older. Smith forwarded all favourable inquiries to Queen's University, which had expressed interest in the admission of women.[10]

Augusta Stowe was one of those who answered the advertisement but she did not go to Queen's. Although the Kingston school offered to create a summer program equivalent to and distinct from the men's winter course in 1880, Emily Howard Stowe rejected this possibility for her daughter, noting:

> ... There is every objection to "summer courses".... No person can study as well then as in cold weather, they cannot dissect, and by the profession generally they would never be recognized as of equal value with the winter courses. There is never the same hospital advantages in summer as winter. With regard to the excessive value of a Canadian degree, it is more imaginary than real, and if obtained from separate or summer courses its value would fall.

Instead she proposed that Elizabeth Smith apply either to schools in the United States or chance the storm at Toronto as Augusta had chosen to do. This rejection, the beginning of Stowe's hostility to Queen's programs did not, however, deter Elizabeth, who found her Kingston choice confirmed by Jennie Trout. [11]

In April 1880, she joined three other candidates, Alice McGillivray, Elizabeth Beatty and Annie Dickson for the first session at Queen's. All four graduated; three in 1884 and Dickson, who was forced to leave school for a time, in 1886.

The first summer term brought the excitement of new knowledge and self-discovery. By the close of classes the women were united and confident. The outspoken McGillivray spoke for all of them when she outlined plans to spread the message of women's medical opportunities.

> Now my dear, we must awaken Ontario this winter to a sense of the needs of her younger daughters. We must hurl the 'Fiery Cross' through hill and dale, and startle something to life, either dissent or assent, the first better than nothing, because then we can have the satisfaction of exposing the meanness and small-mindedness of some of our *modest* fellow-creatures.

The concept of the essentially religious 'mission' of female doctors was influential and very few of the new physicians seriously questioned its validity. [12]

In April 1881, Smith, McGillivray and Beatty returned to Kingston, only to be turned away. The faculty had decreed that because few new students had applied, the course would be postponed until the following winter. That session was conducted partly with male students and partly independently. Although there were occasional problems with ribald remarks, the women generally suffered little harrassment. Their optimism was such that Smith could exclaim:

> I just feel as tho I were really living these days, what with so much interesting study, so much knowledge presented to us, such labyrinths of thought, excited [by] so much to do[,] so little done and such splendid company, really life is active, life is real. [13]

High spirits did not survive the arrival of new scholars in the fall of 1882. Less sympathetic students and unexpected antagonism from one lecturer jeopardized the women's entire program. By November, Smith was driven to write:

And then to know — *they dare* to judge me immodest — indelicate — unwomanly — to know how we are misunderstood, misjudged by most. Oh it is enough to rouse such contending — such violent emotions as to make [the] load too heavy — that *any* should misjudge — that *any* should have other than sympathy for the great sacrifices we make.... Injustice — injustice — injustice rings in my ears and rouses me to bitter thoughts that sometimes I would dearly like to repay them fourfold what they make me suffer now.... I never think of giving up without completing the course.

Such courage attracted its champions. By the beginning of 1883 Dr. Trout was negotiating with Toronto doctors to establish a separate medical school for women. Together with Stowe she pledged $10,000. The sole stipulation was that women be admitted to the governing board and faculty of the new institution. When the Toronto male doctors proved obdurate, she turned to Kingston as an alternate site. There, sympathetic citizens, led by the prominent Liberal, Sir Richard Cartwright and Queen's Principal George Grant, were more receptive. An audience gathered in June 1883 to applaud speakers hailing the unimpeachable record of female doctors, the cruelty of denying the women the full use of their education and the possibility of trained women improving domestic hygiene. Kingston's support was confirmed when Grant, probably the nation's foremost educator, concluded that 'the study of medicine was one of the things for which woman was specially adapted, and as in England and the United States, every facility should be given to her to gratify her reasonable ambitions.' No woman's name appeared on the fundraising committee, but Trout led the list of subscribers with a pledge of $200 a year for five years.[14]

Unhappily for the long-term prospects of the Kingston endeavour, the same month saw a hearing sponsored by the Toronto Women's Suffrage Club. Here Emily Howard Stowe joined with male notables to plan a female college in Toronto. Unlike the Kingston assembly, the majority attending this inaugural meeting were women. The stronger feminist movement of the provincial capital, reflected in the makeup of the audience, would be a mainstay of the young college and its successor institution, the Women's College Hospital. Trout herself, mindful of the resistance to her own very similar proposal a few months previously and perhaps jealous of Stowe's prominence, denounced the Toronto plans as a betrayal of Kingston. Her hostility to Stowe's project was influential, discouraging those like Smith, who had been tempted by Toronto's richer resources, from leaving Queen's. The extent to which the character of the medical pioneers became an issue is suggested by one Kingstonian's rejection of the Toronto initiative: 'I do not care to be a student where Mrs. Stowe has any interest directly or indirectly.'[15]

Such assessments set the stage for the October 1883 opening of the Women's Medical College, affiliated with Queen's, and the Woman's Medical College, affiliated with the University of Toronto and the University of Trinity College. Neither institution was entitled to offer degrees but only to offer the requisite course work. Students wrote the exams of the affiliated universities and graduated with those degrees. After 1895, students of the Ontario Medical College for Women, the successor to the Toronto school, could take the examination of any medical school they chose.

By the last decade of the nineteenth century other universities were also offering women medical training. Dalhousie University (1890), Bishop's University (1890), the University of Western Ontario (1890s) and the University of Manitoba (1891) followed the path which the Kingston and Toronto pioneers had mapped out. The majority of female students now trained in the Dominion but some, like Dr. Eleanore Lennox (Homeopathic Hospital College, Cleveland, 1893) continued to go elsewhere, often for special programs.

Kingston offered separate courses until 1893, when its years of financial difficulty and faltering enrolment exacted their price, and it fell victim to the superior resources of its Toronto rival. The Queen's Medical Faculty did not admit women again until 1943. Toronto, now the only female institution in the country, enlisted the support of all who preferred separate education. Even with this enlarged constituency, its position was not sufficiently powerful to resist pressures to shut down in 1905-1906 when the University of Toronto agreed to permit female candidates in its own medical courses. With the closing of the Ontario Medical College for Women, a unique experiment in Canadian medicine and feminism ended.

Before that date, however, the schools produced 146 students, 34 from Kingston and 112 from Toronto. In addition there were others, like Octavia Ritchie England (Bishops, 1891), who took courses at the Ontario schools but chose to finish their programs elsewhere. Most graduates cannot be traced in any great detail. A few, however, achieved considerable prominence and their lives are well documented. Despite shortcomings in the evidence, it is possible to identify certain general trends. The majority of students, for instance, appear to have hailed from small Ontario towns like Smiths Falls, Merickville, Brockville, Chatham and Port Elgin or farms in their immediate vicinity. The prevalence of consciousness-raising WCTUs in rural areas and small towns is one possible explanation of such origins. At least five families sent two of their daughters, and there are a number of instances of a close female relative in nursing. Most of the scholars seemed to be daughters of ministers, doctors, teachers or farmers, a relationship which placed them, if sometimes precariously, in the middle class. The marginality of that status in some cases is suggested by the considerable number, including Helen Reynolds Ryan (Queen's, 1885), Eliza Gray (Trinity, 1892), Margaret Blair Gordon (Trinity, 1898) and Margaret Wallace Sterling (Trinity, 1898) who financed their medical studies with some years of teaching. It is impossible to know at this time whether Elizabeth Smith's preliminary decision to use teaching as a stepping stone to medicine was typical or whether others arrived at that choice only after first selecting the more common teaching career. Although most students were single, 11 can be definitely identified as having married either before or during their programs. Eventually more than 66 chose marriage, some to other doctors, as did Alice McGillivray (Queen's, 1884). As far as can be judged, most married women such as McGillivray continued with their careers. Even the arrival of children was not an absolute prohibition to employment, a reflection of the flexibility of a medical practice. In contrast, married females were expected or forced to leave employment in nursing, teaching and the civil service. At least 24 former students chose to take up their work in the United States, where a larger number of female institutions — asylums, hospitals and medical schools, for instance — offered greater opportunity for women doctors. Twenty-five graduates went still further afield to missionary work in India and China. This latter choice reflected the deep religious faith and sometimes the British imperialist sentiments which characterized students. With very few exceptions they were Protestants, expecially Presbyterians, Anglicans and Methodists; in addition, many of them seem to have been evangelically inclined, as student branches of the Young Women's Christian Association suggested. Although the majority remained in Canada, the women doctors were generally 'missionary minded' wherever they practiced. Religious faith armoured and comforted them as 'servants of God' in strange lands and as apostles of hygiene in the Dominion. In both arenas they advanced their claim, as women, to a special nurturing role.

Canadians' membership in the expanding British Empire brought with it moral as well as military and economic responsibilities. From the outset of women's entry into medical programs the mission field was considered an unparalleled 'opportunity for the female graduates of our Canadian colleges'. By the mid-nineteenth century the Protestant churches were finding themselves at a serious disadvantage in evangelization. The Catholics reaped considerable benefit from the medical and educational services of their religious orders while Protestants lacked these essential labour resources. The Methodist *Christian Guardian* observed,

> We see more clearly than ever before how next to impossible it is for men to have access, in their Christianizing efforts, to the female population of heathen countries; and how strong is the necessity that Christian women should go.

Increasingly sensitive to such shortcomings, the churches were equally responsive to the demands of middle-class women for a more prominent and meaningful involvement in religious life. Although leading Protestant denominations remained unwilling to accept female preachers, they were eager sponsors of female teachers, nurses and doctors in mission fields. Since the majority of students at the medical colleges were conscientious church-goers, they were receptive to the message that 'the possibilities of medical work for opening the homes and hearts of the women of China, in the hands of fully qualified women doctors and nurses cannot be overestimated.' Branches of such evangelical associations as the Young Women's Christian Association and the Foreign Missionary Society of the Presbyterian Church supplied constant reminders of the possibility, even the obligation, of a foreign field of labour. The Kingston institution acknowledged its religious responsibilities by offering reduced fees to potential missionaries. Its Toronto rival was equally anxious to attract the same type of medical student, advertising that:

> Ladies preparing to undertake the arduous duties connected with missionary work, will find her [sic] special inducements in the study of disease. Too[,] being in a central position and connected by so many lines of railway and steamboats, its hospitals often receive foreigners suffering from disease, indigenous to their respective countries, thus affording to Students a wide field for the study of rare and peculiar forms of disease.[16]

Feminist sympathies strengthened Christian faith in motivating women to seek missionary work. Doubly armoured, then, these women became influential agents of British cultural and political imperialism. However imperfect British traditions and institutions, they remained, in the minds of Canadian physicians, sufficiently superior to justify wholesale subversion of other cultures in Asia and Africa. Women of the non-Christian and non-European world were especially pitied as suffering from the familiar male domination in its most accentuated form. Footbinding, female infanticide, concubinage and purdah were the disabilities which most often scandalized western feminists examining India and China. They made attentive listeners to sermons and missionary letters which depicted '... poor down-trodden sisters in the East' crying out for assistance. These appeals encouraged feminists to carry the message, 'The World is Made for Women Too,' from their own lands to nations across the sea.[17]

Educated Christian physicians would transform heathen lands and uplift their women through example and service. Two graduates of Queen's testified:

> Believing as we do that no better opportunity can be given us teaching our sisters in this country [India] than when they come to us as in-patients, we have made these our first care....

> We have sought to have individual talks with our in-patients on life and death, eternity and salvation.

It was essential to reach the native women; without their cooperation nations would not escape the superstition of eastern faiths. Just as in North America, women and the family unit were the surest guardians of morality. Missionary women claimed that Christianity would give women the authority to fulfill a purifying role within their community. Thus female conversion was the best way of liberating heathens from misogynist traditions and 'backward' practices. As one Toronto woman based in Canton, China urged, 'Think of 200,000,000 women! And then think of the potential power and the budding leadership ... which lies in those strong brown hands and eager, agile minds! These are the women of China today.'[18]

India was the first foreign mission field to attract medical graduates. Only in the 1890s did China emerge as a rival. There was an early tendency for former classmates or graduates of one institution to work in the same location, frequently in the same hospital or dispensary. This was true, for instance, of Elizabeth Beatty (Queen's, 1884), Marion Oliver (Queen's, 1886), Margaret O'Hara (Queen's, 1891) and Agnes Turnbull (Queen's, 1892), all of whom laboured for some time in Indore, India. Common destinations were not all that surprising as denominations and their own particular missionary zones, but they also reflected the friendships which had grown up between classmates. Just as in North

America, these ties would be important in bolstering faltering wills and encouraging further initiatives.

Not unexpectedly, in view of their middle-class upbringing, the first response of such women to their new homes and neighbours was often sheer horror. Margaret O'Hara, who eventually spent 35 happy and productive years on the subcontinent, wrote of her initial revulsion in 1892:

> There is no home life — no *real* home life, I mean — and we are surrounded by sin, suffering and superstition in filthiest and grossest forms. The first few days I was in India seemed dreadful to me.

Nevertheless, like Susanna Carson Rijnhart in Tibet and Pearl Smith Chute in China, O'Hara was quickly drawn to the people she had come to serve. Although she was never completely uncritical of local traditions she did develop respect for them. Her adoption of three Indian children reflected these sympathies. Her response to dolls sent from Canada as a lesson in neatness was also instructive. She rejected their European dress with the observation, 'I firmly believe that Indians should hold to Indian dress; it is far more suitable and graceful than an European dress.' For O'Hara, as for the others, her feminist inclinations played a role in helping her to identify with her adopted land. We do not yet know, however, these women's impact on indigenous feminism.[19]

Doctors were eager to train Indian and Chinese women to minister to their people just as Canadians had chosen to do. In Indore, India, Elizabeth Beatty and Marion Oliver promoted Lady Dufferin's scheme for the medical education of native women. In China, Alfretta Gifford Kilborn (Victoria, 1891) campaigned vigorously for the right of women to enter the Medical School of the West China University. Others, like Jean Hoyles Haslam (Toronto, 1903), Jessie Allyn (Trinity, 1904) and Jessie McBean (Toronto, 1905) were founders and operators of special hospitals for women and children in India and China. In their crusades to establish new institutions and to win entry into older ones, the Canadians must often have recalled their own pioneering experiences. Campaigns against footbinding, child marriage and widow immolation also appeared as regular, if less familiar, additions to their work. The doctors believed that with the elimination of such injustices women would play their essential social role. The full force of womanhood, at last freed of custom's chains, would purify and, incidentally, westernize 'backward' cultures.[20]

The tasks of liberating and reforming other women were not easily undertaken even by adventuresome and earnest Canadians. Elizabeth Beatty, Minnie Fraser Stuart (Queen's, 1890) and Margaret O'Hara were among many to suffer repeated bouts with local diseases. Susanna Carson Rijnhart lost her first husband and child in a futile attempt to convert Tibet. Lucinda Graham (Trinity, 1891) died in Honan. Difficult as it was to endure such hardships, the doctors were certain of the benefits they brought. At a less altruistic level they no doubt appreciated the fact that in foreign fields they were afforded a level of power and authority they could never have had at home.

The careers of other graduates did not usually unfold in such exotic locales, but they too were often dedicated to feminist and reform causes. Medical workers in North America agreed that 'true womanhood' had remained 'dormant' too long. 'Awakened' women should repudiate the senseless frivolity that engaged middle-class women in particular. A distinctly feminine point of view, nurturant, benevolent and moral, must be brought to bear on the problems of the day. [21]

Sensitive alike to the shortcomings of their male colleagues and to the special responsibilities of female healers, new doctors gravitated to the service of women and children in Canada and the United States. Marjorie Ward (Trinity, 1894), for instance, became superintendent of the Montreal Foundling and Sick Baby Hospital; Anna McFee (Trinity, 1897) worked as resident physician to the Infant's Hospital, Randall's Island, New York. Both Jean Willson McDonald (Toronto, 1897) and Jean Cruikshank Bailey (Toronto, 1898) were associated with the New England Hospital for Women in Boston. In Toronto, Emma Skinner Gordon (Toronto, 1896) organized 'incorrigible' boys into a religious and educational association. After 1898, students and graduates laboured in a medical dispensary associated with the Ontario Medical College for Women. It had been founded two years earlier as a separate institution by student Anna McFee. Here female and young patients received the more understanding treatment which was supposedly the prerogative of female physicians. At the same time the clinics maintained by the dispensary gave College students and faculty valuable experience they were frequently denied in city hospitals. The later emergence of the Women's College Hospital from the dispensary was intended to meet the same needs.

Doctors like Elizabeth Matheson Scott (Trinity, 1898) and Mary Crawford (Trinity, 1900) both of Winnipeg, also followed healthier children into the nation's schools. Their appointments as school medical inspectors reflected not only women's own interests but also society's sense of what was appropriate for 'doctors in skirts'. Such prejudices assisted employment in certain restricted fields. Unfortunately there was almost no female penetration of most medical specialities — such as surgery — or institutions — such as the McGill Medical School — where 'maternal' qualities were believed of little importance.

Some women did, however, manage to base powerful careers on their faith in a distinctive female temperament. One leading preacher of this dogma, Dr. Helen MacMurchy (Toronto, 1900) became chief of the new federal Division of Child Welfare in 1919. Although single and childless herself, MacMurchy confessed that 'the dearest wish of a true woman is to be a mother.' Allied with her sister physicians, MacMurchy used her position to educate women in the 1920s to their essential responsibility in reproduction. Her widely circulated 'Little Blue Books' for Canadian mothers set out to inspire and reform their readers. Motherhood was above all the highest form of patriotism, for 'No Baby — No Nation'. Only a dedicated womanhood or better still, motherhood, could make up the losses suffered during the First World War.[22]

Elizabeth Smith Shortt was another influential apostle of the maternal cause. Like MacMurchy, she was not content to limit women's role to childbirth alone. In speeches across the country she argued that 'the mother with the highest sense of her responsibility toward her own children is pre-eminently the woman whose interest, whose "mothering" extends to the welfare of other children and thus becomes inevitably a student of civic conditions.' Smith Shortt and the majority of her classmates divided women into two groups, the competent and the responsible and the incompetent and the irresponsible. More often than not the first corresponded to the middle class and the second to the working class. Not unexpectedly, the 'larger mothering' was the particular trust of middle-class women. They alone had the time, the training and the will to set the world right. Under their direction Canada would be reshaped according to maternally-inspired objectives. In her work with the National Council of Women of Canada, the Young Women's Christian Association and the Mother's Allowances' Commission of Ontario, Smith Shortt laboured to fulfill the stern duty she had set the fortunate of her sex.[23]

Concern for Canadian mothers and the health of the nation in general also led some physicians to examine the advantages of birth control and sterilization. Fewer births would mean better babies, healthier mothers and a stronger country. The precise method of restraint was extremely controversial. Abstinence from intercourse probably had more public advocates, if not private practitioners, than any other means of control. It certainly appealed to those like MacMurchy and Smith Shortt, who believed women to be essentially purer and less sensual than men. According to this viewpoint, abstinence, except when children were desired, was not extremely difficult for normal, that is maternally-minded, women. In fact it could protect them from aggressive male lust. There was an additional dilemma in that birth control was too often adopted by those best-equipped, economically, psychologically and physically, to have children. Legalization of birth control would help bring about 'race suicide'. The influential MacMurchy further argued in her *Sterilization? Birth Control?* (1934) that easy access to birth control would result in sexual promiscuity and debased marriages. At most it should be employed 'in exceptional cases only'.[24]

Some women doctors, however, were more positive about the results of birth control procedures. In Hamilton, Rowena Hume Douglas (Trinity, 1899) and Elizabeth Bagshaw (Trinity, 1905) established Canada's first Planned Parenthood Association in 1930 and encouraged the creation of similar bodies elsewhere in Ontario. Such initiatives suggest a greater willingness to recognize an active female sexuality. Unfortunately, as yet we know far too little about the history of birth control in Canada.

Some groups were considered particularly good candidates for birth control or even sterilization. Investigations of the mentally retarded by MacMurchy, Marjorie Ward (Trinity, 1894), Smith Shortt and Mary Crawford created their own special concern about the unregulated propagation of the 'unfit'. In 1906, MacMurchy, for instance, prepared an Ontario census of the 'feeble-minded' which condemned existing custodial arrangements and described the crime and immorality which were so regularly linked to retardation. Twenty years later another doctor reported that the situation had deteriorated: 'The toll of war took so many of superior stock.... The burden on the superior stock — the so-called normal — is tremendous....' Smith Shortt and MacMurchy saw surgical sterilization as one way of preventing the unwanted proliferation of society's misfits. There was no consensus on this 'final solution' among medical women. The 1930 Convenor of the National Council of Women's Committee on Mental Hygiene, Mabel Mannington (Toronto, 1900), reminded listeners that:

Sterilization of the feeble-minded youth cannot take the place of the training and supervision needed....

> Again, the worst type of psychopathic heredity is often the border-line case, which would not be in an institution, nor available for surgical procedures.[25]

Female doctors pitied mothers with unwanted pregnancies, but many also feared the social problems resulting from the unregulated 'breeding' of the inferior. Sympathy for their own sex went hand in hand with more conservative considerations. As members of a professional elite, doctors shared middle-class hopes for a reformed order in which efficient and rational use of human and material resources would improve, and also control, social development. Sometimes, as in the cases of Smith Shortt and MacMurchy, their views closely resembled eugenics, or the belief that human beings can and should be selectively bred for intellectual and physical improvement. Movements in favour of such programs did exist in the United States, for example, where they were often associated with middle-class fears of social degeneration. The passage of legislation permitting sterilization of the 'unfit' in Alberta (1928) and British Columbia (1933), together with the formation of the Eugenics Society of Canada, revealed similar anxiety in the Dominion. However, no consensus on eugenic policies emerged among the female physicians in Canada.

Female doctors also joined other women in efforts to rectify social conditions and to advance feminist causes. To these ends they enlisted in a multitude of associations, including the Local Councils of Women, the WCTU, the YWCA, the Dominion Order of King's Daughters, the Civic Improvement League and the Dominion Women's Enfranchisement Association. Within these bodies physicians often gave technical and scientific advice. Documenting the need for TB testing of cattle, slum clearance, water purification and free vaccinations, they helped the women's movement keep up-to-date in a rapidly changing society. Their skills identified and eliminated some of the abuses of industrial capitalism. Not surprisingly, the expertise of these middle-class professionals also enabled the same privileged group to maintain control of the emerging welfare state. In this they acted little differently from other reform-minded male physicians.

Mindful of their own experience with male chauvinism and confident of women's equal but distinctive nature, women doctors demanded greater economic and legal rights for their sex. Like other feminists they were divided over the question of equality or protection for the female worker. Many, and probably most, decided, as did Smith Shortt, that women's potential as mothers necessitated somewhat different legislative treatment in the field of business and industry. They did demand, however, that equal effort bring equal reward regardless of sex. They were also unanimous in seeking the removal of all barriers to women in the professions. There middle-class women could presumably take care of themselves.

The franchise issue sparked the same agreement. Female doctors sided with Dr. Mary Crawford (Trinity, 1900) when she catalogued the abuses the vote would cure in her *Legal Status of Women in Manitoba* (1913). Smith Shortt, Helen Reynolds Ryan (Queen's, 1885), Lelia Davis (Toronto, 1889), Bertha Dymond (Trinity, 1892) and Margaret Blair Gordon became leaders with Crawford in the cause of female enfranchisement. Many more were foot soldiers in the same campaign. Smith Shortt supplied a vivid picture of the conditions enfranchised women would have to face:

> I see as in a dream a giant working in a swampy farm. The name of that giant is Humanity, and as ever he works on in the higher levels of his swampy field, the noxious odours and miasmic vapors rise around him and lessen his vitality. As I see drains have been made on the upper edges of the swamp, and I ask, 'Why does he not drain it thoroughly from, and through, its cause and centre?' I am told he cannot, that two giants greater than he control the place and will not let him do it. And as I look I see on the edges of the swampy lane, two giants greater than Humanity, and the name of one is Commercial Interests and the name of the other is Political Expediency.

It was the need for just such 'giant killing' that inspired Blair Gordon to propose the suffrage referendum in Toronto's 1914 municipal election. Clean government, like new legal rights for women, would come with enfranchisement of female voters.[26]

Once the vote had been won, most doctors, like most other feminists, failed to take up roles as active politicians. Caroline Brown (Toronto, 1900) and Minerva Reid (Toronto, 1905) were two exceptions. Brown became president of the Liberal-Conservative Women's Association in Toronto's Ward Five and a city school trustee in the 1920s. Reid, the chief surgeon at Women's College Hospital between 1915 and 1925, ran unsuccessfully as a Conservative candidate in the 1926 federal contest and served on the Toronto Board of Education from 1926 to 1932. These women were exceptions. Most College alumnae appear to have devoted themselves to their practices or local community concerns at most.[27]

Former students of the College did not achieve extensive recognition even in medicine. The first 100 years of the Canadian Medical Association (1867-1967), for instance, saw no woman assume the chief posts of president or general secretary. Nor was any female doctor chairman or honorary treasurer of the Executive Committee and General Council. Nor was any woman editor of the CMA *Journal* or an honorary member during the same period. A survey of other medical/health associations in the years to 1930 also turns up very few female officers. Relatively small numbers, male antagonism and suspicion from the male establishment seem likely explanations for women's absence from leading positions in their profession. They may have attained recognition and status in the course of their private practices, but these roles were much more limited than those envisioned by medical pioneers. [28]

The separate medical colleges offered women advantages difficult to find elsewhere. Their classes provided encouragement which male-dominated programs only rarely matched; their faculties supplied graduates with opportunities for employment, research and influence. Memory of student years fortified female doctors in their subsequent careers, but discrimination existed everywhere outside college walls. Not surprisingly, a large number of students from Kingston and Toronto went on to Europe, Britain and the United States where more numerous institutions offered greater opportunity. Some students, like Elizabeth Hurdon (Trinity, 1895), the author of *Gynaecology and Pathology*, stayed on in the foreign country, in her case as Associate Professor of Gynaecology at Johns Hopkins University. Such losses can be attributed in good part to the conservatism of Canada's medical profession.

The closing of the Ontario Medical College for Women in 1906 deprived female doctors of an important stronghold of psychological reassurance and practical reinforcement. The loss could be offset only in part by the creation, in 1915, of Women's College Hospital, which soon offered residencies and specialist opportunities to women doctors. Inspiration and a reminder of old feminist ideals were also found in the Federation of Medical Women of Canada, created in 1924 by six women, including four graduates of the medical colleges. Dr. Marjory Mac-Murchy became its first president. The Federation was not, however, representative of the earlier outward-looking feminism of female physicians. Its primary aim was to serve as a means of communication between women doctors, not to agitate for new rights. It could not, nor did it intend to act as a substitute for educational institutions which championed the preservation and promotion of women's place in a male-dominated profession. The trend in the number of female physicians as a percentage of all doctors in Canada reveals the marginality of their position. The decline between 1911 and 1921 from 2.7 per cent to

1.8 per cent was not unrelated to the closing of the Ontario Medical College for Women. Although Abraham Flexner's influential report, *Medical Education in the United States and Canada* (1910) concluded that 'women's choice is free and varied' in medicine, the situation was anything but promising. Not until much later, for instance, did the Universities of McGill, Laval and Montreal open their medical schools to female candidates. Even where women faced no overt discrimination in regulations they rarely encountered positive reinforcement. This failure went beyond the universities themselves. Nowhere in Canada's education system were girls encouraged to consider high status professional, especially scientific, employments.[29]

The establishment of a professional medical role for women was dependent on the vitality of Canadian feminism. When this faith faltered so did the cause of female physicians. Ironically enough, medical pioneers, by stressing women's unique nurturing 'instinct', contributed to unfavourable trends. Like other feminists, they had no substantial critique of the 'cult of domesticity' which overwhelmed war-weary Canadians by the 1920s. A renewed emphasis on family life and full-time mothering went hand in hand with a wave of Freudian-influenced popular psychology which emphasized sexuality and female irrationality. Despite the innovative aspects of their individual and collective experience, most female doctors interpreted their lives in terms of unique female qualities. At the same time their indoctrination as medical experts confirmed their membership in a middle-class professional elite. For all their battles with male doctors, the majority finally shared that group's essentially conservative approach to radical social change. A maternalist ideology and a professional orientation are hardly the best guarantees of a feminist revolution.[30]

CHAPTER SIX

Ladies or Midwives? Efforts to Reduce Infant and Maternal Mortality

Suzann Buckley

———————————

Social reformers in Canada, as elsewhere, placed great emphasis on the importance of the stable family for the normal dvelopment of children in an environment that seemed increasingly hostile to the health and welfare of future generations. Children and their problems became an obvious focus for reformers; where hope of change for the older generation faded, expectations of success with children flourished.

The period 1880-1920, as we have seen in the previous article, witnessed the campaign for more women doctors; in this same period nurses organized their profession. Both groups turned some attention to the realm of public health and especially child health. As Neil Sutherland's recently published Children in English-Canadian Society* points out, three areas occupied the public health movement's activists: the health of school children, infant mortality and 'feeble-mindedness'.*

Infant mortality attracted the attention of reformers as part of the general fear of race degeneration. In the late nineteenth century there was widespread public discussion of the poor health of French and English military recruits, destined to fight in imperials wars. In North America the spectre was raised by a combination of an influx of immigrants whose birthrates exceeded those of Canadians and the heavy losses of World War I. Early efforts supported by reform organizations like the National Council of Women of Canada (NCWC) consisted of pure milk depots and the establishment of clinics and public health nursing programs in urban areas. These early programs were eventually adopted by government departments of health.

Suzann Buckley's article adds new dimension to the previous discussions of the problem. In describing the campaign against both infant and maternal mortality she discusses the important effect of interprofessional rivalries. The conflict among doctors, nurses and reform groups focussed on the midwife problem. Despite recognition of poor prenatal and postnatal care in slums and isolated rural areas, health

* (Toronto: University of Toronto Press, 1976).

professionals consistently blocked plans to train or import midwives or obstetrical nurses to Canada. Nurses by and large deferred to doctors in this area and fought to retain their status by refusing to perform obstetrical work since it involved the domestic labour associated with the old working-class image of nurses. The development of public health nursing and the shape of reform efforts was thus severely hampered by the clash between the professions.

There is not very much difference between the murderer and the one who stands by and sees those die whom he could save. The infant mortality rate must be reduced. [1]

This call came from Helen MacMurchy, a Canadian doctor, but it could have been issued by any number of male and female reformers in Britain, Canada or the United States. The incidence of infant mortality seemed to soar during the late nineteenth century as expanding urbanization left in its wake congested cities that were spawning grounds for slums and disease. In Canada and the United States the infant mortality problem was compounded by an influx of impoverished immigrants who flocked to the overcrowded cities or settled in remote rural areas. Unwholesome environments and lack of adequate medical care for infants because of their parents' poverty or isolation meant that a substantial number of children died in infancy. Initially, reformers focussed upon the issue of unsanitary urban environments chiefly because urban problems were more visible. Aware that the infant mortality rate in working-class sections of cities greatly exceeded the rate for the urban middle-class, reformers concentrated upon measures that would mitigate the unsanitary conditions in working-class areas. As part of an extensive sanitary improvement crusade, reformers demanded that governments establish milk depots. They hoped that women who came to the depots would be convinced of the merits of breastfeeding as a means of immunizing an infant. Even if women were not persuaded to breastfeed, the depots could at least provide infants with sterilized cow's milk. The reformers also campaigned for government inspection of milk supplies and started hygiene classes for mothers. [2]

These efforts to reduce infant mortality were in fact part of the general progressive trend to clean up cities. An important factor in this trend was the establishment of social services designed to control urban ills. It was thought that services providing for pure milk and water supplies and

medical inspection of schools and recreational facilities would keep at bay
the moral and physical decay that threatened the existing social order.
Such measures, especially those to improve conditions for infants, would
guarantee a healthy new generation to carry on the work of shaping an
improved society.[3]

The infant mortality question was also related to doctors' determination to professionalize the practice of medicine by strengthening their
pecuniary positions and their controls of medical care. Doctors were
eager to bring childbirth and child care under their control. As Strong-
Boag points out, administering at childbirth often initiated a doctor's
association with a family and its illnesses and it was thus a key to a
doctor's future income. Child care could afford doctors an opportunity to
monopolize a new area of medical treatment. As the purported source of
all knowledge about disease, doctors could claim to be the best authority
on child care. Such rivals as midwives could thereby be eliminated as
competitors.[4]

Shortly after reformers had launched their sanitary improvement
crusade, they realized that these measures would not substantially
diminish infant mortality. They then turned to the question of childbirth
and cooperated with medical men in order to bring it under the control of
doctors by regulating or by outlawing midwives. In Britain the *State
Midwives Act* (1902) set up an instructional program for certification of
midwives. Once certified, midwives could practice, but they were
required to advise a patient to call in a doctor for difficult cases. Many
American states, responding to pressure from the American Medical
Association, either instituted strict controls over midwives or legislated
against the practice of midwifery. In Canada, the issue provoked heated
debate among female reformers. Before examining the midwifery
controversy in Canada, some general comments about Canadian female
reformers during these years are necessary.[5]

In Canada from the 1890s to the 1920s, issues pertaining to the family
were of particular interest to women. Within this context, infant and
maternal mortality were especially important. Many female reformers
viewed these two matters from a personal level. But even those female
reformers not touched directly (in the case of single or childless married
women) took up the cause. Indeed they had little choice if they wished to
be active in reform, because in Canada, as in Britain and the United
States, the respectable female reformer was expected to restrain her
activities to those matters affecting children and mothers. On the basis of
the stereotype of women's intuitive empathy with the weak and dependent, the female reformer, single and married, was socialized to accept the

role of mother of society. As a result, the feminism manifested by most of the female reformers usually did not go beyond 'female' consciousness. As Anne Summers has explained, this involves a heightened awareness among women which might lead to activism, but it is an awareness and activism based on norms imposed by a patriarchal society. The reform-minded woman thus became active in order to ameliorate conditions which threatened to weaken the bourgeois family. [6]

In the case of female doctors and nurses, this type of feminism was further circumscribed by professionalism. Women in both these groups expressed concern about infant and maternal mortality. But their efforts usually remained within the confines of what male doctors judged to be acceptable reform because deviation from the prescribed course would have jeopardized their professional status. Only a comparatively few women were doctors and, in order to be accepted by their male peers, they adopted the male ideology of professionalism. This entailed physicians gaining popular approval by stressing technical competence and training and by emphasizing hospital care and other formalized systems for handling patients. Nurses were even more socialized and constrained. They still laboured under the Nightingale mystique. In the 1860s, during her struggle in England to gain sanction of upper and middle-class women going outside the home and into nursing, Nightingale had defined the respectable and acceptable nurse: an ideal 'lady' who showed 'wifely obedience to the doctor, motherly self-devotion to the patient and a firm mistress/servant discipline to those below the rung of nurse'. Besides this severe limitation on their behaviour, nurses' potential as reformers was further limited. As a newly organized group they were trying to establish nursing as a profession. Their struggle with doctors for acceptance and for adequate training, working conditions and wages made them reluctant to challenge doctors on such other issues as care of infants and mothers. [7]

Within this narrow sphere, for 30 years some women did try to improve the infant and maternal mortality situation. Their efforts were institutional, group and individual. Often their arguments for amelioration focussed on national and imperial goals. Many of the female reformers denounced infant and maternal mortality as a blemish on Canada's image and as a waste of resources that would weaken the connection with Britain. Canada purported to be an advanced nation, but as reformers suspected and as national statistics, which became available in the 1920s, later confirmed, Canada had higher infant and maternal mortality rates than most 'civilized' nations. According to the 1925 figures of 14 countries, Canada's infant mortality rate of 92 per 1,000 live births was exceeded only by Spain (137), Italy (119), Germany (105), Belgium (100) and France (95). The maternal mortality rates for the same year revealed a similar situation. Among 19 countries, Canada's rate of 5.6 per 1,000 live births was only surpassed by the United States (6.6), Scotland (6.2) and Belgium (5.8). Within the national and imperial context, the reformers sympathized with the efforts of the Dominion government to encourage immigration to Canada. They feared, however, that immigration from eastern, central and southern Europe would substantially reduce British preponderance. The reformers therefore wanted the government to spend more money on protecting the health of Canadian infants and mothers and less on immigration schemes.[8]

Because of their concern about preserving the Anglo-Saxon element, many of the reformers subscribed to the popular eugenics and euthenics theories, which maintained that those with hereditary defects should be institutionalized or even sterilized. Greater efforts should be made to uplift economically deprived children to middle-class norms by means of such environmental reforms as child welfare projects and medical inspection of schools. As propounded by reformers these theories usually did not embrace widespread public advocacy of birth control, except for the possible sterilization of defectives. Aside from the fact that such a course would have provoked dissension among reformers because of Roman Catholic opposition to birth control, drastic limitation of family size was contrary to their aim. Disturbed by a steadily declining birthrate and by the immigration threat, the reformers sought the production of healthy Canadian babies.[9]

Organized efforts to reduce infant and maternal mortality began in the 1890s when the problem was taken up by the National Council of Women of Canada (NCWC), which was concerned that medical care was unavailable or unattainable either because of the remoteness of immigrant settlements on the Prairies or because of poverty among western farmers and urban industrial workers. This situation, the NCWC concurred, could not continue. Reform, however, could not involve calls for fundamental changes in immigration and economic policies. For the upper and middle-class women to take such a course of action would, in many instances, bring them into conflict with their husbands, who formulated the policies. By thus promoting familiar discord, the women would undermine one of their main objectives — family harmony and stability. Furthermore, the Council women regarded the problems associated with immigration and industrialization as remediable defects within an otherwise exemplary system. The Council's approach, therefore, was to organize a series of programs designed to ameliorate some of the most blatant aspects of inadequate medical attention. These would involve social mothering schemes intended either to condition immigrants and the poor to the reformers' norms of family stability and self-sufficiency or to provide remedial measures for the children of the unsocialized immigrants and the poor.[10]

On February 2, 1897, Lady Ishbel Aberdeen, the president of the NCWC, announced such a program — the Victorian Order of Home Helpers, which would be financed by a permanent endowment raised by Aberdeen and the NCWC. Women selected as home-helpers would nurse the sick, especially mothers and infants, and would demonstrate techniques of household sanitation. Unlike the regular nurse who only attended specific cases, the home-help would go from house to house 'doing all sorts of mercy and kindnesses' in order to uplift the immigrant and the poor to prescribed middle-class standards of sanitation. To qualify for the order a woman had to be at least 28 years of age and have passed an examination devised by medical men 'and others who under-[stood] the need which had to be met'. Essentially, the examination would entail demonstration of five main items: practical knowledge of midwifery; practical knowledge of first aid and of simple nursing; general knowledge of housekeeping and basic home sanitation; ability to prepare suitable foods for invalids; and 'ladylike' qualities of breeding, tact, courage and self-control. Aberdeen did not specify where she expected to find these paragons of practical and moral virtue. Quite possibly, in view of her earlier efforts to find positions in Canada for distressed British gentlewomen, she intended to draw substantially upon that pool.[11]

There was considerable objection to the scheme from many nurses and doctors. The home-helpers' limited training, opponents maintained, would not enable them to provide adequate medical care. Although this was the most frequently stated objection, there were other reasons given for disapproval. In fact, their concern extended beyond the status of nurses and the pay for doctors. Many doctors regarded midwives as 'untrained, unkempt, gin-soaked harridans'. This representation stemmed, in great measure, from male determination to maintain a monopoly on obstetrics, but the nurses had endorsed it in order to retain favour with doctors and to protect their own precarious status. If the nurses challenged the male doctors by approving of home-helpers, they would jeopardize their position. Furthermore, from the nurses' point of view, the home-helpers were undesirable professional role models. Midwives, of whatever calibre, simply did not fit in with the nurses' Nightingale mystique. Also, midwives were willing to do domestic chores whereas the nurses, in the interest of raising their status, were not. To sanction this type of maternity care might hamper the nurses' struggle to be free from housekeeping duties. From the medical man's perspective, the home-helpers were an anathema because they posed a significant economic threat. They would deny doctors not only the chance for a delivery fee, but also an opportunity to initiate association with a family's illnesses.[12]

Dr. Thomas Gibson, one of the few male doctors who supported Aberdeen's scheme to extend medical services to the poor and isolated, tried to overcome these objections. By April 1897, the draft of a nursing proposal which he had sent to Aberdeen on February 7 had become the model for the Victorian Order. This eliminated the midwives connotation by stipulating that the Order would supply only women who were thoroughly trained in hospital and district nursing. This substantial alteration was reflected in the change of name from the Victorian Order of Home Helpers to the Victorian Order of Nurses (VON).[13]

This major modification allayed some of the opposition. But many male doctors remained hostile. To win their support Aberdeen enlisted the aid of Dr. Alfred Worcester, an American, who in 1885 had founded the Waltham Training Home for District Nurses in Massachusetts. Worcester came to speak to doctors in Ottawa and Toronto and assured them that Victorian nurses would attend only 'the very poor people who [could] not well afford to pay a doctor'. These nurses thus would not seriously threaten doctors' financial interests. Besides relegating Victorian nurses to their 'proper' economically subordinate sphere, Worcester coached Aberdeen on how to disabuse male doctors of their notion of her as a meddlesome moralizer. According to Worcester, he told Aberdeen 'what physicians like to eat, smoke and drink'. These items were supplied in abundance at the meetings and 'the doctors could not conceal their surprise. They had supposed that their hostess was violently opposed both to alcohol and to tobacco.'[14]

Thanks in great measure to Worcester's persuasion and tactics, most of the doctors ceased their opposition. By late November 1897 the VON had begun its work under the direction of Charlotte Macleod, the chief superintendent. Macleod, formerly superintendent at the Waltham school, had been born and raised in New Brunswick. She was, Aberdeen recounts, 'gentle and sweet in manner [but with] plenty of backbone'. Under the tutelage of this 'lady-nurse' the VON slowly expanded its operations. Communities which wanted the Victorian nurses guaranteed a salary of $300 a year with board, maintenance and uniforms. By 1900, 32 nurses were scattered throughout Canada. Also, a cottage hospital scheme had been started in which a Victorian nurse, with the aid of local or district committees, set up a hospital of about six beds to service outlying areas. Lady Minto, Aberdeen's successor as the honorary president of the VON, raised funds for these hospitals by appealing to the public and by applying to the Dominion and provincial governments for grants.[15]

The VON's efforts, however, merely scratched the surface of the infant and maternal mortality problem. The limited number of Victorian nurses and VON hospitals could assist only a small percentage of the population. The lack of care for infants and mothers in urban and rural areas was still an acute problem. With respect to the Prairies, homesteaders' accounts of life in parts of Saskatchewan attest to this point:

> We couldn't get a doctor [to attend to the birth] so we arranged with a woman, who when she was needed was suffering from an attack of gallstones. But she bravely put her pain to one side to help another woman over her emergency. Then she had to go back to her bed and hubbie and I tended the little girlie.[16]

In 1908, Mrs. George Cran, an Englishwoman who had been brought to Canada by the Dominion government in order to assist in promoting the emigration of British women to the Prairies, publicly called attention in Winnipeg to the failure of existing projects to ease the medical problems of western women. Analyzing the situation from the perspective of 'a trained maternity nurse and a mother', Cran concluded that a major difficulty facing western women was lack of medical and domestic assistance during confinement. In the professed interest of alleviating the plight of prairie women, Cran expressed a willingness to send out British women who had received a few months' training in English obstetrical hospitals. In effect, Cran's proposal, like Aberdeen's initial plan, was intended to resolve the different problems of British and Canadian women.[17]

As in 1897 the regular nurses refused to countenance such a scheme. Cran's plan was another threat to their efforts to disassociate nurses from domestic work. Now, however, the nurses discussed means of action. An article in *The Canadian Nurse* argued: 'The scope of the smaller hospitals must be increased and the work of the Victorian Order ... must be extended.' As part of this project, money should be raised to improve the pay for district nurses. Unless salaries for Victorian nurses were increased, regular nurses could not afford to join the Order. 'Many of them not only support[ed] themselves but [had] others more or less dependent upon them.' In addition to supporting expansion of the Victorian Order and improvement in the financial position of Victorian nurses, the article tried to squash completely the idea of the nurse-domestic. 'The domestic side of the question should not be shouldered off upon the nursing profession entirely. They have sufficient responsibility already.' The correct approach was for the women's organizations to convince the government to appoint a Royal Commission to deal with the domestic servant shortage. After all, the article contended, the problem of domestic help was 'as important as the building of railways or the conservation of forests, only it takes a long time for a male government to see it in quite that light'. Besides getting the government to realize the seriousness of insufficient domestic help, the article recommended that:

> Every western hospital be compelled to take obstetrical cases, especially such as cannot afford to pay, and also, that the Provincial Government make a grant to the hospitals to cover the expenses of such patients, and if necessary assist the municipality with funds for the erection of a building to accommodate them.

While waiting for action along these lines, women throughout Canada should 'counsel together ... to help our sisters'. By being forced to defend themselves against Cran's proposal, the nurses had been drawn into the reform effort. Once having taken a stand, however, they were content to leave the thrust for change to women who were less constrained by professional concerns. [18]

Many women and women's organizations were in fact expanding their reform activities. Examples abound, but it is sufficient to cite three: the work of Dr. Emma Gordon in Toronto, the efforts of the Women's Service League in Winnipeg and the efforts of the VON to expand services in sparsely settled areas. In 1906, Gordon 'realized the need for clinics where poor women could receive prenatal and natal care'. With the aid of Dr. Jennie Gray and Dr. Skinner Gordon, she founded the first out-patient clinic, staffed by women, for women. In 1909 in Winnipeg, the Women's Service League started clinics for infant care. At the same time, the VON, as part of its expansion of district nursing into isolated areas, encouraged its nurses to select

> desirable women and girls to go out as Home Helpers. These would be called upon when needed, would go with the nurse to patients' homes, look after the house, do the cooking, washing, etc. under the nurse's guidance, and be left in charge of the patient and home after a time while the nurse passed on to a more urgent case. [19]

Women's activities apparently generated some provincial responses. In 1909, the Saskatchewan commissioner of public health, Dr. M.M. Seymour, used his position in order to further his commitment to governmental responsibility for improved health services. He informally instituted a maternity grant program which involved giving public money to pregnant women who met two criteria: remoteness from a doctor and lack of money for maternal medical care. Sums of approximately $25 were allocated to assist in preparation for confinement and to subsidize the doctor's fee. In Ontario in 1910, the government asked Dr. Helen MacMurchy to compile a report on infant mortality.[20]

MacMurchy's entrance into the infant mortality realm introduced to the reform world a new variety of woman professional. Unlike many of the NCWC women, she was single. Unlike the nurses, she belonged to an established, high prestige profession. Despite these differences, MacMurchy shared their national and imperial goals and was careful to maintain 'all the fine and essential qualities of womanhood'. Like many women professionals in the early twentieth century, MacMurchy endorsed the professional monopoly in the name of science and efficiency, while advocating creating special female roles within the profession to compensate for its deficiencies. Thus, MacMurchy could support a doctor's monopoly of obstetrics while campaigning against infant and maternal mortality.[21]

MacMurchy's limitations are clearly evident in her report to the Ontario government on infant mortality. It set out reasons why nearly 7,000 infants (under one year) died in 1909 in Ontario. The chief explanations involved the interrelated factors of poverty and unsanitary living conditions. Although MacMurchy sharply critized the situation, her main emphasis for reform was not on substantial economic change. In keeping with her roles as professional and female reformer, she stressed measures which would bring the infant under institutionalized medical care. Part of this involved convincing women to breastfeed their infants. Breastfeeding would avoid the risks of unpasteurized milk and provide an infant with some immunity to an unhealthy environment. In order to encourage women to breastfeed, a mother's qualms about the cost of such a procedure had to be overcome. A working woman who could not adjust her schedule to a breastfeeding routine should have a pension, if necessary, to take care of the family. Until this change enabled women to make motherhood their sole occupation, one means of partially overcoming the economic hurdle to breastfeeding was for a provincial grant of $.14 a day for an infant nursed by its mother in a hospital or infant's home and $.07 a day for an infant not nursed by its mother in such institutions. By paying more for an infant nursed by its mother within an institution MacMurchy evidently not only hoped to entice poor women to leave the unsanitary conditions of their homes in order to give birth in more antiseptic surroundings, but also to persuade them to breastfeed their infants. Other recommendations in MacMurchy's report, which she expanded in 1911 and 1912, suggested education about sanitation, registration of births and deaths of infants in order that public health officials could contact cases, provincial grants of one-third the salary paid to a doctor or nurse exclusively employed in infant welfare work in any municipality and the establishment of a bureau of infant welfare within the provincial board of health.[22]

MacMurchy's report implicitly urged other women reformers to increase their efforts to reduce infant mortality. Various women's organizations responded by increasing their pressures for government action and expanding their educational programs. To cite only two examples, the Women's Institutes in Ontario continued their efforts to get local governments to supervise the quality of milk, and the NCWC encouraged women to deal with the problem in various ways. On the educational level, the NCWC specifically emphasized 'Little Mother Classes' in schools. These were intended to stimulate girls to help with babies in their homes and neighbourhoods, to encourage them to direct their mothers to medical care and to prepare themselves for the eventual career of motherhood.[23]

However notable all of these efforts, they were piecemeal and plodding. It remained for the experiences of World War I to vitalize the work of the NCWC and other women's groups. As various articles in *Women's Century* stressed: 'The war has intensified the child welfare problem and the solution of this must be taken up and solved.' In 1916 the NCWC petitioned the Dominion government to establish a bureau of child welfare and to appoint 'a competent woman' to direct it. The NCWC's concern lest infant mortality continue to compound the war-induced loss of human resources was shared by the VON and by the Nurses Association. The VON sent a memorandum to all local councils of women pointing out that 'more babies die in Canada yearly, under one year old, from preventive causes than soldiers have been killed during the war.' In a paper presented to the Canadian Nursing Association, one nurse deplored the fact that in 1918, in Canada's three largest cities, 3,985 infants died from preventable causes at a time when 'never before was human life so valuable to the nation as at present.'[24]

But healthy infants required healthy mothers, and so women's organizations increased their efforts to deal with the maternity situation. Lack of maternity care for women in sparsely settled districts still preoccupied the NCWC and in this concern they were not alone. In June 1916, at the fifth annual meeting of the Canadian Nurses Association, the Ontario Graduate Nurses Association called upon the national Nurses Association to appoint a committee to work with the NCWC to resolve the problem. In subsequent discussion at the same meeting many nurses revealed a different emphasis from the NCWC. While the NCWC had focussed on the lack of any type of care, many nurses accented the issue of unskilled care. If something were not done about this, it was argued, lives would continue to be lost 'by the inexperienced and unskillful attention of midwives.'[25]

Despite the fact that midwifery was illegal in most provinces, it was difficult to stop it. The burden of proof lay with doctors, who found it extremely difficult to acquire the necessary evidence. One speaker at the nurses' meeting reported that:

> Every month in British Columbia we have these cases coming up; but the medical profession cannot prove it. The midwives always arrange it so they cannot be found out. The patient does not want to say anything. The midwife says, 'I will take the case for such and such a price, and do all the work. If you have a doctor, you will have to pay him $25, and you will also pay me $25.' The patient of course says, 'We will not bother about a doctor, if everything is all right.' It cannot be averred then that the midwife actually said she was not willing to have a doctor.[26]

If midwives were to be checked, the meeting concurred, nurses had to change their attitudes and tactics. Many nurses were antipathetic to all obstetrical cases because they involved more work than the average surgical case. Other nurses merely did not want to go to outlying areas. Unlike the Victorian nurses, many of whom were willing to go miles in the face of disagreeable conditions, many regular nurses refused. One nurse vividly illustrated the point:

> I have been out in the country in a shack; and when I would go 50 feet from the door to get ice, I would hear the coyotes howling around. Nurses do not like to take these cases away out in the country.

The meeting could not come up with any specific means of dealing with the midwifery question. Instead, a committee was appointed to meet with the NCWC in order to ascertain if expansion of the VON could eliminate the midwife.[27]

By June 1917, the NCWC committee concluded that the 'very great and urgent' need for skilled maternity care in sparsely settled areas could not be met by the VON. The Order's slow rate of growth and its inadequate financial resources precluded its doing more than touching 'the fringes of the problem'. In fact, the report argued, inadequate maternity care was only part of the problem. 'Rich and poor of whatever nationality, in the thinly settled places of Canada, need more, better, and speedier medical and nursing care.' No private organization could provide it. The VON and organizations of that type could 'greatly relieve the situation', but to be successful a scheme required 'the authority of the Government as well as its financial aid'. The report concluded:

> The solution of the whole problem ... is the provision of small country hospitals with qualified and competent nurses in charge, and medical skill available. The hospital to furnish both nursing accommodation to all patients who can come in, and a home for a staff of visiting nurses who can go out to patients who from varius [sic] causes are unable to leave their homes.

Representatives of the NCWC and the Canadian nurses had combined to urge some of the reforms mooted in 1909. Now, however, with the wartime experiences of government intervention into private spheres, the time was right to propose government responsibility for an elaboration of the VON's cottage hospital and district nursing projects. [28]

This report and a paper by Mary Ard MacKenzie, chief superintendent of the VON, were presented to the sixth annual meeting of the Canadian Nurses Association in June 1917. MacKenzie's paper indirectly supported the NCWC's report by trying to dispel any lingering suspicions about the VON's attitude towards midwives. The answer to the problem of inadequate infant and maternal medical care in sparsely settled areas did not, she argued, lie in permitting 'the Old Country people who know nothing of our conditions to dictate a solution of our problems by dumping on to our prairies people they wish to get rid of'. It could be found with the fully trained nurse and with the increased knowledge of doctors and nurses in obstetrics. [29]

With the red herring of midwives seemingly removed, discussion turned on how to implement the NCWC's proposal. One nurse wanted to force the government, which had 'the money bags', to build homes large enough to accommodate three times the existing number of nurses. Others urged more immediate remedies. Failure to do something specific at once for the western problem could have disastrous effects for nurses.

It might revive the midwife question, and it might prompt the laity to assume total responsibility for resolving the issue. By 1917, with the anticipated increase of government participation in public health, the situation was crucial for nurses. They decided to take the first step in branching out. They agreed to have the Association recommend to provincial associations that 'a large, strong committee be appointed to interview the Governments of each Province, and to state through them that the nurses are willing to supply nurses ... if they will supply the funds and get the hospitals ready.' Once again in order to protect their professional position, the nurses were forced to consider reforms. Unlike previously, however, they intended to be more active in bringing about change.[30]

At the same time, a report on the question of midwifery in relation to district nursing in Canada and Britain had been prepared for the VON. It was the work of Dr. Thomas Gibson, who had been instrumental in founding the Victorian Order and who was now an honorary secretary to the VON. His chief conclusion was that well-trained midwives could be useful in district nursing. Many of the VON branches interpreted Gibson's conclusion as an endorsement of the importation of British midwives. As a result there ensued 'considerable unrest and disappointment among all the Branches – not only among the Boards but among the nurses, and many nurses ... resign[ed]'. The arguments against such a course of action were similar to the professional ones which regular nurses had been advancing since 1897. As Mrs. J.B. Laidlaw of the Victorian branch in Whitby, Ontario complained:

> The women who take midwifery as a separate course and not in connection
> with any of the training schools of England, are quite a different stamp,
> [and] unfortunately, have not the social standing that women in the nurs-
> ing profession deem necessary.

In sum, only a fully trained nurse could maintain the high standards of a lady, and vice versa.[31]

Gibson assured Laidlaw and others that the VON had not approved the plan, but this did not end debate about either the immigration of British women or midwives. In September 1917, Charlotte Hanington, who had replaced Mary Ard MacKenzie as chief superintendent of the VON, proposed that fully trained nurses should be brought over to take a four-month course in public health work. Writing to Amy Hughes, general superintendent of Queen's Nurses in London, Hanington argued:

[I]t would be to our mutual advantage. The war has taken many of our best nurses, and from the same cause comes an awakened public consciousness which has led to a great extension of all Social Service work, and nurses were never in such demand. I believe in our great Canadian West lies one of the finest fields for National Service open to the women of the Empire today, and I can imagine no greater opportunity than is offered to the highly educated nurse to carry on what is *her* service to the pioneer mothers of Canada who are doing the greatest service of all, filling the cots with British born Citizens — and in some measure making good the wastage from this war. Surely the services of our men so gloriously and freely given, should result in good for the dear land for which they so freely gave their lives.[32]

Hanington hoped to get about 100 British nurses, but her plan encountered opposition from Canadian nurses. In 1919, at the annual meeting of the Canadian Nurses Association, Hanington tried to convince the members that they need not fear the arrival of British nurses. They would be comparatively few in number and partially trained in Canada. Equally important, they would not practice obstetrics 'unless it was a case of absolute necessity and a matter of relieving their sisters in their hours of distress'. The Canadian nurses were unreceptive. Despite their professed concern for prairie women, other factors, especially professional needs, were more important. In this instance, sisterhood was narrowly defined in terms of the economic bonding of Canadian nurses. With the anticipated return of approximately 1,800 nurses from war work, it was expected that 'the palmy days for nurses will probably never come back again.' They therefore did not want to risk possible competition from group immigration of British nurses. They would only concede not to object to individual British nurses emigrating to Canada.[33]

But Hanington was not easily deterred. Besides being from New Brunswick and from the Waltham Training Home for District Nurses, Hanington resembled Macleod, the first chief superintendent of the von, in another way: she had 'plenty of backbone'. An account of Hanington's early experiences in a mining camp attests to her determination:

One winter night, soon after the arrival of the evening train, a young man came to beseech her help. She dressed and hurried to the unfurnished shack, where, during his absence, twin sons had been born! Mrs. Hanington looked at the terrible emptiness of the room, less concerned with the problem of working than preventing her patients from freezing to death.

Have you no stove? she demanded.

Yes, said the miserable young father, but it ain't unpacked. Besides we ain't got a stovepipe.

Go back to the house and tell my husband to take down our stove and give you the pipe.

I daren't gasped the man. He'd shoot me.

[She rejoined:] And if you don't, I'll knock your few brains out.[34]

By the 1920s Hanington intended to 'knock a few brains out' in order to bring immediate relief to western women. 'The Prairie women,' she warned, 'are tired of waiting for help. They would like the highly trained, but if they cannot get it, then they are going to get help of some kind.' Hanington agreed with Saskatchewan women that a nurse attendant might be of some use. Under the Saskatchewan plan the Red Cross would supervise a year's training for nurse housekeepers. In effect, women who were already 'nursing' in the province would be able to receive theoretical and practical instruction. Hanington, however, realized that nurse attendants would not offer a substantial, immediate solution to the problem. For her, the answer was trained midwives. This was, 'for the present, the only practical way of dealing with this problem, having for its object the temporary safe-guarding of helpless women and children'.[35]

Hanington convinced many NCWC women of the reasonableness of her argument. She was not so successful with the nurses. They thought the introduction of nurse attendants had been sufficient. The attendants would, they assumed, put an end to the midwifery controversy, and they would 'not do any of those things we all seem to dread, that they will not put on a white uniform or not charge a nurse's fee'. Failing to win the nurses' support for midwives, Hanington tried to provoke them into undertaking obstetrical work. In an appeal to nurses to challenge the doctors' monopoly of obstetrics, Hanington focussed upon the nurses' subordinate position:

> We make an attractive setting for a good obstetrician and an unwilling and critical collaborator with a poor one. The medical profession is responsible for this condition. They do not fear the competition of the nurse in any other department of the practice of medicine.[36]

This call for action merely stirred up the midwifery issue again. Ignoring the subordinate status point, the nurses simply marshalled an all-out effort to end the debate. Dr. Elizabeth Smith Shortt, one of the first women physicians and a notable champion of mothers' allowances, dismissed midwives on economic grounds:

> The trained midwife ... would only be available in sufficient number if she were allowed to charge sufficiently large fees to ensure a good income. If this were so, the majority of those now without trained service at time of delivery would be still so because of the fact of the increased charge.

Kate Mathieson, the first vice president of the Canadian Nurses Association, ridiculed the ideas as irreconcilable with the modern prairie woman's desire for the best medical care.[37]

Having exhausted virtually all of the arguments against trained midwives, the nurses concluded that the solution of the maternal and infant care problem in sparsely settled locations lay mainly in the Red Cross outpost hospitals, which had been established since the end of the war. In these small, four or five-bed hospitals scattered throughout Canada, a registered nurse handled maternity cases, a system which was, in essence, an extension of the program provided for in the *Alberta Nursing Act* of 1919. This legislation allowed any trained nurse, if she had taken a course in obstetrics and had obtained the consent of the government, to practice midwifery in those areas of the province that did not have a doctor's services.[38]

Pleas for the use of trained midwives continued, but lacked the same force. In September 1923, Hanington threatened to resign as chief superintendent of the VON. She complained to Charles Macgrath, president of the VON, that the Order was poorly managed. It had placed:

> a highly developed technical nursing service in the hands of lay people who, with the best intentions, cannot know the needs, the nursing personnel have no point of contact with the policy, added to the placing of a medical man in control of the nursing service — they go back to the old stand that no matter how able a woman takes charge it will break her — and it is not worthwhile to encourage nurses to take up this work.

Greatly offended by this criticism, Macgrath made sure that Hanington's threat became a reality. Following Hanington's removal from the scene, the midwifery issue ceased to be a source of major debate in the 1920s.[39]

The departure of the feisty reformer did not put an end to efforts to reduce infant and maternal mortality. In 1918, the NCWC succeeded in persuading the Dominion government to establish a Department of Health to deal, among other things, with the well-being of children and mothers. By 1919, the Department and its Division of Child Welfare had begun to function, although their duties were carefully circumscribed and limited virtually to an advisory capacity. Essentially the Division's role was to gather information and to aid local associations which wished to carry on child welfare work. This narrowness did not disturb the head of the Child Welfare Division, Dr. Helen MacMurchy. The gathering and presentation of data was suited to her reform approach. From 1919 until her retirement in 1933, MacMurchy diligently struggled to make people aware of the problems of infant and maternal mortality. Through documentation of a high infant and maternal mortality rate from the recently established Dominion Bureau of Statistics, she verified earlier claims of reformers that the Canadian situation was worse than in most other 'civilized' nations.[40]

In addition to stirring up Members of Parliament, provincial governments, women reformers, nurses and doctors, MacMurchy tried to stimulate reform from below. One of her chief projects involved the free distribution of pamphlets about infant and maternal care. Commonly known as the Little Blue Books, the pamphlets were written in understandable, patriotic prose. They captured the attention of thousands of Canadians, who enlisted in MacMurchy's ranks simply by adhering to the pamphlets' guidelines. This adherence was to have extensive ramifications for reform, as the following letter by a distraught mother indicates:

> As stated in the Canadian Mother Book:
>
> If the baby has three or four stools per day, do not hesitate and call the doctor. This is what I did as soon as I was aware of this fact. Why did my physician assert that this was not serious? and in whom can one place her confidence? Noticing no improvement, I called a second physician who immediately told me a baby suffering from diarrhea should be placed on a diet. This was done, but it was too late. If great are the responsibilities of the mothers (I nursed my child) those of the doctors are of the same degree, although some of them seem to ignore this fact.

This letter and others like it demonstrate that the impetus for reform was no longer limited to Canadian 'ladies'.[41]

By the time of MacMurchy's retirement, the infant and maternal mortality rates had decreased. Although Canada still had higher rates than most industrialized nations, the gap had narrowed between 1925 and 1933. For example, in 1925 the infant mortality rate for Britain (England and Wales) had been 75 per 1,000 live births; for the United States, 71.7. In 1933 the rates were 63 per 1,000 live births for Britain, 58.1 for the United States. Canada's reduction from 92 per 1,000 live births to 73 was a significant change. To a lesser extent this was also the case with respect to maternal mortality rates – Canada went from a rate of 5.6 per 1,000 live births to 5.0, whereas the reduction for the United States was from 6.6 to 6.2.

Some of the credit for these reductions must go to the various reform efforts of the NCWC, the VON and MacMurchy. Operating within the limitations of the accepted roles for 'lady' reformers and 'lady' professionals, they brought improvement. Amelioration was no easy task. Besides great opposition from many male doctors and indifference from governments, there was the stumbling block of the nurses. Most nurses were too unwilling to threaten their economic well-being and their professionalism to do much to mitigate the problems of infant and maternal mortality.

Despite sympathy for the constraints on the NCWC, the VON, Mac-Murchy and the nurses, it must be recognized that their efforts were circumscribed by class and professional interests. Their ameliorative measures, which barely touched upon such issues as poverty, were inadequate to deal with the problems. Certainly these measures were hampered by the complex professional rivalries played out in a male-dominated medical world, but the women deferred to male-determined norms for professionalism and medical care in their efforts to create a respectable, middle-class nursing profession. Hanington's efforts to provoke the nurses into action and her outspoken criticism of the doctors went unheeded. On her own she could not convince Canadian women to depart from 'their proper sphere' in order to support substantive change. The nurses refused and the middle-class women demurred. Consequently, in the short run, the lack of trained midwives resulted in the loss of life for many Canadian infants and mothers; in the long run the exclusion of trained midwives ensured that future generations of women would be denied an alternative to the gynecological and obstetrical monopoly held by a predominantly male profession.

The WCTU: 'For God, Home and Native Land': A Study in Nineteenth-Century Feminism

Wendy Mitchinson

For reformers, one of the most troubling problems of Canadian life in this period was the increasing consumption of alcohol. It had worried some citizens as far back as the 1820s when the first temperance societies were formed in the Maritimes. But in the late nineteenth century two new organizations (the Dominion Alliance and the Woman's Christian Temperance Union) carried the message of abstinence to members of the Canadian and immigrant working class, who were considered the primary offenders. The WCTU differed from the earlier organizations not only in its targets but in its methods; persuasion and education dropped into the background and were replaced by the drive to obtain prohibition through legislation.

The women's organization which is the subject of this paper was formed as a national body in 1883 and claimed a membership of 10,000 by 1900. The Woman's Christian Temperance Union had a much larger following than the suffrage movement, whose national organization was essentially Toronto-based. Yet historians have largely ignored the WCTU in Canada in favour of writing about suffrage. This article provides a preliminary study of this important women's organization.

By the time the WCTU was founded, temperance was no longer a personal concern to the largely Methodist and Presbyterian segment of the middle class to which these reformers belonged. Alcohol use was severely disapproved of by these churches. The organization's main impact was on the lives of working-class families. The WCTU particularly abhorred the suffering alcohol caused for women and children. More broadly, the Union traced a perceived breakdown in the social order to intemperance. Reformers linked alcohol with pauperism, mental illness and crime, ills they also associated with urbanization and immigration. Thus, the thrust of the temperance movement was toward social control, which would ensure the creation of a stable, disciplined work force.

Mitchinson's study is an intellectual biography of the WCTU that traces the *politicization process of its members. She argues that women's increased involvement in the public sphere arose from a need to protect the home, and that support for the suffrage, which was a radical cause in the late nineteenth century, did not in any way contradict domestic values. Integral to her analysis of the* WCTU *is the moral-ethical dimension of temperance. Although the evangelical approach to the individual remained a small part of the program, Mitchinson stresses the strong alignment with the Methodist church and the general religious framework which encouraged women to practice an active Christianity.*

Other studies of the WCTU *in the United States and in Toronto demonstrate that in the twentieth century the composition of the membership changed to include more working-class women. This suggests that we need to know more about the later phases of the temperance movement in Canada. If the membership did become more working class, what does this tell us about the impact of social control on the lives of the working class?*

————————————————

The organizational woman is a familiar phenomenon today whether she belongs to a feminist group, a church society or one of a myriad of other women's organizations. But this was not always the case. In the early part of the nineteenth century women were seldom organized, prevented by distance, poor transportation facilities and lack of time. Only the more privileged could overcome these obstacles and those who did tended to form local church and benevolent societies. By 1900, however, this situation had altered greatly. Women's organizations had increased in number: many continued the work of the church and benevolent societies which had formed earlier in the century; others formed to provide new expressive outlets for women; still others organized to reform what women saw as problems in society. All represented the ability and desire of many Canadian women to become active outside the domestic sphere.[1]

Several reasons account for this extraordinary expansion of women's activities: transportation had improved, making it easier for groups of women to meet together; towns and cities were growing in size, thus enlarging the membership potential of women's groups; and the increasing affluence of Canadian society meant that more middle-class women had leisure time to devote to women's organizations. In 1871, 81.2 per cent of the Canadian population lived in areas classed as rural. By 1901 this had declined to 62.5 per cent. The greater population density of cities heightened the need for institutional responses on the part of society — orphanages, refuge homes and hospitals — philanthropic areas in which women had long been involved. Cities also accentuated the problems of poverty, crime and intemperance. Many Canadian women realized such problems could not be offset through traditional benevolent activities and responded by searching for the causes of these problems. The result was the formation of reform organizations designed to eradicate the source of a specific social ill and not simply to ameliorate its symptoms. The willingness of many women to become so involved reflected an important change that was occurring in their lives.[2]

Throughout the latter half of the nineteenth century, Canada was slowly emerging from a commercial to an industrialized society. At the same time it was becoming more urbanized. As both these processes occurred, the workplace became separated from the home, where women were increasingly isolated. The domestic isolation of women was complemented by what historians have referred to as the 'cult of domesticity', the dominating image of which was 'woman as mother'. Ironically, as woman's prestige in society was being enhanced by her maternal role, the actual fertility of women was declining. In 1871 the registered legitimate fertility rate in Canada was similar to what it had been in the eighteenth century, 378 births per 1,000 women aged 15 to 49 years. By 1891, however, it had declined by 24 per cent to 285 births per 1,000 women aged 15 to 49 years. This decline was especially extreme in urban areas. Although women were having fewer children than had been the case earlier in the century this did not necessarily lessen women's commitment to the domestic sphere; indeed, through an intensification of the mother-child relationship it may have increased it. Women were becoming, in fact as well as in ideal, the emotional centre of the home and family.[3]

Women may have had influence within the home but the ideal of domesticity certainly limited them outside it. The emergence of women from the domestic sphere through women's organizations was a response to their dissatisfaction with this situation. Many women wanted to preserve their status within and control of the family by becoming active in society. As well, the seeming increase in power and prestige that women had gained through the rise of the domestic ideal led to a desire to publicly assert and extend that power outside the home. The easiest way to accomplish this, given the context of Canadian society at the time, was to rationalize it by an appeal to domesticity.[4]

Women's reform organizations were one way in which Canadian women hoped to protect the family and assert themselves in an acceptable way. Each organization was initially formed to right a specific wrong, but once formed, each tended to involve itself in a number of reform enterprises. The Woman's Christian Temperance Union was such an organization. It provides an example of the emergence of women from the domestic sphere to an active participation in society.

FORMATION AND PLATFORM

The first local WCTU was formed in Ontario in 1874, the first provincial union in 1877 in Ontario and the Dominion Union in 1883. By 1900, the Woman's Christian Temperance Union had approximately 10,000 members. This made the WCTU one of the largest women's organizations of the time and certainly much larger than any of the suffrage societies. As well, the WCTU was a truly national organization and was located in both small towns and urban centres across Canada, whereas the Dominion Women's Enfranchisement Association, the one national suffrage organization, was essentially based in Toronto.

The Union very early adopted prohibition as its main platform. While most reform organizations in the nineteenth century emphasized the importance of adjusting the individual to the existing norms of society, temperance organizations emphasized the adjustment of society to create an atmosphere of temperance for the individual. By mid-century, temperance advocates had concluded that voluntary appeal did not work. When the state of Maine introduced a compulsory temperance law — that is, prohibition — Canadian temperance advocates quickly followed its lead. Consequently, by the time the WCTU was formed in 1874, prohibition had become *the* weapon against intemperance. But because it depended on government support, its adoption by the WCTU paved the way to an eventual confrontation between the temperance union and the elected representatives of male society, if and when the latter refused to adopt prohibition.[5]

The WCTU had few qualms about supporting prohibition. Its members believed it to be a radical reform but an essential one. The atrocities of war were negligible beside the atrocities of the liquor trade. As a foe of morality 'it turns men into demons, and makes women an easy prey to lust.' Because the majority of convicted criminals were known to drink, the WCTU concluded that alcohol caused crime and argued that supporting such a criminal population was uneconomical. Intemperance was ruining the physical health of Canadians as well, one member of the WCTU even linking the spread of cholera with the consumption of alcohol. The statistics of alcohol consumption served only to increase these fears. In 1871 the total alcohol consumption per capita, 15 years of age and older, was 1.19 imperial gallons, rising to 1.29 in 1873 and in

1874, the year in which the WCTU formed, to 1.42. WCTU members were convinced something had to be done to prevent the terrible toll in human suffering that this increase represented to them.[6]

They believed women, as innocent victims of an invasion of alcohol into their homes, suffered most from the liquor trade, and they exploited this appeal to the fullest. 'How can Christian women sit still and be quiet while women's cries for help are in their ears?' they asked. Children's cries were also heard. The Children's Aid Society in Vancouver noted in its first annual report that, with one exception, 'Every case which has been brought before us had been brought about through drink.' Temperance women felt they had a special duty as women to protect these children. Certainly men did not seem willing to do anything about alcohol abuse, perhaps because they were the main consumers of alcohol and profiteers from the liquor trade. The WCTU believed most women did not drink. Where men were seemingly unable to act, then, women could and would. A social ill such as intemperance could not be kept isolated; it reached out and affected temperate and intemperate alike. It had to be stopped.[7]

The WCTU was not particularly concerned about the individual inebriate — the union had neither the resources nor the time to help individuals. They were more concerned with the effects of intemperance on society, the way in which the inebriate hurt innocent people such as his wife and children, and the way in which he undermined the strength of society.

Blaming alcohol for society's ills was a comfortable belief. It did not threaten the economic status of the temperance women or their families because they did not talk about intemperance in personal terms. In fact, their belief in prohibition was a reflection of their class status. Most executive members of the WCTU were married to lawyers, businessmen, doctors, journalists and clergymen. Considering the connection temperance women made between intemperance, crime and sexual immorality, it is not surprising that they saw in intemperance a challenge to their middle-class way of life. It was the foreign element in an otherwise ordered society.[8]

THE POLITICIZATION PROCESS

Only the state, through legislation, could ensure a temperate society. To persuade the various levels of government to respond, the WCTU became actively involved in the public sphere. Its members believed they had a responsibility as *women* to protect not only their own but all homes.[9]

One of the WCTU's methods was the use of petitions. They were circulated for signatures, then forwarded to the appropriate level of government in the hope that once officials realized there was a good deal of support for prohibition, they would act. This naive view of the democratic process assumed a common morality for all and, in fact, the existence of an absolute 'right' in society, a notion which derived from a fundamentalist interpretation of Christian morality and the members' own political inexperience.[10]

These petitions did have limited success. Through them, governments became aware of the demand for prohibition, and usually responded by granting a plebiscite on the question. The plebiscite was a good tactic, for it allowed Canadians to inform the government of their views on a controversial problem on which the government was hesitant to act. If supported by an overwhelming majority, plebiscites permitted the government to act with few fears of political reprisals. Prohibition was undoubtedly a controversial question. It not only attracted opposition from the liquor interests, but also from those opposed to government intervention in the day-to-day lives of individuals, especially in a practice that was as widespread as drinking was in the nineteenth century.

Petitions and plebiscites were the high points in the preventive public work of the WCTU. They both legitimized temperance work and forced Canadians to consider the question of control. Generally the WCTU's activity was more mundane. Members painstakingly distributed literature and called on electors to vote for temperance advocates. They appealed to 'their fathers, husbands, brothers, sons and friends who possessed the right of suffrage to exercise this right in the interest of temperance and total abstinence'. The WCTU approached clergymen, church members, teachers of Sunday schools and public schools and heads of organizations such as the Knights of Labor, requesting them to use their influence to dissuade people from drinking. It asked doctors to stop prescribing liquor as medicine. Members tried to persuade anyone in a position of prestige to recognize their work, or any part of it, thus using their influence as women in a very traditional way, that is, through moral suasion.[11]

Yet they did not limit themselves to this tactic. The WCTU was so determined to achieve prohibition that it even gave guarded support to a new political party. In March 1888, through the efforts of male temperance organizations, Canada's New Party was formed. Soon afterwards, in the WCTU publication, the *Woman's Journal,* Mrs. Rockwell, a prominent member of the union, appealed to her readers to use their 'influence with husbands, fathers and brothers, for the first and only Political Party committed to the accomplishment of the prohibition of the liquor traffic'.

The Dominion WCTU resolved to give 'individual support to the party which will unequivocally put the plan of Prohibition in its platform'. This resolution could only apply to the New Party; however, the party floundered. Old party loyalties remained entrenched and, as the corresponding secretary of the Ontario WCTU reported, 'Politics first, politics last, politics everytime, each party afraid of the temperance question.'[12]

This was proven again and again. In provincial plebiscites in Manitoba, Prince Edward Island, Ontario and Nova Scotia, prohibition seemed, to the WCTU, overwhelmingly endorsed; yet the respective governments did nothing. Unfortunately for the temperance women, greater disillusionment lay ahead.

In 1896 the Liberal Party under Wilfrid Laurier promised a national plebiscite on prohibition. Great excitement pervaded the temperance forces. As the president of the Nova Scotia WCTU declared,

> The question of Prohibition is at last a Political issue. Not as a weak, struggling Third Party, but a live question with which both parties feel that they must deal whether they will or not.... The world is turning to our country today, with great interest for a solution of the Liquor Question. It is nearer a solution with us than anywhere else on earth.[13]

The women naturally felt they should be able to vote in the plebiscite. When this was refused, even the Nova Scotia WCTU, usually more quiescent than others about the enfranchisement of women, showed its exasperation.

> Dear women, are we free and intelligent citizens of a civilized country, or are we the irresponsible nonentities that our government reckons us? If the former in the name of all that is just and right in the name of all that is pure and lovely and of good report; in the name of God and home and humanity, let us rise and claim the citizen's heritage – the right of self-government! If the latter then may we write 'failure,' not only of the cause of prohibition, but of every other righteous reform for the stream never rises above the mothers of men. If they be 'small, slight ... miserable,' how shall we grow?

Once again the women argued that they should be allowed to enter society in order to protect their homes; moreover, as the domestic force in society they should be encouraged to do so. Many of these women were becoming increasingly frustrated and bitter about being dependent on men to determine the nature of the society in which they lived. They used all the power they had as women to obtain a favourable result, but in the end they could only watch while men voted. The plebiscite took place on September 28, 1898. Every province with the exception of Quebec voted for prohibition, for a net majority of 13,687. The temperance forces felt this was a victory; the government, whose support lay in the province of Quebec, did not.[14]

With this defeat the women of the WCTU lost their faith that governments act in the best interests of the people. In their eyes, prohibition was never a question of individual rights but of moral rights, and it believed no government had the power to make what was morally wrong a legal right. The state was an active agent in society and as such had a responsibility to do 'not what shall punish wrong-doing so much as what shall tend to right doing'. The Canadian government legalized the liquor trade and, 'for a price, for revenue, makes the whole nation, women and all, party to its own degradation.' The only solution was for temperance women to have representation at all levels of government.[15]

One reform essential to this process was the enfranchisement of women. Appealing to the good will of men in power had failed. The alternative, then, was for women to represent themselves. By supporting a controversial reform, the WCTU women had confronted their own lack of power as women. With their espousal of suffrage they went on record as supporting two of the most controversial reforms of nineteenth-century Canada. From a desire to protect their homes through the protection of society, these Canadian temperance women had come far. One way in which they met the challenge was to hold fast to the traditional concept of themselves as women, that is, they did not support suffrage as a right owed to them as individuals, but as a useful means by which to meet their feminine responsibility — the care of the family.

THE WCTU, WOMEN'S SUFFRAGE AND A SENSE OF IDENTITY

The WCTU had not always supported the enfranchisement of women. In the early years of organization Letitia Youmans, WCTU president, deliberately avoided the issue of women's rights and stressed the protection of home and children. In this way she hoped to gain support for the union.

> So strong was the opposition in Canada to what was commonly termed 'women's rights,' that I had good reason to believe that should I advocate the ballot for women in connection with my temperance work, it would most effectively block the way, and it was already uphill work for a woman to appear on a public platform.[16]

In the 1870s, the suffrage question had been a divisive issue. By the 1890s, after the WCTU had come face to face with government intransigence, it was acknowledged as *the* weapon against the liquor interests.

The WCTU stressed the good that would result if women were given the vote. Mrs. Jacob Spence, first superintendent of the Ontario WCTU's Franchise Department and mother of Canadian temperance leader F.S. Spence, explained the reasons best:

> It is not the clamor of ambition, ignorance or frivolity trying to gain position. It is the prayer of earnest, thoughtful, Christian women in behalf of their children and their children's children. It is in the interest of our homes, our divinely-appointed place, to protect the home against the licensed evil which is the enemy of the home, and also to aid in our efforts to advance God's kingdom beyond the bounds of our homes.

> It is only by legislation that the roots of great evils can be touched, and for want of the ballot we stand powerless in face of our most terrible foe, the legalized liquor traffic. The liquor sellers are not afraid of our conventions, but they are afraid of our ballots.

The appeal to woman's maternal role attracted many women who might otherwise have rejected such a reform. Home and family were the cornerstones of society; an attack on one was an attack on the other.[17]

The connection between prohibition and votes for women was made clear. Where it was not, support for the franchise was weakened. In the Maritimes, for example, there seemed to be little concern over the ballot except among the WCTU unions, and even this was negligible when compared to other provincial unions. One reason was that the Maritimes, more than the other provinces, took advantage of the *Scott Act*, the local option law, with the result that they had the lowest per capita alcohol consumption in Canada. Because of this virtual prohibition in the Maritimes, the connection between temperance and the enfranchisement of women could not be easily made. There, only the justice argument for suffrage remained. It was a political appeal, one that suggested a challenge to the established order that would force women out from behind their concerns of home and family into the world. Few women in the nineteenth century identified with this concept, for it negated the altruism which was seen as the source of their influence in Canadian society.

The struggle for the franchise was the epitome of the temperance women's confidence in themselves, a confidence which had emerged only slowly. In the early years they were very hesitant, even to the point of discussing whether a woman should lead a public prayer unless careful scrutiny of the audience revealed the absence of men. Such timidity was understandable. The WCTU had formed at a time when women were not used to speaking in public, and although this timidity lessened as the women learned to run meetings and publicly express themselves, it never disappeared. Certainly their attitude toward working with men remained ambivalent. On the one hand, they encouraged men's support through honorary memberships and the occasional men's auxiliaries. On the other hand, men were not allowed to vote in their meetings. There were other men's-only and mixed temperance organizations, but there was only one *Woman's* Christian Temperance Union. Its members formed a wholly female society in which they were comfortable and in which their individual efforts were recognized.[18]

The campaign for prohibition was a significant one for the temperance women. The liquor interests represented 'the heaviest monied monopoly on the continent. It has an outpost in every town. It cows legislation. Its grip is upon the throttle valve of all political enginery.' To counter such evil, the women of the WCTU had to be strong. Their special mission allowed no compromise, even to attract new members.

> I have heard it hinted by some, by both within and without our fold, that our burning need was an influx of the upper tendom, 'to give tone to the movement,' to popularize it. If the money and influence secured in this way were not counter-balanced by some shrinkage of our principles, to accommodate the less rigid notions of those educated to a polite tolerance of wrong, we would doubtless be the gainers. Yet, the 'if' is a large and serious one. It is to be feared that the Dons would have more to get than to give. The common people have ever been the bond and sinew of successful revolutions, whether in morals or estates.[19]

The revolution they wanted was one of morals and attitudes. It was a world where their position as leaders would be recognized and where they would receive the accolades which normally went to 'society' women. As one member explained, 'While we believe there are many good women leading a social life, yet we believe no true woman whose spiritual sensibilities have not been benumbed by habit and custom, finds in this a satisfying portion.' A woman was to be admired for what she did herself and not for her husband or family connections. This belief provided these organizational women with a feeling of unity and devotion to one another and to their leaders.[20]

This feeling of solidarity is evident in the following description of Frances Willard, president of the American and World WCTU. One member of the Canadian WCTU recalled with quiet reverence her first contact with Miss Willard.

> At the first appearance of her calm sweet face, I was enraptured and before she had closed, her thrilling words and the spirit within her had so filled my heart that I too would have been more than willing to have left all and followed her.... As I look back through the vista of years to this first knowledge of Miss Willard, I think I have a dim realization of the feelings of the disciples when our Master and Saviour stood revealed to them in all purity and truth of His manhood and called to them 'come and follow me.'

Feminine friendships were particularly strong in the nineteenth century because women were expected to remain within their own, separate sphere. In the rarefied atmosphere of women's organizations, women could find congenial company and develop friendships which, as revealed by the love shown to Frances Willard, were very deep. Such devotion and trust in one another and their leaders was also necessary. WCTU members faced great opposition to their advocacy of prohibition and suffrage and they undoubtedly found needed support in these friendships.[21]

THE STRUGGLE FOR A MORAL SOCIETY

Support for women's suffrage did not negate the belief in separate spheres for men and women. Temperance women made it clear that their espousal of suffrage did not make them 'new' women. 'A man is to a woman and a woman is to a man, a stronghold; a completeness such as no two women or two men ever can be to one another,' they declared. Mothers were urged to train their daughters in the duties of housekeeping. The Union stressed the adoption of manual training in schools to ensure that children received the practical skills requisite for their future careers; in the case of girls this meant domestic science. Better fulfilment of the domestic role even justified support for higher education. The WCTU also advocated the appointment of female school trustees, factory inspectors, physicians at girls' reformatories, matrons, bailiffs and police matrons. The limited acceptance of these demands resulted in the creation of new work roles that extended women's participation and involvement in society and did so on a premise which most could accept, that is, the domestic ideal of woman.[22]

The women of the WCTU also wanted to protect children. The British Columbia WCTU endeavoured to secure a Children's Protection Act similar to the one in Ontario; the Dominion WCTU supported the establishment of cottage homes as reformatories for boys and girls so that juvenile offenders could be reformed in a home atmosphere; and several provincial WCTUs tried to institute curfew bells which would ring at a certain hour, usually nine o'clock, after which time no child was to be on the street unless accompanied by parent or guardian. The WCTU hoped a curfew would prevent late hours, 'that most subtle of stimulants', and thus lessen the number of children who would be tempted to drink. It began to realize, however, that curfew bells only controlled the actions of children to a limited extent, whereas education encouraged them to voluntarily restrain their actions, and in 1896 the women of the New Brunswick WCTU supported compulsory education for this reason. Education for its own sake was not their goal, but it could offset a bad home influence and teach children to be well-behaved.[23]

The WCTU was equally concerned about young girls and women. Its members felt that all girls did not have the advantages of a decent home life and a loving and protecting mother, and as mothers themselves they wanted to help them. They believed that young girls kept ignorant about the beginnings of life were especially vulnerable and urged that mothers and educators be honest about sex, arguing that ignorance was not a protector of purity but a weapon against it. Society was seen by them as dangerous to women; man was the seducer, woman his victim, and unfortunately, the law favoured the former. The WCTU of British Columbia pointed out that the law did not appear concerned with the protection of girls since it allowed them to give sexual consent at the age of sixteen, yet did not prosecute the seducer until the age of twenty-one. The WCTU protested that when police raided houses of ill fame only the names of the prostitutes were published. It demanded that the names of the men be published as well, so that respectable women would know which men to shun.[24]

In many areas the WCTU was over-zealous, its members responding in a drastic way to what appeared harmless to most Canadians at the time. Concern for the moral health of society led them to condemn certain styles of evening dress, round dances, nude art, gambling, theatre, prize fights and the use of women as bar maids. For members of the WCTU these were serious problems which had dire consequences.

What has produced the almost numberless bands of young thieves, murderers, and train-wreckers, of whom we read in every day's paper? Dime novels, indiscriminately sold....

Why are there so many divorces among young married people, now-a-days, where they have not the Bible ground of excuse to plead. Distorted views of life gathered from the trashy novel, where the heroes are all strong, tender and wealthy, and the heroines are beautiful, pure, and loving. Real life proves a different thing, and there is no strength of character to meet and bear the common discipline of plain human nature.

The WCTU invited confrontation in its advocacy of prohibition and suffrage. Because of the continued rejection by the majority of Canadians of their two central reforms, WCTU members developed a siege mentality. They saw the foundations of their world — that is, the sanctity of the home — attacked on all sides. As a result, they became more entrenched in their own principles.[25]

Any compromise in the struggle for a moral society was unthinkable. The WCTU protested vehemently when the British government reintroduced the *Contagious Diseases Act*, whereby brothels were legally licenced. When Isabella Somerset, vice-president of the World WCTU, apparently approved of the Act, she was criticized severely. At the quarterly meeting on February 4, 1898, the Stanstead County WCTU resolved, 'That we have no sympathy with the propositions of Lady Henry Somerset in relation to the C.D. Act and we reaffirm that the first plank in our platform is no compromise with sin.' Dr. Amelia Yeomans, a vice-president of the Dominion WCTU, condemned the re-election of Somerset by the World WCTU and urged the Canadian union to resign from the international body. By this time, however, Somerset had recanted and the Dominion executive, with the exception of Dr. Yeomans, voted full confidence in her.[26]

The WCTU accepted the view that woman was and should be the moral guardian of society and so took a particular interest in the campaign for purity. Its campaign emphasized a single standard of sexual morality for both men and women, the standard being that dictated to women — control. This standard would not only help individuals, but would safeguard the future of the race. 'Impure living', whether represented in sexual promiscuity, reading licentious novels (any novels) or the 'secret vice' (masturbation) had, the WCTU believed, horrendous results on subsequent generations. The WCTU held that a mother's thoughts could influence her child before birth, warning that 'sensuality may be transmitted to the yet unborn child by ... want of care in this respect.' The new science of eugenics confirmed it. Heredity was important physically and morally and therefore men and women had a responsibility to choose their spouses wisely. Intemperance itself was hereditary, they thought, and its consequences reached out to maim the innocent, as the 1892 Report of the Department of Heredity and Hygiene was meant to illustrate.

> Recently a friend of mine was urging a little boy two years of age to join the Band of Hope, when he startled her by saying, 'You don't know what you are asking of me. *Never drink any more liquor?* I love it better than my life, I could not live without it.' Think you that was an acquired taste with that child? No, no; his parents are responsible for it. 'A corrupt tree cannot bring forth good fruit.'

The purpose of this obviously fantastic story is clear.[27]

The belief in heredity created a problem. If intemperance was inherited, the WCTU could do little to prevent it, and this would mean defeat, a negation of its entire educational and preventive program. Fortunately, the members of the WCTU had a strong belief in the spiritual power of man. As upholders of morality they were upholders of the Christian faith. The two were inseparable in their eyes and so to fully understand their determination it is important to understand the source of it.

THE WCTU AND THE CHURCH

The WCTU wanted a Protestant Christian society. For most of its members, faith and temperance went hand in hand. The fight for prohibition was part of a religious battle, and one which women were determined to win. In the early years of its existence this religious strain probably did much to attract the initial WCTU membership and make it a respectable organization. Certainly the WCTU was closely aligned with those churches which endorsed prohibition, as revealed by the religious affiliation of its executive. Forty-three per cent of its executive were Methodist, 18 per cent were Presbyterians and only 10 per cent were adherents to the Church of England. Methodists had long disapproved of the consumption of alcohol and had been active in condemning it, although Presbyterians had not. Except for the more evangelical among them, Church of England supporters were uncomfortable in an organization which disapproved strongly of their church's use of wine as part of its religious service. The WCTU, then, was aligned to the church most active in its social involvement and strongest in its encouragement to women to become involved, to accept personal responsibility and to follow Christ's teachings.[28]

The Union patterned itself after the church. Its meetings opened with a prayer and a hymn and ended with a benediction. During the meeting there was more hymn singing, a collection and often an address by a minister. The WCTU believed that religious faith was the cornerstone of a temperate society and supported anything which strengthened the church. It firmly endorsed the movement to maintain Sabbath Observance and devoted a department to this end. Sunday law allowed families to be united by granting workers one day of rest, but Sunday laws also made it difficult for the working man and his family to have outings together. In the same way that curfew bells limited the freedom of children, Sunday laws limited the freedom of working men on the one day they had to call their own.[29]

The WCTU's religious faith was strong. Uppermost in its members' minds was the spiritual welfare of the people they were trying to help, for although they rejected the denominational exclusiveness of missionary societies, they still retained the 'spirit of Faith and Prayer' which characterized them. They believed that they could help men stop drinking if they could only bring them back to the Christian faith. They did not advocate temperance as simply a rational economic philosophy, but as a moral ethical one which was necessary if man was to live through Christ. Because reform of men's temporal state came only through Christ, the WCTU wanted 'to carry the Gospel cure to the drinking classes'. Its only approach to the individual inebriate, then, came through an evangelical commitment.[30]

Many work departments reflected this evangelical tendency: Flower Mission, Work Among Sailors (Immigrants, Lumbermen, Railwaymen), Sabbath Observance and Sabbath Schools, and Work in Jails. The women attempted to comfort those in need with the solace of religion. They often visited the inmates of prisons, hoping to win these men and women away from their former intemperate habits by bringing them the word of God. Yet when faced with prison conditions, they were led to demand prison reform. They became the advocates of prisoner classification, work for the incarcerated, the indeterminate sentence (an open-ended sentence which would terminate only when the individual had reformed), the parole system and schoolrooms within the jail. However, the women of the WCTU were worried that prison reform might take the spotlight away from their evangelical work and so continually stressed the need to remember the power of prayer and maintained a vigilance over their own spiritual well-being.

The church was the one institution in which women had been permitted and encouraged to work, even if only in a subordinate role. More importantly, the women of the wctu believed a common Christianity bound them together as women, allowing them the freedom to think and act. They were convinced that Christianity and its handmaiden, the Protestant church, recognized women as being equal to men. Believing this, their involvement in public agitation to support prohibition and suffrage was not a denial of their proper sphere but a fulfilment of it. Their activism was justified by faith.

wctu members were part of a movement to rectify wrong. As individuals they counted for little; as part of a great crusade they believed they became worthy of Christ.

> The Woman's Christian Temperance Union is no accident, but one of God's special creations. Throughout the ages since the fall of man Divine Love has been raising up instrumentalities for the restoration of our race to its original standard of moral rectitude.[31]

CONCLUSION

The Woman's Christian Temperance Union played a significant role in the lives of many Canadian women in the nineteenth century. Its advocacy of prohibition necessitated state intervention, which meant the wctu was forced to appeal to the public in order to persuade the government to implement such a controversial policy. This made the union much more visible than most other women's organizations and hastened the time when its members would be faced with their own powerlessness as women. Through this politicization process the members of the wctu confronted the reality of their lives in nineteenth-century Canada — they had little concrete power. As a solution they advocated women's suffrage, not so they could represent themselves as individuals, but so they could extend their domestic power as women in their effort to protect their homes by protecting society from the problems within it that could undermine both. They did not reject society's view of women, but argued that what made them different from men and what made them the centre of domestic life necessitated their involvement in temporal society. Their belief in an active Christianity supported them in this endeavour. That their actions and beliefs might appear contradictory did not concern them. They were practical women; they did what they felt had to be done and rationalized it by any means possible.

The rationales they used were the domestic ideal of woman and Christian duty. These were successful because the members really believed in them and these were also two supports which could not be attacked by those disapproving of women's activism. There were limits to what women could do using the ideal of domesticity to justify their actions. It meant an acknowledgement that woman's role was to care for the home. However, few Canadian women in the nineteenth century perceived this as a limitation. For them there was no contradiction between their actions and belief. Their interpretation of the domestic ideal of woman-hood was a dynamic one, one that could and did encompass the women's rights movement. They were social feminists, not feminists.

As a precursor for the experience of other women's groups the WCTU's significance is great. It exposed the importance of the domestic ideal and Christian duty for women in the nineteenth century and demonstrated how Canadian women were able to use what some historians have seen as restrictive concepts to extend and exert their power in society.[32]

CHAPTER EIGHT

'Transplanting from Dens of Iniquity': Theology and Child Emigration

Joy Parr

———————— ·•◆•· ————————

The economic, social and political upheavals of the late nineteenth century in Great Britain affected as well as parallelled those in Canada. Although the same general downturns in the economy from the 1870s through the 1890s were experienced in Canada, the dimensions of the resulting poverty and unrest were far greater in Britain, especially in metropolitan areas like London. Particularly in the decades of the 1860s and 1880s, London was thrown into turmoil by the spectre of 'Outcast London', that lowest strata of the poor which survived on the intermittent wages of casual labour. The 1880s in particular, challenged the middle-class explanation of pauperism as a moral failing, not only of the poor themselves, but also of the rich who refused to develop a 'scientific' mode of charity. Drink, idleness, improvident marriage and lack of religion were still associated with poverty, but a new explanation emerged. As Gareth Steadman Jones remarks in his seminal study, Outcast London,* the middle class only then discovered that 'at the root of the condition of the poor lay the pressures of city existence.'

Emigration provided an obvious solution to the problem. Even before the 1880s, however, emigration was a safety valve for excess British population and a labour supply for Canada and Australia. Beginning in 1869 and continuing for a half century, British pauper children were shipped to Canada as apprentices and domestic servants. The emigration of most of these 80,000 children was the responsibility of a group of nondenominational evangelicals under the pioneering auspices of Annie Macpherson.

Joy Parr's paper distinguishes these evangelicals from the later social gospel people, who, under the influence of rather heterogeneous humanitarian goals, questioned the social inequalities and misery wrought by industrial capitalism. She argues that the choice of this particular social policy, that is, emigration, was influenced by the particular doctrinal views of the evangelicals. Their belief that salvation was personal

* (London: Penguin, 1976).

and experiential and corruption individual and not communal led them to moral rescue work that ignored the effects of the economic and social environment. Parr's paper helps us to distinguish between reform, which views social problems as the result of larger social, economic and political forces, and moral rescue work, which aims at individual salvation.

In nineteenth-century Britain and North America, social concern proceeded almost without exception from Christian concern. In the Lord's name liquor and lice were condemned, votes for women and vacations for children were condoned, and expeditions were launched to explore the branches of the Nile, the brothels of Bethnal Green and the back kitchens of North Winnipeg. Manifestations of the Lord's will characterized by such variety and vitality could not but be contradictory. No change in the existing social order was too small or too large to be a fitting challenge to accept in His Name.

Although secular allegiances and assumptions also helped the character of particular social works, theology influenced the way in which Christian concern was transformed into social action. Differences in religious beliefs led Victorians of similar social backgrounds to very different conclusions about the Christian's role in the world. Dogma filtered social reality and circumscribed the range of acceptable social remedies. In particular, Christian social policies emerged from divergent theological disciplines which had markedly different effects upon the working-class children, women and men who were the principal objects of home mission programs. Because of the influence of doctrinal preoccupations, the social action of Victorian middle-class Christians lacked the single-minded purpose which their common backgrounds in commerce and the liberal professions might suggest.[1]

For students of Canadian reform, the suggestion that doctrinal differences crucially influenced individual believers' selection of social issues and the formulation of social policy may seem odd. The Christian social movement about which we hear most, the social gospel, was indeed a 'movement in search of a theology', an escape from 'outworn dogmas'. Social gospellers, responding to a vaguely construed 'gospel mandate' to minister to 'concrete human needs', went out from the vestry in search of the needy, leaving theological preoccupations to those who remained within the chapel walls.[2]

The reason for social gospellers' retreat from theology is readily apparent. By the early twentieth century the evangelical creed, which lay at the core of most English-Canadian Christian religious practice, no longer offered meaningful direction for church members who wanted to complement their faith with works. Its doctrine of spiritual change emphasized the individual at a time when the sources of material and moral regeneration were increasingly being found in a social context. Its conception of the nature of the church was atomistic during a period of rapid industrialization and urban growth, when models emphasizing the corporate nature of society and an ethos of cooperation and harmony seemed most fitting. The incompatibility between the counsel of the church and the crisis in the streets led Canadian Methodist and Presbyterian evangelicals to discard doctrinal direction and embrace reform. The campaigns upon which individual social gospellers embarked show remarkable heterogeneity because they were influenced by an ill-defined set of 'humanitarian aspirations' ungoverned by either religious or secular ideology.[3]

But as yet we know little about the process by which brotherly and sisterly concern was substituted for a system of belief. The standard study of the social gospel movement in Canada begins after this conceptual change has taken place. It does seem that within this increasingly secular movement vestiges of dogma continued to direct church members' energies. We know that doctrinal differences placed the Anglicans and the Baptists on the periphery of, or outside, the social gospel, and that these denominations and smaller evangelical groups, notably the Salvation Army, were engaged in home mission and social service programs of their own.[4]

In Britain the forces of Christian charity were arrayed differently. The 'anchorage in Christian doctrine' of the mid-century English discussions of Christian socialism came from Frederick Denison Maurice, a High Church Anglican. In the last third of the century, high church priests inclined more toward social reform than their broad or low church evangelical colleagues. The evangelical leaders of late nineteenth-century Britain, from the most rigid doctrinal followers among the Plymouth Brethren and the Quakers through the more moderate Methodist and established church groups, generally held less radical social ideals. They were prominent in Christian philanthropy but their work is usually better characterized as rescue than reform, moral rather than social. A group's position along this policy continuum was determined by doctrine rather than denomination.[5]

Thus, although some theological disciplines were atrophying in the late nineteenth century, they remained extremely important for many Christians acting upon social concerns. Preoccupation with dogma sheltered substantial numbers of believers from the influence of shifting secular ideologies. This means that ambitious turn-of-the-century social programs with a powerful impact upon the lives of the poor are often entirely bewildering outside a particular doctrinal context. To the student looking back from an assertively secular world these policies seem wrong-headed, inefficient, inhumane, a peculiar species of charity edged by cruelty. None in the Canadian context seems more malevolent than the transportation and apprenticeship of British children to labour-short regions of the Dominion. This policy is a fitting place from which to begin an exploration of the links between theology and the formulation of Christian social action.

I.

Throughout the period from 1869 to 1924, a half century in which ideas about the legitimate scope of government action and the rights of the labouring poor underwent substantial change, British youngsters from refuges, workhouses and industrial schools were sent to Canada to be apprenticed as domestic servants and agricultural labourers. Some of these 80,000 children had no known kin, but more often than not, the young emigrant left at least one living parent behind in Great Britain. The path toward emigration began with the decision to admit a girl or boy to a British philanthropic institution. Prospective emigrants entered charitable children's shelters either because their families could not afford to care for them, or because the Christian workers who ran the institutions thought that on moral grounds their kin ought not to be allowed to do so. Parents were required to consent to emigration before their children were granted admission. Home officials then decided whether and when the youngsters should emigrate. Under the *Custody of Children Act of 1891* parents could retrieve their children from the homes only if they reimbursed the institution's costs.[6]

Most young emigrants stayed in British institutions for several months, some for several years, before being selected for Canada. Girls were trained for domestic service, but were encouraged to think of this introduction to household skills as preparation for their adult role as mothers as much as for their adolescent rank as maids. Boys' instruction in institutional workshops generally emphasized habits of personal discipline and pride in craft rather than skilled technical instruction which might be transferable to the Canadian workplace.

Twice as many boys as girls were chosen for emigration. The services of young maids were valuable in Great Britain, and with good reason officials suspected that their female wards might be particularly vulnerable in Canada. For boys and girls, emigration was seen as an extension of admission and training policies; distance made family partition more thorough and the Canadian environment was presumed to make stable family formation and economic self-sufficiency more likely.

Within a few days of their arrival in Canada, the 'Home Children', as they were known in Canada, were dispatched to rural or village households. Their period of apprenticeship was to provide them with an introduction to work and social patterns in the Dominion and a small sum at the age of majority with which to establish themselves in a marriage or an occupation. The labour requirements of their indentures made it unlikely that young apprentices could substantially augment their British schooling after emigration.

In adulthood, they found themselves most often among the ranks of manufacturing and service employees and their spouses. Materially, they were likely to be more prosperous and secure than their siblings who remained behind, approximately to the degree that economic conditions in Canada and the United States were more favourable than those in the United Kingdom. But the emotional effects of emigration were often devastating. Their precipitate uprooting and marginal apprentice status clouded the childhood memories of many with mystery and bitterness.[7]

The juvenile emigration policy thus entailed an intervention in the child's family life more drastic than institutional admission alone. It placed the child in a family setting but outside the family structure and at substantial risk. The program radically altered the circumstances of the individual by change of place. It had no wider discernible ramifications in Britain and few in Canada. In whose interests was it to enforce a policy with such a large but localized impact?

Forty-seven agencies are listed in the Canadian Immigration Branch statistical survey of the movement, and this inventory is by no means complete. The social assumptions and doctrinal orientations that directed philanthropists and government officials toward child emigration were so motley as to defy generalization. The Children's Friend Society, which sent children to the Canadas before the Rebellions of 1837, was a secular organization concerned primarily with the suppression of juvenile vagrancy. For Maria Susan Rye, the most publicized pioneer of the larger and longer-lived late nineteenth-century movement, work with girls developed as an extension of an earlier emigration program for single women, which had emerged in turn as a branch of the London-based feminist Society for Promoting the Employment of Women. Early in the twentieth century, plans such as those of Elinor Close to develop children's shelters in the Maritime provinces as low-cost annexes to the English workhouse system received wide publicity. Committees of the Royal Colonial Institute and the Royal Commission following upon the 1911 Imperial Conference lauded child emigration as an enterprise which would promote imperial unity. More than one enterprising Briton looked no further than Canadian immigration cash bonuses for incentive to mount a colonial apprenticeship scheme. But fully 70 per cent of the children who came to Canada between Confederation and World War 1 were sent by evangelical nondenominational children's shelters, institutions which did share a common theological orientation and religious practice.[8]

The evangelical pioneer in child emigration was Annie Macpherson, a Scots-born Quaker who began to take parties of youngsters from her Home of Industry, Spitalfields, East London to eastern Ontario in 1870, using Belleville as her base. Her sisters, Louisa Birt and Rachel Macpherson Merry, expanded the work in succeeding years to include a children's shelter in Liverpool and distributing homes in southwestern Ontario and the Eastern Townships of Quebec.

Macpherson, either personally or through her correspondence with the widely circulated evangelical weekly, the *Christian*, persuaded the founders of Britain's largest nondemoninational homes, Dr. Thomas John Barnardo, William Quarrier, Leonard Shaw and J.W.C. Fegan, to experiment with juvenile emigration. It was doctrinal affinity among the revivalist Christians which led them to place greater emphasis than any other group upon this kind of Christian social action, and which left these sensitive and concerned Christians unresponsive to the glaring weaknesses of this child-saving policy.

The prominence of women in the program is not surprising. The Society of Friends had long recognized women ministers. Revivalists accepted that divine guidance might be as effectively revealed through women as through men. In accordance with broadly held Victorian conceptions of 'proper spheres', evangelicals thought women particularly fitted for rescue work, since they were

qualified by nature to enter into the deeper mysteries of pain, and with an instinctive adaptation for comforting the sufferer their feet have travelled further to soothe and to save than those of their more rugged brothers. With a delicacy of touch and a strength of nerve they prove themselves

natural nurses and the best of surgeons. Like sunbeams they penetrate
into foul dens and keep their purity unsullied. Their presence in the
fever-ward is as cold water to the thirsty traveller; their smile charms
away melancholy and their cheering words stimulate hope.

As Lord Shaftesbury affirmed in his speech opening Macpherson's British training home for emigrants, the last decades of the nineteenth
century were a 'generation of women's work', particularly revivalist
women's work. In these circumstances the absence of women leaders in
juvenile emigration would have been more remarkable than their
presence.[9]

II.

The appeal for these agencies of the drastically interventionist policy of
child emigration bears examination, for here the strongest affinity
between policy implications and theological doctrine must lie. The
evangelical nondenominational homes persisted in their emigration
work through half a century in which significant reappraisal of social
conditions and social policy was taking place among Christian welfare
workers. The Methodists, Anglicans and Roman Catholics practiced
juvenile emigration, but less extensively, with more reservations, and in
the case of the Catholics, for substantially different reasons. The evangelical revivalists, whose doctrinal descendants we know as fundamentalists, grasped the policy as their own and shaped it substantially to the
dictates of their religious beliefs.[10]

Most Christians on both sides of the Atlantic who were engaged in
social work inside and outside the established denominations were
evangelicals, that is, they shared the belief that salvation was personal
and experiential. The aspiration to replicate their own experience in
others drew these converts into the streets, the meeting halls, the soup
kitchens and the brothels. Quite understandably then, the broadening of
social concern among nonconformists and established church members
alike in the second half of the nineteenth century found its theological
foundation in an alteration in doctrine concerning salvation. Christians
who accepted Calvinist tenets conceived of salvation as the happy fate of
a limited number of humankind whose election was predestined. Within
this system of belief wide-ranging missionary activity was inappropriate
and irrelevant. But as more Protestants came to believe that salvation
was accessible to everyone, and more conditional than absolute — a
doctrine called Arminian after a sixteenth-century Dutch Protestant

theologian who disputed Calvin — it became reasonable, indeed, necessary for these Christians to develop an evangelizing work which might reach the limitless mass of potential converts.[11]

The transition to Arminianism, then, led to an expansion in the amount of Christian social action during the nineteenth century. Arminians were not, however, unanimous about the aims of this heightened activity. For some, belief in the possibility of universal salvation combined readily with an emphasis upon the environmental rather than the original roots of sinfulness. If sinfulness was environmental then mortals could be made more godly through environmental, that is to say social, change. Christian socialists and some social gospellers came by this route to think of social change as the Lord's will. For others, among them the evangelicals who chose child emigration, the Arminian conception of salvation was grafted onto persisting beliefs in the individual rather than the communal nature of corruption. It led to no consideration of social change, but rather to an expansion in missionary work directed toward personal spiritual renewal.[12]

These missionaries did live among the unconverted and worked to alleviate physical as well as spiritual distress; but this species of concern for material well-being must be carefully distinguished from the welfare impetus which spawned Christian socialism, the social gospel movement and concern for basic reform. When an evangelical such as Annie Macpherson went into the back courts and rookeries of East London, urging temperance and offering women and children wage work in her Home of Industry, she did not see herself in confrontation with an environment which induced sinfulness. She acted upon a doctrine of personal holiness and perfect love. In her work she hoped to prove herself to be 'by every simple and loving act ... earnestly seeking the welfare of all with whom we are brought in contact'. Each charitable act was a personal demonstration and affirmation of divine love.[13]

The foundation for the broad appeal of child-saving is readily apparent. The evangelical reverence for childhood developed through an identification of all children with Jesus. Helping children was an honour akin to sheltering the Christ-child himself. To turn away from a child in distress was to deny the Lord, who too had entered this world in lowly circumstances.[14]

High birth and death rates in late nineteenth-century cities created a large number of orphans. Low wages, irregular employment and inadequate housing eroded domestic stability and forced early independence upon children among the labouring poor. The popular image of these street children emphasized their discernment, forethought, love of liberty and cunning business sense. But the evangelical child-savers, among whom were the juvenile emigration workers, viewed the street children's acuity with less admiration than did the popular press. Painful as the physical deprivations of waifs and many working-class children were to evangelicals, it was the youngsters' strain and anxiety, their precocity and sharpness in pursuit of a living which evoked most worried comment, and which made their childhoods 'unnatural'.[15]

The family had become in many ways the church for the individualistically-minded evangelicals, the place where moral lessons were taught to innocent, receptive youngsters. Children who were not afforded protracted family shelter might never learn to exhibit family feeling, would rather 'dread and hate those who ought to be nearest them', and 'grow in evil, until the fruits of evil are prized as the best things in the world'. The evangelicals thus saw it as imperative not only to shelter children from the physical deprivations of life on the streets, but also to unschool them of their street experience, to return them to a child-like condition of dependence and receptivity. The conventional barrack-style orphanages and industrial schools of mid-nineteenth-century Britain and North America imposed order through rigorous discipline. But submission to force developed a kind of mental numbness in children. The evangelicals wanted the children to exhibit not numbness, but pliancy before enlightened example, a pliancy which might only be engendered through a sense of affection, which required a family setting. This setting would render a 'mixed mass of children ... obedient and well-conducted' and as 'nice and well-behaved as our own children would be at home'. Their well-chronicled position as leading advocates of institutions organized in family groups, of boarding out, and of emigration is closely linked to this particular emphasis upon the household as the place where children were introduced to the power of 'Christian love at work'.[16]

The training programs within institutions which practiced juvenile emigration bore many traits common to the North Atlantic child-saving movement. Instruction in the scriptures was emphasized not only to prepare a more fertile bed for the seeds of conversion in each young ward, but also to train knowledgeable lay workers who could guide new converts after revivals, canvass neighbourhoods in preparation for them and, through their examples among the poor, lead others to a Christ-like life.[17]

The industrial training programs in evangelical, philanthropic homes shared many of the policy assumptions of state-run industrial schools. The practice of manual skills taught moral lessons: 'In mastering his tools, a boy always to some extent *masters himself*; and thus our shops teach him not merely to be a good tradesman, but also a good man.' The acquisition of manual skills made it possible for a wayward youngster to earn an honest living. The particular authority of 'handicraft labour' as a religious and moral lever was enhanced by the tradition that Christ and the Apostles were artisans.[18]

The evangelicals who practiced child emigration were thus following a well-trod path through an Arminian conception of salvation and the Wesleyan doctrine of personal holiness to an extensive proselytizing program which saw practical helpfulness toward individuals as a demonstration of Christian love. The appeal of children's work was similarly broadly based upon an identification of neglected youngsters with the suffering Christ-child. The emphasis upon family setting and industrial and scriptural training for reclaimed juveniles grew from prevalent evangelical characterization of the household as church, the workplace as moral proving ground. What then distinguished the evangelicals, who employed emigration extensively in the Lord's name, from those who chose less drastically interventionist routes toward child-saving?

III.

Annie Macpherson first resorted to emigration in 1869 out of despair with the futility 'of relieving misery from hand to mouth'. The reasons why she and her colleagues should have turned to this program as a substitute for domestic piece-meal relief, rather than to reform, seem to lie in some resilient adhesion of theological to temporal assumptions about social order. Clearly these women bequeathed upon social inequality in Great Britain some potent moral worth. The writings of Ellice Hopkins, an English evangelical intermittently associated with and generally admired by juvenile emigration workers, suggested this combination of earnest questioning in matters spiritual and of reasoned acquiescence in matters temporal.

> Has not God put us into different ranks that each may supply what is lacking in the other, that we might learn our most precious lessons in faith, in endurance, in contentment and self-denial from the poor, and that they, in their turn, should learn from us lessons of refinement, of modesty and decency, of carefulness in little things in the training of the young, and the fulfilment of our great common task of bringing up the children of God? Has not the Master given us our larger homes and separate bedrooms, our good localities, our greater education and knowledge, and the purifying and refining influence of our lives, as a trust for the good of the many, in order that we might diffuse a high standard of living, and keep our human

life from being forced down by the conditions of back-streets, as it inevitably would be if we were all of us ugly and filthy and ignorant together in those back-streets?

Inequality, then, was thought to be instructive. Change which reduced it robbed Christians of important moral insights.[19]

The premillenarian strain in the evangelicals' theology also influenced their response to the suffering which surrounded them in the slums. The premillenarians believed that Christ would return to earth before the dawn of the millenium, that is, before a godly human society had come into being on earth. Social distress in Britain was thus part of divine preparation for the Apocalypse. Unlike the postmillenarian radical social gospellers, who saw social reform as part of the divine plan to make this world a more fitting place into which the Lord might return, most evangelicals involved in child emigration viewed reform as a challenge which would subvert the ordered sequence of events leading to the Second Advent. The evangelical rescue workers were as pained and angered by the suffering they saw around them as were the reformers. But it was this sense of the divine ordering and ultimate transitoriness of social distress which allowed Macpherson, for example, in the 1880s, to restrain her outrage with the 'grasping capitalists and the oppressors of the poor, the grinding task-masters who cannot wring another farthing out of the toilers'.[20]

Many women and men engaged in juvenile emigration saw the Lord's hand at work not only in the direction of human society as a whole toward the millenium, but also in the most minute of daily events. Their beliefs were dispensational, that is, they saw the Lord's will being progressively revealed through signs. The conviction that it was necessary to wait upon God's initiative before commencing any work 'in His Name' placed evangelical children's homes in a peculiar financial predicament for which emigration offered particular relief. Annie Macpherson, William Quarrier of Bridge of Weir, Renfrewshire, and J.W.C. Fegan of Deptford and Southwark, placed their needs regularly before the Lord in prayer but would not solicit the general public for financial support.

> Feeling we had no direction in Scripture to state our wants to the world by newspaper appeals, and trembling lest in our desire to aid thousands in our great cities going fast down to darkness, we might lose Our Father's blessing by any step of ours in getting the public gaze upon our feeble efforts and the virtue go therefrom.

Transplantation provided a way in which the compulsion to reach ever more souls awaiting salvation could be accommodated to the persistent penury and intermittent destitution which dispensationalist financial policies forced upon the revivalist homes. The outfitting, transport and aftercare of each emigrant child cost the equivalent of one year's maintenance in a British institution. Emigration could take place at least two and sometimes as many as nine years before orphaned and deserted children could be released into the British labour force. By substantially reducing the length of stay of each child, emigration markedly decreased the cost of rescuing each youngster and increased the turnover through any given facility. For evangelicals dependent upon the support of the faithful for the continuation of their work and obsessed by the sheer number of the 'lapsed masses', the opportunities in Canada for children were viewed, quite literally, as a godsend.[21]

Within the existing social order in Canada there was a place for needy British children, a position in many ways vulnerable, in some aspects harshly exploitative, but one which met the evangelical child-savers' key requirement. Devout and temperate rural families, 'Christian hearts yearning for God' in their search for labour were willing to incorporate British children into their households, to instruct them through enlightened example, 'to receive an orphan in His Name'. Even though the emigration workers early recognized that the differences between British street children and the rural Canadian-born would make generalized adoption unfeasible, they anticipated that young apprentices would 'associate continually with the family of the employers, all eating at the same table and occupying the same sitting room'. Children would be called by name, and so long as the 'transplanting' implied a transition 'from the wretched, impure, immoral dens of iniquity here to straight paths of usefulness in loving Christian families there', the emigration workers were willing to trust the Lord for the rest. Appropriately devout families were selected by soliciting letters of reference from clergymen. So firm was the evangelicals' confidence in the beneficence of the Christian household, that despite evidence from the courts, the press and British parish officials that Canadian apprenticeship harmed young emigrants in many ways, the program persisted for half a century essentially unreformed.[22]

Juvenile emigration offered one further merit which attracted the evangelical child-savers. Transplantation to Canada assured a partition from kin more thorough than any high orphanage wall or visiting restriction. Emigration was the ultimate safeguard for the process of practical helpfulness which Thomas Barnardo candidly described as 'philanthropic abduction'.

The extraordinary optimism with which evangelicals viewed children as receptive candidates to enlightened example and good works was not parallelled in their dealings with parents. The plight of the widow attempting to raise her family alone was the object of much sympathy. But the economic insecurity, which deprived other children of the period of dependence thought natural to childhood and which forced them into work in domestic industry, the street trades, or child care at an early age, was attributed to neglect, intemperance and lack of natural affection on behalf of their parents. Some hope was expressed for the reformation of mothers who deserted their domestic duties in order to work in factories. Although the evangelicals expressed considerable regret about reward-ing brutality by 'relieving parents of a primary obligation of humanity', there seemed little alternative to the partition of families if the reformation of children were to take place.[23]

The fear of unworthy relations who were less susceptible, in their later years, to reformation and conversion and who might induce youngsters to leave their situations provided evangelicals with their most compel-ling argument for juvenile emigration. Even rescue organizations, which felt strong obligations not to remove children from their roots or from their role in the British labour force, sent to Canada children who would otherwise be 'dragged back to their vagrant, drunken and vicious sur-roundings'.[24]

Contemplated closely, the child emigration program is not a very appealing demonstration of Christian charity. Youngsters were removed from Britain too young to understand the implications of their consent and separated from kin so thoroughly that family reunions were rarely possible. Emigration truncated their schooling, set them down in isolated farmsteads where their origins were suspect, their work was poorly paid – if paid at all – and their good treatment was dependent upon the good will of their employers. Too many children were brought to Canada and dispersed over too wide an area for effective supervision. As a result, the young apprentices were vulnerable to sexual, as well as economic, exploitation. Few look back fondly upon their period of indenture in Canada. Many say that they were happier in the orphanages of Britain where they had less food to eat but more that was friendly and familiar around them.

Many children's homes thought emigration and apprenticeship too drastic a change to impose upon young boys and girls. They restricted the number of admissions into their institutions rather than make room for more youngsters through emigration, or they sent abroad only adolescents who had completed their schooling and were better able to fend for themselves. Christian charitable workers became increasingly ambivalent about sending the children on their own. Secular attitudes toward childhood were changing and policy-makers increasingly argued that the children of working-class parents should be allowed the fourteen years free from onerous labour long afforded the offspring of the upper classes.

The evangelical institutions which had pioneered the juvenile emigration work persisted in their Canadian programs despite sustained criticism originating from both Canadian and British observers through the late nineteenth century. They expanded their Canadian branches as the socialist critique of children's work gained credibility early in the twentieth.

In many respects it seems odd that this group of women and men should have been so blind to weaknesses in the program that they continued to make life difficult for so many children. They are not noticeably different from other child-savers in their class backgrounds. They were, if anything, more sensitive than most to individual children's needs in the administration of their British homes. They were social conservatives but not definably more conservative than Charles Spurgeon, the Baptist preacher who never emigrated children from the institution which bore his name, or Edward de Montjoie Rudolf of the Church of England Waifs and Strays Society who placed severe restriction upon the categories of children who might be sent abroad.

The most meaningful distinction between children's homes which practiced emigration and those which did not is a theological one. The child-savers who ran emigration homes placed greater emphasis upon the premillenarian and dispensationalist doctrines of evangelical theology, or in the case of Dr. Barnardo, had boards who believed they ought to follow dispensational precepts even if the actual conduct of the institution revealed greater theological suppleness. Premillenarian expectation made them wary of any significant social ramifications of their rescue work. Dispensationalist guidance made their financial predicament exceptionally precarious. The child emigration policy was well adapted to conform to these key constraints.

In this respect the study of child emigration is instructive. So often the historical analysis of turn-of-the-century reform and rescue movements in both Britain and North America proceeds without reference to theology. Yet the women and men whom this literature describes were devout

Christians and looked to theological doctrine for direction in the conduct of their daily lives.

CHAPTER NINE

'A Work of Empire': Canadian Reformers and British Female Immigration

Barbara Roberts

While emigration took on special significance during the troubled 1880s, it was not the first effort to solve the problem of poverty and overcrowded trades in Britain. One special aspect of the problem, the increasing number of single, impoverished women from the lower middle class, had attracted the attention of philanthropists since the 1840s. Family colonization schemes in mid-century were supplemented by plans to increase the population of the colonies with the emigration of domestic and home-help. Generally the various organizations used the appeal of a genteel domestic situation and the incentive of marriage to attract young women. One notable exception was the Female Middle Class Emigration Society, which abandoned the two-tier (working-class and middle-class) emigration system of Maria Rye in the mid-1860s, in favour of a single group of impoverished 'gentlewomen' suitable for governess positions. This policy, feminist in its insistence on independent labour for middle-class women, underlined the real impetus behind the emigration schemes, that is, the colonial need for domestic labour and the oversupply of educated, British, middle-class women seeking genteel work.*

In the late nineteenth and early twentieth century, the female emigrationists framed their endeavours within an increasingly social imperialist context. 'Imperialism' in this context does not connote the highest stage of monopoly capitalism; rather it denotes an upper middle-class concern with the development of the British empire and Canada's place within it. Emigration was compatible with both the imperialists' desire to strengthen Canada's agricultural resources and with their distaste for industrial capitalism. The social imperialists worried a great deal about the degeneration of the empire not only as a political entity, but also as a biological organism. Emigration promised to rebuild the British stock in a healthful

---

* A study of the FMCES appears in Martha Vicinus, *A Widening Sphere* (Bloomington: Indiana University Press, 1977) under the authorship of A. James Hammerton, 'Feminism and Female Emigration,' pp. 52-71.

environment, while solving the problem of imbalanced sex ratios in both Britain and Canada.

Barbara Roberts' article examines the main sending organization after 1880, the British Women's Emigration Association, which developed a complex and tightly controlled network of protection for emigrants. Unlike the FMCES, the BWEA was not a feminist organization; its chief characteristic was its imperial point of view. The BWEA established links with other voluntary and reform groups that took over responsibility for the emigrants once they arrived. An extension of the network was the founding of 'Homes of Welcome', which functioned as employment agencies as well as temporary shelters. Some of these hostels eventually received government support, a first step toward the public administration and control of female immigration and the professionalization of immigration work.

Roberts' article delineates the development of these networks and firmly situates the female emigration movement within the imperial context. Unlike the previous author, she places emigration work within the social reform tradition, rather than in the category of moral rescue work. Despite the existence of these immigration networks, the labour needs of Canada were not filled; impoverished single women of the middle class envisioned more independent employment and domestic servants chose to remain at home when faced with less favourable wages and conditions in Canada.

The emergence of female immigration as a field for reform work coincided in Canada with a period of great changes and great social and economic upheaval. Between 1880 and 1920, Canada built a nation. For most, that nation was to be British in outlook as well as in character. The highest level of citizenship was based on love and loyalty to Canada and to the British empire; the two were inseparable. The nation that the reformers confronted was not solely an economic entity, not, as traditional historians often seem to imply, merely a matter of railroads, national markets and entrepreneurship. To the reform-minded, it was rather the embodiment of a certain spirit in a developing human community. The building blocks of this nation were to be her people, her families and her homes.

If the family were the cornerstone of the nation, the woman's role as wife and mother was the cornerstone of the family and thus the key to building the nation. On her shoulders rested not only the nation, but the empire and the future of the race — or so thought the Canadian reformers involved in female immigration work. They were aware of the part played by women in the development of a country and thought that the best way to express their patriotism was to assist and encourage the 'best classes' of British women to come to Canada. They insisted that:

> [I]t would be impossible to speak too strongly about the need of a wife and mother for the settler's home. As a sympathetic companion, an economical manager, an actual helpmeet in the farm work, as a mother of future citizens, and as a standard bearer of civilization, she will always be invaluable.

For them, the ultimate significance of their work was in the safeguarding of the future of the race.[1]

Prominent immigrationist reformers were notably imperialistic, not only in the sense that Canadian historians traditionally use the term, that is, concerning imperial defence, imperial economic development and imperial preference. Their imperialist interests also lay in the social and cultural spheres and it is upon this aspect of imperialism that this study focusses. It was not guns and butter that preoccupied these empire builders, but babies — the potential offspring of the female immigrants who were the objects of their reform work. Yet despite their focus upon women's concerns and women's domain, and their analysis of social problems in these terms, immigration reformers were not staunch feminists. Their feminism, if it existed, was subordinated to their imperialism and to their bourgeois interests.

Like many reformers, the area they chose to work in was not threatening to them as individuals. Female immigration work was compatible with their class position. It did not challenge their economic and political interests, nor those of the men in their families; indeed, it complemented them. Female immigration reform work in an imperial context was not itself a controversial issue and offered an umbrella under which women as reformers could function respectably. This is clearly seen in the work of women in the National Council of Women of Canada.[2]

The majority of Canadian reformers working in female immigration were associated with the National Council of Women. This is not surprising, as many women reformers in Canada were so associated, either as individuals or through their organizational affiliation. But the involvement of the Council itself in female immigration reform was considerable, in part because of its ability to provide a network for such work. Shared concerns were expressed within several often-complementary frameworks: the patriotic, the reforming and the pragmatic. Veronica Strong-Boag characterizes the 'mainstay of the Council's immigration policy' during its early years as little more than a 'search for servants'. Undeniably this was the case, yet the policy had wide ramifications. The reforming aspect of the Council's activities was slightly more complex, and was based on its maternalistic and bourgeois self-serving approach for improving the lot of women and the moral tone of society. Most members of the Council shared the Victorian belief that the family was the basis of society and that one of the most effective ways to promote a sound society was to promote a 'pure and holy family life'. What Strong-Boag has called the 'armour of professional motherhood' — maternal feminism — protected reformers' sensibilities and helped them to carry out their work. They believed that the 'Dominion's future would be safeguarded by actively virtuous women'. The patriotic component of their reformist raison d'être was inseparable from their belief in the pure, virtuous and well-staffed home as the cornerstone of a morally sound society.[3]

Work in female immigration was admirably suited to fulfill a number of requirements. First and foremost, it was practical, supplying domestics to the middle-class women of Canada — and it must be remembered that it was considered very difficult, if not impossible, to maintain a home without a domestic servant. Immigrant women had to be selected, protected and supervised, so that they could become more than servants — the pure and virtuous mothers of the ideal Canadian home and the foundation of the moral Canadian nation. Female immigration was also patriotic; these women were the stuff of which nations were built. To most reformers, the emigration of British women to Canada was a method of 'relieving over-population at home while simultaneously improving [the emigrants'] own chances for worldly success'. Strong-Boag describes Lady Ishbel Aberdeen, the founder of the Council, as a 'benevolent imperialist'. Many, if not most, of the reformers working in female immigration were, and remained, 'benevolent' imperialists, long after the Council ceased to see itself as an imperialist organization.[4]

In the 1890s, the National Council functioned as a sort of 'imperial federation' and displayed a spirit of liberal progressivism. Before the Boer War (1899-1901), rhetoric characteristic of political and military imperialism was not uncommon at Council meetings and evoked no criticism, even from those who might not be expected to agree with it. After the Boer War, the rhetoric softened. The 'imperial fragment' remained, but the imperialism to which it was committed increasingly tended to be cultural and social imperialism, which was expressed in concerns about the importation of only the 'best type' of British women immigrants, the necessity for an even more stringent selection and protection procedure, and especially in the reiteration of the commitment to the best of 'Anglo-Saxon ideals' — that Canada should be a 'nation of homes'. There were occasional conflicts between the quantity-versus-quality factions among the immigrationists, but nearly all agreed that the most desirable immigrants were 'virtuous' British women who were willing and able to do domestic or other work initially, but who were of the right character to become and to produce the future citizens of the nation and of the empire.[5]

After the Boer War period, the situation began to change. The pioneers in female immigration work were being replaced by younger women. On some matters the older generation were seen as either 'grand old ladies' or the 'old guard', yet conflicts between the two groups do not seem to have been a serious problem. Carrie Derick is perhaps representative of the new professional woman reformer in the Council. She was the first woman professor at McGill University, an ardent suffragist and an equally ardent eugenist. Despite her commitment to the belief that hereditary defects could not be eliminated by environmental change, Derick was a pioneer worker for educational reform and special education, as well as for a host of other causes. In 1897 she collaborated with the most blatant imperialists in the Council in female immigration work.[6]

The cultural and social imperialism underlying the efforts to transplant the bourgeois Victorian family ideology to the colonies was compatible with the feminine and reforming consciousness of not only the old-school imperialists, but also with the more modern reformers. The fundamental values of the immigrationists were tied to the domestic ideology, which, in the broadest cultural sense, was British. Female immigration offered a cause and a great work of reform for nearly everyone.

The work was carried out along the lines set down by the pioneer reformers in female emigration who had worked in Britain and the empire from the earlier years of the Victorian period. In one sense, the work of the emigrationist reformers during this forty-year period can be seen as a continuing campaign to organize and implement ever more stringent and effective protective measures and networks.

The main sending organization between 1880 and 1920 was the British Women's Emigration Association. The BWEA was the granddaughter of the mid-nineteenth-century British Ladies Female Emigrant Society, which had been founded by women seeking to ameliorate conditions for female emigrants by providing matrons to superintend and train them.

Visitation committees counselled, befriended and assisted the 'young and friendless', and distributed suitable materials and work baskets, so that 'the voyage might be made a season of industry and employment, and not of idleness and demoralisation'. The BLFES established a system of corresponding committees in the colonies to take over the job of supervision and protection after arrival. A stepdaughter organization, the Female Middle Class Emigration Society, formed in 1862, aimed to promote and assist the emigration of distressed gentlewomen doomed to spinsterhood and starvation at home. The founders would have preferred to lessen sex discrimination in the job market so that gentlewomen could support themselves in respectable occupations in their own country, but saw that expansion of work opportunities for women at home was a monumental task, and realized that emigration to the colonies was a viable alternative. In the colonies work existed; a gentlewoman who was willing to undertake 'respectable' work (usually some variation on domestic service or the care or teaching of young children) could live in dignity and eventually marry and found a family and a British home. Some of the organizers of the FMCES were feminists as well as reformers. Some of them were independent women running small businesses, like writer and publisher Emily Faithful. By the 1880s, several like-minded female emigration societies had merged to form the BWEA.[7]

The Association was similar in some ways to its predecessors. It shared the same ideological heritage, including the same notions about the necessity of supervision and protection of female emigrants, and the necessity of peopling the empire with respectable British women. As Victorian wives and mothers, they would civilize and christianize the colonies and transform them into British communities abroad. The Association saw itself as 'working ... from an Imperial point of view' to build the empire by facilitating the transfer of women who were 'superfluous' at home but not 'as far as the Empire is concerned'.[8]

Immigration was believed to be opportune for both the women who went and those who stayed behind. The BWEA reasoned that if there were fewer women in Britain, they could not be as easily used as sweated labour and a lessening of the supply also meant that women's labour would not be so cheap. There were moral considerations too. The disproportion of the sexes in the colonies and at home was always unfortunate morally, and some theorists argued, economically as well. There were not enough suitable, respectable women for men to marry in the colonies, and 'a man is never settled until he is married,' Ellen Joyce of the BWEA explained. Although the women who emigrated came for work, the 'ultimate destiny of most of them – marriage', was the BWEA's main object.[9]

The surge of interest in female emigration in the 1880s was due in part to increased general interest in emigration as a remedy for economic and social problems in Britain. The depression of the mid-1880s created pressure upon the British government to promote emigration as a means of relieving working-class distress. At the same time, there was renewed interest in emigration as a component in an empire-building program. The notion that redundant Britons would somehow be transformed, mid-Atlantic, into sturdy, productive colonial subjects was not a new one, but it found new favour in this decade. As well, there were economic conditions in Canada tending to encourage emigration, and a barrage of often-misleading propaganda suggested to Britons that employment and other opportunities awaited them here.

Although the demand for men's labour fluctuated in Canada throughout the century, the demand for the labour of women remained constant. Reports from travellers, immigration agents and others almost invariably referred to the need for women as domestics, farm-helps and home-helps. Often these reports made explicit the demand for other work women performed: as home-builders, wives, mothers, socializers and educators of children and moral influences in the community. This latter need was of particular importance from the point of view of the creation of a stable society. Many agreed that 'the great want of the country is the mangement of women. Many young Englishmen of rather good quality are out there, but they never become anchored until they marry.'[10]

The main factors which promoted the more systematic sending-out of these nation-builders by the mid-1880s were not related to changes in the demand for women's labour, but to the more efficient organization and amalgamation of the work of individuals and societies involved in the field in Great Britain, and to similar changes in women's reform organizations in Canada. The contact between the British and Canadian reformers was formalized by a visit from Ellen Joyce of the BWEA to Canada in 1884. She came to investigate the emigration traffic in which she and other emigrationists had been involved for several years and she was not pleased with what she found. After discussions with Canadian reformers and federal immigration officials, a more satisfactory system was developed.

The system required the following of careful selection, protection and supervision procedures. The selection of suitable emigrants was based on an elaborate information-gathering network in Britain. The reformers claimed they could get 'personal information about anything' to do with an applicant, by contacting acquaintances or members of sister organizations in every part of the British Isles.[11]

Applicants were scrutinized to determine their moral character and respectability, job performance, attitudes, intelligence and physical health. Complete dossiers were forwarded to the colonial correspondents so the receiving groups would know exactly what to expect. The Canadians were sometimes able to place the immigrants in jobs before their arrival, on the basis of these dossiers and testimonials.

The emigrants were sent out under the supervision of matrons, who were generally from the upper classes, and who were supposedly able, by their breeding, experience and strength of character, to take their charges firmly in hand. The women travelled in parties of fifty to one hundred, in second or third class accommodations. These parties were carefully watched during the voyage and were not supposed to idle away their time or to form unsuitable acquaintances. Generally speaking, unsuitable meant male, but the matrons feared their charges might also be lured away from their parties by women. Sometimes a woman, appearing to be a lady of benevolent intention and good character, might actually be an 'emissary of Evil'. Sometimes evil meant 'white slavery', sometimes merely a destination and a destiny different from that chosen by the sending organization.[12]

Upon arrival in Canada, the women were sorted into groups by destination. They were taken to temporary shelters or hostels at the ports, usually approved or supervised by women's groups, then taken onto the trains by matrons and supervised as carefully by rail as they had been at sea. The trip from Montreal to Vancouver took five days and nights. Women who were travelling unescorted or unprotected were exposed to danger due to the long period of time spent in close quarters with other (male) passengers. While they expressed these fears, the reformers from the BWEA and other female emigration societies were quick to point out that their women were generally safe, but there were rumours that women had disappeared from the train between Quebec and Toronto, never to be seen again — no doubt into 'white slavery' or some other fate 'worse than death'.[13]

All those immigrants who had managed to remain safely under the care of the matron would be dropped off at distribution centres across the country: the major ones were at Montreal, Winnipeg, Calgary, Regina, Edmonton and Vancouver. They were met by representatives of local women's groups and signed into the registers of the receiving societies. From there, the women were escorted to respectable boarding houses, private homes or immigrant hostels and handed over to the supervisors of these establishments. From these temporary quarters, they would either be forwarded to their final destination in smaller or more remote locations, or immediately referred to work situations selected for them by the local receiving groups.

Canadian correspondents were chosen in a variety of ways. Some of the main contacts were made when Canadian women involved in reform work made visits to Britain and were referred to the British emigrationists and interviewed by them during their visits. Other contacts were established through personal networks; the suitability of a prospective associate could be established through mutual acquaintances or organizational ties. In some instances, reliable government officials were consulted by reformers to establish the character and credentials of women who had offered to work with them. In other cases, the screening of workers was left to the organizations to which they belonged. There was a good deal of cooperation between groups in the Canadian West, made necessary by sparse population and possibly by common patriotic goals. The Young Women's Christian Association relied upon local subcommittees which received lists of incoming immigrants, who would be met by Y members. Newcomers were escorted to safe lodgings or welcome homes or hostels. They were helped in finding employment, and indeed, were sometimes placed in advance of their arrival. They were put in touch with church members and appropriate social groups. The system was efficient and apparently effective. By the end of World War I, it was in operation in many of the smallest centres, managed by church missionary societies, ladies' aids, women's institutes and home economics groups, where Y groups did not exist.[14]

After 1910 part of this work was institutionalized by Travellers' Aid. A badged TA worker would meet all ships and trains and keep a watchful eye out for women travelling alone or unprotected. On arrival, women were given cards of introduction and directed to the local YS or to approved hostels or lodgings. Any information that could be obtained about the women was sent on to the Y or other association in the receiving locations so that women could 'be tracked down by the Association' should they fail to appear.[15]

To facilitate tracking down their charges, the Y attempted to persuade local businessmen to place Y notices at workplaces and employers to provide the Y with the names of all new female employees. The Y also supported the efforts of reformers to get the government to institute compulsory matrons rather than stewardesses on all steamship lines. Although some lines provided matrons, others did not. The reformers felt that, as a member of the crew, a stewardess would identify with the interests of the men on board rather than with the ideology of the reformers and would not have the authority or the moral outlook necessary to enforce strict segregation and protection. They proposed instead that matrons (who must be 'refined' women of education and 'strong character') be given a rank of ship's officer, so they would have sufficient authority to give effective 'guidance' to women passengers. [16]

Y reformers, like their colleagues, more and more enacted a comprehensive program of control and minute supervision over every aspect of the lives of female immigrants, whom they presumed could not be relied upon to choose a morally pure path. Most groups felt that more government assistance was needed in order to increase their power and financial resources. The Y proposed, for example, to establish compulsory government registration and reception centres in all city stations so that each female immigrant 'may be located and guarded'. The reformers' imperative to build the nation upon culturally imperial lines — their patriotism — was far stronger than their commitment to the development of women's independence and autonomy — their feminism. The reformers' class position combined with their imperialism to give their maternal bent this rather authoritarian edge. [17]

Thorough supervision was not always successful. Some immigrants 'failed' in morals, health or job performance and some had to be deported. Some of the immigrants managed to elude the grasp of the societies and the reformers. Nevertheless, the system was thorough, patronizing and maternalistic. Although about one-fifth of the immigrants were classified as gentlewomen in the years preceding World War I, the system was still based on the Victorian assumption that the working classes — particularly the women — were incapable of choosing how to live their own lives. [18]

The patriotic work of the reformers was immensely useful to the business community. Immigrant nation-builders were desirable passengers on steamships and railway lines not only because of the profit they brought, but also because they were well controlled. Herded onto the lines and shepherded and supervised during the trip by the ubiquitous reformers, these immigrants were not only relatively trouble-free cargo, they also maintained the transportation companies' veneer of bourgeois respectability. By their presence and gentility (real or apparent) the women helped to conceal the harsh reality of colonial exploitation.

The Home of Welcome movement was a logical outgrowth of the desire of the reformers to increase their control over the immigrants and provided a vital link in the female emigration networks created by Canadian and British reformers. Several of the most committed empire builders opened homes as part of their work as 'philanthropic emigrationists', as Miss Fowler of the Winnipeg home called herself and her colleagues. They believed their work provided a greatly needed service to the nation and to the empire, as well as to the immigrants. Essentially protective in nature, the service was generally two-fold: the provision of a respectable and carefully controlled environment for the new arrival and the provision of an employee for the employer — usually, but not always in domestic service. The facilities undoubtedly met the immigrants' need for safe, cheap shelter, but it is clear that the terms upon which this service was rendered rigidly enforced 'respectability', docility and other traits considered characteristic of the 'right sort' of British female immigrant. As well as agencies of social service, the homes were agencies of social control. [19]

The first such home was founded in 1882 by the Women's Protective Immigration Association of Montreal. These women were members of the families of the economic, political and social elite. The second home in Canada was the Girls' Home of Welcome in Winnipeg, founded in 1896 by Octavia Fowler, daughter of the former Lord Mayor of London. (She originally intended to call it the Exiles' Home of Welcome to illustrate its role in receiving more or less voluntary expatriates, long absent from home.) Like most of her colleagues in the BWEA, she was most interested in helping educated women. Yet the bulk of the work was to supply the Canadian demand for domestic servants. She believed that this work was 'thrust upon them and was done as a matter of duty rather than of choice'. Fowler had wanted to place gentlewomen in positions here, following the traditions of her British predecessors. However, by 1900 she was reporting that she could no longer recommend the position of home-help or lady-help to her friends and other women of her class, as they would 'lose caste' except in perhaps a few small prairie towns. She attempted to promote the idea of Canadian agricultural training colleges for the daughters of the British 'impoverished gentry' so that they might have a dignified alternative to what was ill-disguised as domestic service. Frustrated, she returned to London in 1901. [20]

By far the most remarkable figure in the home movement was a redoubtable Canadian named Mary Agnes FitzGibbon, who was born in 1851 into the mainstream of the Upper Canadian imperialist tradition. She was the granddaughter of Susanna Strickland Moodie and spent many of her formative years in close association with her grandmother. In the early 1880s she acceded to the request of her great-aunts Agnes and Jane Strickland to stay with them in England through their closing years. Back in Canada by the 1890s, she became increasingly active and prominent in women's reform work. She was a writer as well as an activist. She wrote about her Western travels in *A Trip to Manitoba, or Roughing It Along the Line*, which was as popular in Britain as her grandmother's work of a similar title had been decades earlier. Her next book, a Loyalist hagiography of her grandfather Colonel James FitzGibbon, *A Veteran of 1812*, was also very popular.[21]

FitzGibbon's work in female immigration was consistently imperial in its orientation. Her most significant endeavour was the establishment and management of the Toronto Women's Welcome Hostel. She became involved in placing newly-arrived women in safe lodging houses in the city and gradually drew the members of the Local Council of Women into this work.

The Hostel was in a sense a joint British-Canadian venture. FitzGibbon's speeches made in England during her visit there in 1902 attracted the notice of British emigrationists, who asked her to serve as a liaison for them in Canada. She persuaded the Local Council to form a subcommittee to oversee more formally the placement of BWEA and other female immigrants in Canada. The subcommittee persuaded the Ontario Director of Colonization, Southworth, to help support a reception home to aid in their placement work. Southworth was privately as well as publicly enthusiastic and appears to have approved of the connection between FitzGibbon, the Local Council and the BWEA. He attempted to aid FitzGibbon in her quest for federal funds for the home. The federal government at first was unresponsive, but, funded by private donations and a provincial grant, the Hostel opened its doors in 1906, for the 'reception of immigrant women of a respectable class'. The lobbying of influential friends like Senator (later Speaker of the Senate) Kerr, the husband of one of the Hostel supporters, persuaded the federal government to change its mind, and after 1906 the Hostel received some federal support.[22]

Shortly after the opening of the Hostel, FitzGibbon arranged to go to Britain (partially at government expense) to organize immigration parties and to coordinate Canadian and British immigration activities. Her recruiting trip was the beginning of the relationship between the federal government and the Hostel, the most important part of which was financial. Each year, the government supplied an annual grant of $1,000. Senator Kerr and various influential friends usually wrote letters citing imminent bankruptcy or the closing of the home to elicit the money, since the procedures for allocation and disbursement of the grant were lengthy and the home was not a high priority. Despite constant financial crises, the Hostel expanded its work and eventually its facilities, and provided an important reception and distribution centre for Ontario and the West for many years.

The Hostel received immigrants from a variety of sources. Chief among them was the BWEA. Between 1884 and 1914 the BWEA sent about 8,500 women to Canada. In addition to its own women, the BWEA provided protection for parties from other British groups, such as the Girls' Friendly Society. As female emigration work became better coordinated and more rationalized, organizations often referred applications from prospective female emigrants to the BWEA for screening and selection, rather than sending these women themselves with a BWEA escort. The Hostel was open to other women immigrants if there were space for them, and received referrals from such diverse sources as Travellers' Aid, train station employees, church groups and individuals. Not all of its suppliers were satisfactory. Passenger agents in Britain were not always scrupulous in their selection of emigrants or in disseminating information about what they should expect in Canada. In 1910, a Miss Wileman, a duly certified and supposedly reputable agent, had badly misinformed a group of women, who were understandably annoyed when they got to Toronto, and FitzGibbon acquainted them with the realities of wages and working conditions. She calmed the irate women and managed to place them all satisfactorily. But because of experiences like these, FitzGibbon was cautious about working with agents not personally known to her or to her friends and she attempted to verify the integrity of new contacts, who she feared might let their desire for bonus payments overcome their scruples.

FitzGibbon saw the bonus system as a threat to the integrity of immigration work, although she and many of the other organizations depended on it for partial funding. She feared it would result 'in the wrong class coming to Canada and its being filled with undesirables instead of those who are likely to get on here'. She advocated ending the bonus payment system, to help 'weed out those irresponsible agents who are not careful in their selection'. She believed that as long as the prospect of financial rather than moral gain was a motivating factor in the selection of immigrants, Canada's real needs were unlikely to be met.[23]

FitzGibbon always relied upon women friends as well as the federal and provincial governments for support in the enterprise. While the governments gave more financial support, the women's work was of far greater importance. FitzGibbon's friends donated money and a startling variety of goods to the Hostel. Each annual report gave thanks to donors of such things as a new hot water boiler, hams and other foodstuffs, reading materials, furnishings, a piano and other musical instruments. The women also gave their time and skills. FitzGibbon's workload was staggering, and at times she was heavily dependent upon volunteer labour to help her keep the Hostel functioning.

During the War, the Hostel was busy rather than overwhelmed. The BWEA and other parties continued to arrive, although in lesser numbers and the Hostel still placed women as domestics in the West as well as in Ontario. The dearth of women domestics was due partly to the slowdown in immigration, but also to the attractiveness of the alternatives of war work, marriage or return to the 'old country'. The Hostel also provided lodging and employment referrals to 'old girls' who were changing jobs or recuperating. It continued to lobby the federal government about the importance of adequate reception facilities for female immigrants, both for the needs of the present and to receive the expected flood of postwar immigrants. Despite a threat in 1916 to reduce the grant, the government continued to lend its support. However, reorganization of female immigration reform work was imminent.[24]

In 1919, the Canadian Council of Immigration of Women for Household Service was organized as a central coordinating body to oversee the immigration of female domestics. It was comprised of representatives from the provincial government, the various hostels, the YWCA, the churches, the WCTU, the Girls' Friendly Society, Business Girls' Clubs, the Council of Women, the IODE, the Women's Institutes and the Patriotic League — all of which had been involved in female immigration work. One of its first objectives was to assure proper accommodation for all immigrant women in Toronto. The facilities of the Women's Welcome Hostel were utilized. It was proposed that domestics would receive free board and lodging for 24 hours, paid for by the Council, while all others would pay modest rates. The groups on the Council agreed to accept responsibility for various tasks. The provincial representatives agreed to meet all boats and trains and to send information on all arrivals to the Hostel. The federal grants formerly given to the Hostel were to be given to the Council and allocated by it to the various societies.

The scheme appears to have worked well, with minor exceptions. Chief among these was the problem of the differential fee policy. Women who were not domestics complained about not also having the free twenty-four-hour period given to domestics. The government and the Council were both uncertain about how to deal with this complaint. The government was eager to keep all women under the auspices of the Hostel until they were safely placed in their new jobs and homes, but was not willing to pay for this service. Eventually a compromise was reached and the work of the Council continued.[25]

The Council represented a transition between private and public control of imperial female immigration, a transition which was complete with the advent of the *Empire Settlement Act* in 1922. The Empire Settlement scheme was the brainchild of Leopold Amery, Colonial Office Undersecretary, and was intended to shift the labour force of the empire from Britain, where it was often redundant, to the colonies, where it was needed. The Canadian government was sold on the idea by the promise of a flood of selected British settlers, especially domestic servants. The reformers saw in it the culmination of decades of work and the promise of the application of their principles on a truly imperial scale. The promise was not honoured. Trained domestics were as much in demand in Britain as in Canada. There was little purely economic incentive to come to Canada. Those who came were snapped up by the well-to-do and remained in the cities instead of going to the developing areas of Canada and making the transition from helper in another woman's home to mistress in their own. Immigration to Canada came increasingly to be seen as what it was — a move into another domestic service job, often at lower wages and under worse working conditions than at home.[26]

Instead of a flood, there was a trickle. Women still emigrated, found jobs and husbands. But with the advent of public administration of female emigration schemes and the lessening of the exclusivity of supervision over them by the imperial emigrationist reformers, the fervour was leaving the movement. 'Maternal feminism' was dissipated by a passionless bureaucratic modernism. Immigration 'workers' more and more frequently became paid professionals.

The strong connection among the 'maternal feminism', the moral imperialism and the bourgeois reformism of the earlier women is partly explained by the theory that their 'political' ideology, their imperialism, was an important determinant of the direction of their reforms. Yet the connection is even more fundamental. Carl Berger argues that there is a direct relationship between imperialism and social reform and describes some of the components of imperialist social thought: the perception of Canada as an agrarian country, the distaste for urbanization and industrialism and the perception of the West as an agrarian paradise where the essence of British civilization could be transplanted, and finally, the hope that a simpler society free of the overcrowding and social pressures of a decadent and decaying Britain could be produced in Canada. Although Berger discusses the relation between imperialism and social reform in terms of economic policies, he explains that even these policies were based on a general non-economic conception of the national interest and were 'intended to realize objectives which were essentially non-economic in character'. He explains the connection between Canadian imperialism and social reform in terms of the expression of a sense of mission, which was based partly on the notion of British racial superiority. As another writer explains,

> Even the more rabid Imperialists ... did not believe that the British were necessarily more brilliant or more attractive than other races. But they felt that they were somehow more *moral*; firmer, less excitable, juster, more humane, more practical, and reliable.

Imperial duty called forth the highest moral qualities of the Anglo-Saxon race. The embodiment (as well as the agent) of these qualities was the British 'lady' building British societies in the far-flung colonies of the empire, reforming the working classes in the new land as local imperialists attempted to reform them at home. The truest imperialism was that based on the 'extension of British institutions and wholesome influences', argued Lord Carnarvon, Disraeli's Colonial Secretary. As founders of British homes in Canada, as daughters of the empire and mothers of the race in social as well as in personal terms, the Canadian 'philanthropic emigrationists' were the real imperialists. For these women, 'imperialism was based on a fine enthusiasm for what is now known as the English way of life.'[27]

The English way of life was based on certain sex and class assumptions. 'The Victorian cult of domesticity' in Canada and the rest of the settled empire 'endowed Home, Woman, and Mother with transcendent moral force.' This moral force, based on a view of women as 'the conservors of life, the natural guardians of the young, the creators of the home', justified the social reform activities of women, activities that were eventually institutionalized and taken out of the control of women, although many of the bourgeois feminine values held by the founding mothers of social welfare in Canada have been retained. Women were to be confined to the home, their influence reduced to producing good citizens who would accept the values of the ruling classes, and whose actions as workers and consumers would reflect that acceptance.[28]

Although the Canadian experience was unique, its broad outlines were shaped by the economic and social conditions of colonial nation-building under capitalism. Rapid economic development, urbanization and industrialization created tremendous social problems; they also created tremendous opportunities. The Canadian reformers were responding to both. By more systematic, selective and supervised immigration, they expected to eliminate some of the worst abuses and dangerous conditions in Canada. At the same time they hoped to shape the future development of the nation upon the soundest, most rational and most moral principles. For them, these principles were embodied in the Victorian home. The nation was the home and the home was the woman; all were best British.

Notes

INTRODUCTION

1 'A Girl of the Period,' Rose-Belford's *Canadian Monthly*, Vol. IV (1880) pp.624-27, cited in eds. Ramsay Cook and Wendy Mitchinson, *The Proper Sphere* (Toronto: Oxford, 1976), pp.65-69.

2 Paul Rutherford, 'Toronto's Metropolis: The Urban Reform Movement in Canada, 1880-1920,' Canadian Historical Association, *Papers*, 1971, p.203; Rutherford, *Saving the Canadian City* (Toronto: University of Toronto Press, 1974), p.89.

3 For a discussion of the 'imperialists', see Carl Berger, *The Sense of Power* (Toronto: University of Toronto Press, 1971); social gospel attitudes to race are discussed by Marilyn Barber, 'Nationalism, Nativism and the Social Gospel: The Protestant Church Response to Foreign Immigrants in Western Canada, 1897-1914,' in ed. Richard Allen, *The Social Gospel in Canada* (Ottawa: National Museum of Man, Mercury Series, History Division, Paper No. 9, 1975), pp.208-10.

4 Richard Allen, 'The Background of the Social Gospel in Canada,' in Allen, *The Social Gospel*, pp.3-4; 13-14; 28-30.

5 Robert Craig Brown and Ramsay Cook, *Canada 1896-1921* (Toronto: McClelland and Stewart, 1974), Ch. 7; on Bourassa and anti-feminism, see Susan Mann Trofimenkoff, 'Henri Bourassa and "the Woman Question,"' in eds. Trofimenkoff and Prentice, *The Neglected Majority* (Toronto: McClelland and Stewart, 1977), pp.104-15.

6 Deborah Gorham first commented on the definition of feminism; for 'social feminism' see Aileen Kraditor's two books, *Up From the Pedestal* (Chicago: Quadrangle, 1970) and *The Ideas of the Woman Suffrage Movement, 1890-1920* (New York: Anchor, 1971). See also William L. O'Neill's *Everyone Was Brave* (Chicago: Quadrangle, 1969).

7 Daniel Scott Smith, 'Family Limitation, Sexual Control, and Domestic Feminism in Victorian America,' in eds. Mary Hartman and Lois Banner, *Clio's Consciousness Raised* (New York: Harper, 1974), pp.123-24.

8 Jill Conway, 'Women Reformers and American Culture, 1870-1930,' *Journal of Social History*, v, No. 2 (Winter 1971-72), p.167.

9 *Globe* (Toronto), March 22, 1883.

10 Mary Ryan, *Womanhood in America* (New York: New Viewpoints, 1975), p.183.

11 Edith M. Luke, 'Woman Suffrage in Canada,' *The Canadian Magazine*, 5, No. 4 (August 1895), pp.328-36; Catherine Cleverdon, *The Woman Suffrage Movement in Canada*, 2nd ed. (Toronto: University of Toronto Press, 1974).

12 Ellen DuBois, 'The Radicalism of the Woman Suffrage Movement: Notes Toward the Reconstruction of Nineteenth Century Feminism,' *Feminist Studies*, 3, No. 1/2 (Fall 1975), pp.63-71.

13 Alice A. Chown, *The Stairway* (Boston: Cornhill Comp., 1921).

CHAPTER ONE

I would like to thank Ellie Kirzner, Gene Homel and Glen Frankfurter for their criticisms of an earlier draft.

1 G.E. Denison, 'The Evolution of the Lady Cyclist,' *Massey's Magazine* (Apr. 1897), p.281.

2 S.F. Wise, 'Sport and Class Values in Old Ontario and Quebec' in eds. W. Heick and R. Graham, *His Own Man, Essays in Honour of Arthur Reginald Marsden Lower* (Montreal: McGill-Queen's University Press, 1974), p.113; G.E. Denison, 'Lady Cyclist'; *Canadian Epworth Era* (June 1899), p.163, cited in G. Homel, 'James Simpson and the Origins of Canadian Social Democracy' (Ph.D. dissertation, University of Toronto, 1978), p.22; W. Roberts, *Honest Womanhood, Feminism, Femininity and Class Consciousness in Toronto Working Women, 1896-1914* (Toronto: New Hogtown, 1977), p.32; *Canadian Practitioner and Review* (Nov. 1896), pp.848-49; *Memoirs*, Augusta Stowe-Gullen Collection, Victoria College Library, University of Toronto (hereinafter ASG).

3 Sarah Jeanette Cotes (Duncan), *A Social Departure* (New York: Appleton, 1893), pp.91-92.

4 *Canadian Courier* (June 21, 1913), p.21; Lily Dougall, *The Madonna of a Day* (New York: Appleton, 1895); H.J. Morgan, *Canadian Men and Women of the Time* (Toronto: W. Briggs, 1898), p.279.

5 R.T. Lancefield, *Tim and Mrs. Tim, A Story for the Club and Society Man and the New Woman* (Toronto: Rose, 1897); Lottie McAlister, *Clipped Wings* (Toronto: W. Briggs, 1899), p.25.

6 L.E. McCully, 'A Critical Study of Milton's Theory of Divorce' (MA thesis, University of Toronto, 1908), pp.12-13. For additional information on McCully, see the *Star*, Apr. 26, 1907; *Torontonensis* (1907), p.72; J.W. Garvin, ed., *Canadian Poets* (Toronto: McClelland, Goodchild & Stewart, 1916), p.422; H. Morgan, op. cit. and L.E. McCully, *Mary Magdalene and Other Poems* (Toronto: Macmillan, 1914).

7 *The Ontario Woman* (Dec.-Jan. 1911-12), p.50; cf. the report of the conversation in Augusta Stowe-Gullen typescript in Box 2, Flora MacDonald Denison Collection, Thomas Fisher Library, University of Toronto (henceforth FMD).

8 Cf. Peter Cominos, 'Innocent Femina Sensualis in Unconscious Conflict,' in ed. Martha Vicinus, *Suffer and Be Still* (Bloomington: Indiana University Press, 1972); see Leonore Davidoff, *The Best Circles* (London: Croom Helm, 1973) for discussion of these themes in other countries.

9 Margaret Browne, *My Lady of the Snows* (Toronto: University of Toronto Press, 1908), pp.26, 99, 131-32, 517.

10 For participants' surveys of the suffrage movement, see Flora MacDonald Denison, *Woman Suffrage in Canada* (Toronto: Toronto Suffrage Association, 1917); Edith Luke, 'Woman Suffrage in Canada,' *Canadian Magazine* (1895), pp.328-36; E. Stowe, 'Report of the Dominion Woman Enfranchisement Association,' *Women Workers of Canada, Being a Report of the First Annual Meeting and Conference of the National Council of Women of Canada* (Ottawa, 1894); H. Ridley, 'Woman Suffrage in Canada' (n.p., n.d.).

11 Clipping, ASG Scrapbooks (n.d.).

12 Clipping, op. cit.; National Council of Women of Canada (henceforth NCWC) *Minutes*, Mar.-July 1898, NCWC Collection, Public Archives of Canada (henceforth PAC).

13 J.T. Saywell, ed., *The Canadian Journal of Lady Aberdeen, 1893-1898* (Toronto: Champlain Society, 1960), pp. xviii, xxi.

14 *Women Workers of Canada*, pp.10-11; cited in Veronica Strong-Boag, 'The Parliament of Women: The National Council of Women of Canada, 1893-1929' (Ph.D. dissertation, University of Toronto, 1975), p.142; Aberdeen to Cummings, Jan. 13, 1894, NCWC, Box 65. See also Fidelis, 'The Women's National Council and Certain Critics,' *The Week*, Sept. 6, 1895, p.968.

15 *Women Workers of Canada*, pp.29-31; Bessie Pullen-Burry, *From Halifax to Vancouver* (Toronto, 1912), pp.147-48. (My thanks to Gene Homel for bringing this to my attention.) For examples of the NCWC's work, see *Star*, Dec. 6, 1898, June 17, 1911, Jan. 22, 1914, Mar. 30, 1914; *News*, Dec. 21, 1907, Feb. 15, 1908, July 25, 1908; memo to executive members, Mar. 13, 1898, NCWC; NCWC *Minutes*, Oct. 1906, pp.41-43, typescript in FMD, Box 2.

16 Emily Stowe, 'Domestic Problem, Cause and Cure,' *Women Workers of Canada*, p.165. See also *Citizen and Country*, Sept. 30, 1899; Flora MacDonald Denison, 'Vocational Training for Women: An Appreciation of Dr. Robertson's Address,' FMD Scrapbooks; J. Hoodless, M. Watson, *Public School Household Science* (Toronto: Copp Clark, 1905), Intro.; 'Lillian Massey School' (Brochure, University of Toronto Archives), p.4; *News*, Nov. 13, 1901. See also *World*, Oct. 6, 1910.

Notes

17 Clipping (n.d.), FMD; B. Pullen-Burry, op. cit., pp.147-50; *Star*, Jan. 10, 13, 1912; Clipping, Jan. 13, 1912, FMD.

18 *World*, Oct. 1909, FMD.

19 Stowe-Gullen typescript in Box 2, FMD; *Globe*, Dec. 9, 1897; *Star*, Dec. 9, 1907; Clipping, Dec. 9, 1907, FMD.

20 *Star*, Mar. 5, 8, Dec. 4, 1912; *Telegram*, Mar. 5, 1912; *Globe*, Mar. 5, 1912; *Star*, Dec. 17, 26, 1912; *Industrial Banner*, Jan. 10, 1913; *Star*, Nov. 27, Dec. 11, 13, 1913; *World*, Sept. 22, 1913; Canadian Suffrage Association, 'Municipal Referenda on Votes for Women,' in ASG Scrapbooks.

21 *Star*, Mar. 16, 24, Apr. 29, May 13, 1914; *Star Weekly*, Mar. 21, 1914. See, for example, 'Women and The War,' *Canadian Annual Review for 1916*.

22 On the radical essence of the suffrage movement, see E. Dubois, 'The Radicalism of the Woman's Suffrage Movement: Notes Towards Reconstruction of Nineteenth-Century Feminism,' *Feminist Studies* (Fall 1975), pp.63-71, cited in M. Evans, 'Oliver Mowat and Ontario, 1872-1896: A Study in Political Success' (Ph.D. dissertation, University of Toronto, 1967), p.282. On the importance of property, see *Mail and Empire*, Dec. 5, 1905; M. Evans, op. cit., p.276; *Star*, Mar. 24, 1909; *Telegram*, Mar. 25, 1909; *Mail and Empire*, Mar. 29, 1909; ASG Scrapbooks, p.93.

23 NCWC *Minutebook*, May 1903, Box 8, NCWC Collection, PAC; *Star*, May 9, 1913. For patrons and friends, see, for example, letterhead in Box 6, NCWC Collection; International Council of Women, *Who's Who at the Congress* (Toronto, 1909); E. Cummings letter, Jan. 15, 1902, Box 106, NCWC Collection.

24 F.M. Eaton, *Memory's Wall* (Toronto: Clarke, Irwin, 1965), p.108; *Star*, Oct. 28, 1913. Members of the anti-suffrage league are listed in the *Star*, Feb. 5, 1914. (Names were crosschecked with Toronto street directory.) H. Morgan, op. cit.; Charles G.D. Roberts, Arthur Tunnill, eds., *A Standard Dictionary of Canadian Biography* (Toronto: Trans-Canada Press, 1934-38); J.E. Middleton, W.S. Downs, eds., *National Encyclopedia of Canadian Biography* (Toronto: Dominion Publishing Co., 1935-37). Supplementary information on one member not cited here, Mrs. Van Koughnet, is in *World*, Dec. 7, 1911.

25 *World*, Nov. 26, 1908, Apr. 27, 1913. See also C. Derrick, 'Professions Open to Women in Canada,' *International Council of Women* (London, 1900), Vol. 3, pp.30 ff.

26 See statistics presented by M.C. Urquhart, *Historical Statistics of Canada* (Toronto: Macmillan, 1965), pp.59-60. See also N. Meltz, 'The Female Work: Occupational Trends in Canada,' *Changing Patterns in Women's Employment* (Ottawa: Queen's Printer, 1966), p.40.

27 It should not be thought that these ladylike prescriptions matched reality. See, for instance, the British study, Patricia Branca, *Silent Sisterhood*

(London: Croom Helm, 1975). For a description of the socialization in Canada, see Isabel Bassett, *The Parlour Rebellion, Profiles in the Struggle for Women's Rights* (Toronto: McClelland & Stewart, 1975), Ch. 1; G. Eggleston, 'The Education of Women,' *Canadian Educational Monthly* (1883), p.382, cited in N. Thompson, 'The Controversy Over the Admission of Women to University College, University of Toronto' (MA thesis, University of Toronto, 1974), p.1. For the controversy over women's admission, see also John Squair, *Admission of Women to the University of Toronto and University College* (Toronto: University of Toronto Press, 1924); *Queen's College Journal,* Dec. 16, 1876, cited in eds., R. Cook and W. Mitchinson, *The Proper Sphere* (Toronto: Oxford University Press, 1976), p.123.

28 For Wilson's full speech, see N. Thompson, op. cit., pp.131-33, see also p.54. See 'The Need For Ladies' Colleges for Higher Education, 1885,' in Cook and Mitchinson, op. cit., esp. p.141.

29 'The Sweet Girl Graduate,' in Sarah Curzon, *Laura Secord, the Heroine of 1812* (Toronto: C.B. Robinson, 1887), p.122.

30 Ibid., pp.131-32.

31 Augusta Stowe-Gullen, 'Women in the Study and Practice of Medicine,' in ed. B.F. Austin, *Woman: Her Character, Culture and Calling* (Brantford: Book Bible House, 1890), pp.122-24. For similar views, see 'Professions for Women, 1879,' in Cook and Mitchinson, op. cit., pp.135-39.

32 I. Bassett, op. cit., Ch. 5.

33 Cited in C. Dyhouse, 'Social Darwinistic Ideas and the Development of Women's Education in England, 1880-1920,' *History of Education* (Feb. 1976), p.54; for the US parallel, see Robert H. Wiebe, *The Search For Order, 1877-1920* (New York: Hill and Wang, 1967), pp.122-23.

34 *The Week* (July 1884), cited in N. Thompson, op. cit., pp. 135-36.

35 Cited in T.R. Morrison, '"Their Proper Sphere" Feminism, The Family, and Child-Centred Social Reform in Ontario, 1875-1900,' *Ontario History* (June 1976), p.65.

36 B. Austin, 'What Knowledge is Most Worth to Woman?' in Austin, op. cit., p.340.

37 A. Carman, 'Strength and Beauty in Woman's Character,' in Austin, op. cit., pp.358, 364.

38 Mrs. Dr. Parker, 'Woman in Nation-Building,' in Austin, op. cit., pp.454 ff.

39 *Star,* Jan. 4, 1908; *Canadian Home Journal* (Aug. 1897), p.1.

40 *Massey's Magazine* (Feb. 1897), pp.82-83; *Star,* Oct. 13, 1897, Jan. 10, 1910; M.E. Addisson to Burwash, 'Report of Annesley and South Halls 1909-1910,' Mar. 10, 1910, Burwash Papers, University of Toronto; E. Macpherson, 'Careers of Canadian University Women' (MA thesis, University of Toronto, 1920).

41 *Mail and Empire*, July 20, 1908; on McCully, see fn. 6 above; *Star*, Jan. 6, 1913; E.S. Kelley, *The Devil's Hand* (Carbondale: South Illinois University Press, 1974), esp. p.291; *Star*, Sept. 17, 1973, Feb. 24, 1914.

42 'Report of the Committee Appointed to Enquire in Regard to a Possible College for Women,' Mar. 10, 1909, in G. Wrong, Miscellaneous Correspondence, University of Toronto Archives; University of Toronto Senate, *Minutes* (Vol. 10), pp.212-13; ibid. (May 1909), p.268; *Star*, May 19, 1909. Falconer also charged that women were driving men out of languages — see *Star*, Jan. 10, 1910. For a later reflection of women students' opinion, see *Telegram*, Nov. 21, 1911.

43 *Globe*, Nov. 29, 1913.

44 Cited in A. Bowker, 'Truly Useful Men: Maurice Hutton, George Wrong, James Mayor and the University of Toronto, 1880-1927' (Ph.D. dissertation, University of Toronto, 1976), p.330; *Canadian Home Journal* (Mar. 1896), p.180; *Torontonensis* (1910).

45 Maud Edgar, 'The University Women's Club,' *University of Toronto Monthly* (Dec. 1905), pp.42-43; M. Waddington, 'The Woman Student in Toronto,' *Arbor* (Mar. 1913), p. 237; *Star*, Apr. 18, 1914.

46 'Manual Training for Girls,' *Sesame* (1901), p.18.

47 'The First Women Medical Students, Queen's University, 1916,' in Cook and Mitchinson, op. cit., p.156.

48 Ibid., p.162.

49 This discussion draws on unpublished material from Women's College Hospital Archives. I would like to thank the hospital director for making these records available to me. Ontario Medical College for Women, Ltd., *Annual Calendar, 1903*; 'The History of Women's College Hospital' (mimeo, n.d.); E.L. Skinner-Gordon, 'Information regarding the growth of the Women's College Hospital, Toronto, from 1896 to 1922' (n.d.); *Women's Work for Women's Need* (1912), (1914); G. Maloney, 'The Women's College Hospital as a Teaching Institution' (n.d.); Ontario Medical College for Women, *Annual Announcement* (1896), p.6. See also Augusta Stowe-Gullen, *A Brief History of the Ontario Medical College for Women* (1906), ASG; L. Edward, 'The Woman Doctor in Canada' (Toronto Academy of Medicine Archives, n.d.); C.M. Godfrey, 'The Origins of Medical Education of Women in Ontario,' *Medical History* (Jan. 1973); *Women's Journal*, May 1, 1899.

50 'Submission of the Ontario Medical College For Women,' in Royal Commission on the University of Toronto Papers, University of Toronto Archives.

51 J. Gibbon, *Three Centuries of Canadian Nursing* (Toronto, 1947); 'The T.G.H. Training School for Nurses,' *The Canadian Nurse* (Mar. 1905); M. Snively, 'Trained Nursing in Canada,' ibid. (Aug. 1909); 'A Great Canadian Nurse,'

Notes

ibid. (Jan. 1910); 'Employment For Women, 1876' in Cook and Mitchinson, op. cit., p.171.

52 E. Shortt, 'The First Women Medical Students,' Cook and Mitchinson, op. cit., p.163; cited in T.R. Morrison, op. cit., p.71.

53 *Massey's Magazine* (Jan. 1896), p.50; Jessie Lawson (Kerr), *Dr. Bruno's Wife, A Toronto Society Story* (London, 1893), p.66.

54 *Canadian Practitioner and Review* (July 1897), pp.532-33; ibid., (Jan. 1898), pp.45-46; Lady Aberdeen, *We Twa, Reminiscences of Lord and Lady Aberdeen* (London: Collins, 1926), pp.124-31; *Canadian Practitioner and Review* (Nov. 1897), p.830, see also 'correspondence'.

55 *The Canadian Nurse* (Nov. 1969), p.695; (Aug. 1916), pp.331-51; (Jan. 1914), pp.32-33; (Mar. 1910), p.110.

56 Ibid. (Mar. 1913), pp.169-71; (July 1913), pp.461 ff.; (July 1911), pp.335-40; (July 1912), pp.401-406; *Fifteenth Annual Report of the Nursing at Home Mission,* Dec. 31, 1901 (University of Toronto Rare Books); *The Canadian Nurse* (Jan. 1908), pp.11-12.

57 The assessment of nurses' backgrounds is based on lists of The Ontario Graduate Nurses' Association, cited in *The Canadian Nurse* (Mar. 1905), p.48. These were crosschecked with the Toronto Street Directory. Only three of the 64 lived with parents whose occupations were listed: they came from families of skilled workers or clerks. Most of the rest lived in residence. See also *The Canadian Nurse* (June 1912), p.296; 'The Toronto Nurses Club,' ibid. (Dec. 1906), pp.19-20; 'The Story of the Toronto Graduate Nurses Club,' ibid. (Aug. 1913).

58 H. Morgan, op. cit., p.250; *Scrapbooks: Biographies of Men,* Vol. 16 (Toronto Public Libraries), p.38; *Canadian Courier,* Feb. 17, 1912, p.18. The writing of this section on journalism has benefited greatly from a reading of C. Fox, A. Klein, 'An Examination of the Writings of Pioneer Women Journalists in Toronto' (Unpublished undergraduate paper, 1974).

59 *Mail and Empire,* Nov. 20, 1897; Oct. 23, 1897; Jan. 16, 1897; Oct. 26, 1901; July 25, 1896.

60 Ibid., Mar. 20, 1897; June 15, 1901; May 23, 1896; Mar. 16, 1895; July 4, 1896.

61 Ibid., July 6, 1895; *Sunset* (Mar. 1916), p.16, FMD.

62 *Canadian Courier,* Jan. 27, 1912, p.13; Madge Macbeth, *Over My Shoulder* (Toronto: Ryerson Press, 1953), pp.56-57; M. McMurchy, *The Canadian Girl at Work, A Book of Vocational Guidance* (Toronto: A.T. Wilgress, 1919), preface; 'The Work of Canadian Women Journalists,' *Women Workers of Canada,* op. cit., Vol. 1, pp.396-400; *Mail and Empire,* May 14, 1921, as cited by Fox and Klein, op. cit.

63 Ross Harkness, *J.E. Atkinson of the Star* (Toronto: University of Toronto Press, 1963); J.H. Cranston, *Ink On My Fingers* (Toronto: Ryerson Press, 1953), pp.83-84.

64 *Star*, Oct. 23, 1909; Feb. 27, 1909; see also Mar. 22, 1902; Oct. 15, 1904; Harkness, op. cit., pp.44-45.

65 *Star*, Dec. 23, 1911.

66 *Star*, June 15, 1913; Apr. 26, 1907; *Globe*, Feb. 17, 1910.

67 Ibid., Feb. 21, 1910.

68 *Star*, Dec. 9, 1913. For a more detailed discussion on the problem of working women's organization, see my *Honest Womanhood*, op. cit.

69 Toronto District Labor Council *Minutes*, June 20, 1902 (PAC); ibid., Mar. 4, 1909; *The Canadian Labor Party Bulletin*, Apr. 3, 1911, p.4.

70 *News*, Sept. 2, 1913; 'Woman Suffrage,' *Women's Century* (n.d.), FMD Scrapbooks; *Industrial Banner*, Jan. 2, 1914.

71 Ibid., Dec. 26, 1913.

72 Ibid., Feb. 14, Apr. 11, Mar. 21, Mar. 14, Apr. 11, Feb. 21, 1913.

73 *Western Clarion*, Sept. 12, 1908; Oct. 10, 1908.

74 Ibid., Sept. 26, 1908, Oct. 17, 1908; *Globe*, Jan. 5, 1909. I am grateful to Veronica Strong-Boag for directing me to this.

75 *Star*, May 1, 1902; *Mail and Empire*, May 19, 1902; May 30, 1902; *Globe*, May 30, 1902; Nov. 8, 1901; *Cotton's Weekly*, Sept. 22, 1910; *Industrial Banner*, Dec. 19, 1913.

76 *Citizen and Country*, May 13, 1899; Cotton's Weekly, Nov. 24, 1910. The editor had been pro-suffrage before becoming a socialist. Cf. *Observer*, Nov. 5, 1908.

77 Unidentified clipping, FMD Scrapbooks; torn clipping (n.d.), Box 2, FMD.

78 See, for example, the discussion in J. Kornberg, 'Feminism and the Liberal Dialectic: John Stuart Mill on Women's Rights,' Canadian Historical Association *Historical Papers*, 1974. Kornberg sees Mill's ambiguity as a personal rather than a structural-ideological problem.

CHAPTER TWO

I should like to thank my friends Cyril Greenland and Wayne Roberts, and the staff at the Thomas Fisher Library, University of Toronto, for their help with this paper.

1 From 'The Position of Women in Society,' a speech in manuscript (n.d.) in Box 2 of the Flora MacDonald Denison Papers at the Thomas Fisher Library, University of Toronto. (All subsequent references to these papers will be indicated by FMD.)

Notes

2 For the history of Picton, see *Illustrated Historical Atlas of the Counties of Hastings and Prince Edward Ontario* (Toronto: H. Belden and Co., 1878). The quotation is from an article entitled 'Our Girls' from an unidentified Picton newspaper, n.d. but probably late 1890s, in Newspaper Clipping Scrapbook, FMD. Information about Flora MacDonald Denison's early background is scattered in several places. Besides her papers at the University of Toronto, there is some information in the papers of Merrill Denison, her son, in the Douglass Library, Queen's University, Kingston, Ontario. There is also her thinly disguised autobiographical novel, published under the pen name she often used, Flora MacDonald, *Mary Melville: The Psychic* (Toronto: Austin Publishing Company Ltd., 1900). There is also information in the Merrill Family Papers at the Public Archives of Ontario. See also Dick MacDonald, *Mugwump Canadian: The Merrill Denison Story* (Montreal: Content Publishing Limited, 1973). Cyril Greenland, who has done work on Denison's sister Mary (Cyril Greenland, 'Mary Edwards Merrill 1858-1880: "The Psychic,"' *Ontario History*, XVIII, No. 2 (1976), pp.81-92) kindly let me use some family papers in his possession. James Hayes, Denison's nephew, kindly spoke to me about his aunt in June 1975. Her niece, Grace Wiren, talked to me on the telephone in June 1975.

3 From her 'Open Road' column, *The Sunday World*, June 18, 1911, in Map Case Clippings, FMD.

4 'Open Road' columns, Aug. 21, 1910 and Aug. 14, 1910, ibid.

5 On her early days in Michigan, see a *Toronto News* clipping of March 10, 1919, in possession of Cyril Greenland, who also has her autograph book. Howard Denison was not a member of the powerful Denison family of Toronto. Information about his background is in a folder marked 'Biography' in M. Denison Papers, Kingston, Box 81, Subject Files Personal. (All subsequent references to the M. Denison Papers will be indicated by MD.)

6 For information on women in the clothing industry, see several of the articles in *Women at Work: Ontario 1850-1933*, eds. Janice Acton, Penny Goldsmith and Bonnie Shephard (Toronto: Canadian Women's Educational Press, 1974). See also Greg Kealey, *Working Class Toronto at the Turn of the Century* (Toronto: Hogtown Press, 1974) and Michael Piva, *The Condition of the Working Class in Toronto, 1900-1921* (Unpublished Ph.D. dissertation, Concordia University, Montreal, 1975).

7 When writing for *Saturday Night* in the 1890s, Denison used the name 'Flora MacDonald'. Both these articles are in the Newspaper Clipping Scrapbooks, FMD.

8 The information about the store is from James Hayes, who remembers delivering dresses. Also see a column Denison wrote for *The Sunday World*, Oct. 19, 1913. She paid her ordinary sewers from five dollars to ten dollars a

week. Skilled cutters received eighteen to twenty dollars. She paid the cleaning woman one dollar for four hours' work. Clipping in Map Case Clippings, FMD. For average wages see Piva, op. cit.

9 The description of Denison's 'creation' is from *The World,* Dec. 18, 1898. Clipping in her dressmaking notebook in Box 5, FMD. Denison wrote extensively on servants. One version of 'The Servant Girl Question,' a piece she used several times, is in Box 2, FMD. The speech on dress reform (written c. 1913) is in 'Lectures Given at Suffrage Meetings,' Box 2, FMD.

10 The full text of this speech on 'Burns and Whitman' is in Box 5, FMD.

11 For information on the Whitmanite movement, see Gay W. Allen, *Walt Whitman as Man Poet and Legend* (Carbondale: Illinois, 1961).

12 See 'Under the Pines,' *The World,* Oct. 24, 1909. Newspaper Clipping Scrapbook, FMD.

13 The program is in Box 2, FMD.

14 The full text of this speech on the militants is in longhand in Box 5, FMD.

15 A copy of the pamphlet is in Box 2, FMD.

16 Denison was apparently never paid by *The World* (see the 'Tribute' given to her by the Canadian Suffrage Association on her resignation in 1914, Box 2, FMD). A draft of a letter she probably never sent indicates that she was dissatisfied with this situation — she calls the paper's treatment of her 'abusive' (see a notebook in Box 5, FMD). For the 'People's Press' see P.F.W. Rutherford, 'The People's Press: The Emergence of the New Journalism in Canada, 1869-99', *CHR,* LVI, No. 2 (1975).

17 I have discussed the connection between the English militants and the Canadian suffragists more fully in 'English Militancy and the Canadian Suffrage Movement,' *Atlantis: A Women's Studies Journal,* Vol. 1, No. 1 (1975).

18 For her financial contributions, see a *Star Weekly* story of Mar. 21, 1914.

19 See a letter to Denison from her intimate friend Hazel Wagner, dated Sept. 28, 1906, which suggests that both Wagner and Denison had reason to believe Dr. Gullen was jealous of the publicity Denison received after her Copenhagen journey. Letter in Box 9, MD. But there is plenty of evidence that Denison and Dr. Gullen were close (see letters in FMD). Personal letters from Margaret Gordon are in Box 9, MD.

20 This quotation is from Lady Ishbel Aberdeen's 'President's Message to the Fourth Quinquennial Meeting,' June 1909, National Council of Women Papers, Vol. 20, Public Archives of Canada. For information on the National Council see Veronica Jane Strong-Boag, *The Parliament of Women: The National Council of Women of Canada, 1893-1929* (Ottawa: National Museum of Man Mercury Series, 1976).

21 For the NCWC and the suffrage, see Strong-Boag, pp.275 ff., ibid.

22 The quotation is from 'Under the Pines,' *The World*, Nov. 21, 1909. Scrapbooks, FMD.

23 See Strong-Boag, Appendix III, p.429, for more on the 'women's platform'. For Denison's public views, see the letter printed in the *Women's Century* and elsewhere (see Map Case Clippings, FMD). The Canadian Suffrage Association and the Medical Alumnae were on record against the 'flogging' resolution (see Denison's open letter to the president of the Council of May 2, 1913; NCWC papers, Vol. 67, Public Archives of Canada (PAC)). Apparently this aroused the Council's hostility not only to Denison but also to Dr. Gullen. In private, Denison was bitter; she wrote on Jan. 17, 1913 to Mrs. Torrington, president of the Council, in defence of Dr. Gullen: 'It was Dr. Stowe-Gullen who proposed Lady Aberdeen for first National President of Canada. Dr. Gullen has been connected with both National and local work ever since. She has carried the banner of Women's Suffrage in all seasons, till today your organization stands for the reform ...' and in her own defence said: 'For myself — I understand the smug snobbery existing in Toronto Church and Social circles and do not look for courtesy but for my position as President of the Canadian Suffrage Association, I will certainly ask for justice ...' The letter is in NCWC papers, Vol. 67, PAC.

24 The anonymous letter is in Box 2, FMD.

25 See 'Stray Leaves from Suffragette's Notebook,' 1913, Map Case Clippings, FMD.

26 This quotation is from scattered notes in Notebooks, Box 5, FMD.

27 Other Canadian feminists — like the early women's page editors of the *Grain Growers' Guide* — were also influenced by Gilman, but few took her statements concerning the future of the family as seriously as Denison. Ramsay Cook in 'Francis Marion Beynon and the Crisis of Christian Reformism,' *The West and the Nation: Essays in Honour of W.L. Morton,* eds. Carl Berger and Ramsay Cook (Toronto: McClelland and Stewart, 1976), analyzes the life and work of one of these women's page editors.

28 'Under the Pines,' *The World*, Jan. 23, 1910, Scrapbooks, FMD.

29 Ibid.

30 Ibid., Nov. 21, 1909.

31 'Women's Sphere,' Oct. 19, 1913.

32 There are literally hundreds of letters from this correspondence in the MD. There are also many in Box 4, FMD.

33 Denison's friendship with James L. Hughes, Toronto's unusually progressive school inspector, influenced her ideas about children.

34 The review was entitled 'Life and Love and Books and Other Things,' and appears to be from *The World*, n.d., Map Case Clippings, FMD.

35 The comment on birth control is from 'Under the Pines,' Nov. 14, 1909, in Scrapbooks, FMD. For a discussion of birth control and abortion in Canada during this period, see Angus McLaren, 'Birth Control and Abortion in Canada, 1870-1920,' *Canadian Historical Review*, LIX, 3(1978). The comment about the 'dual-sex principle' is from a speech in Box 3, FMD, entitled 'Mental Over Physical Conditions,' n.d. but probably post-1913.

36 Drafts of the novel are in Box 5, FMD.

37 Letters concerning her work in New York are in Box 2, FMD.

38 'War and Women' has been reprinted in Ramsay Cook and Wendy Mitchinson, eds., *The Proper Sphere* (Toronto: Oxford University Press, 1976), pp.249-52.

39 Grace Wiren remembers the dinnerware. Andrew Glen, who worked with her in the Social Reconstruction Group, remembers being asked to contribute. Personal communication with Andrew Glen, June 1975.

40 Among others, J.W. Bengough and A.E. Smythe wrote for the *Sunset*.

41 Information about the Social Reconstruction Group can be found in the papers of Andrew Glen in the Douglass Library, Queen's University, Kingston, Ontario. It should be noted that although the Social Reconstruction Group thought that Denison attended the Labour Party convention as a delegate from their group, James Simpson did not agree. In a letter to Glen of Apr. 13, 1918, he wrote: 'The acceptance of Mrs. Flora McD. Denison as a delegate at the Good Friday convention was more a recognition of her good work in the Women's Suffrage movement than a recognition of the group referred to.'

CHAPTER THREE

This research is chiefly based on documentation from the archives of the Fédération Nationale Saint-Jean-Baptiste and from the personal papers of Marie Gérin-Lajoie at the motherhouse of the Communauté des Soeurs de Notre-Dame-du-Bon-Conseil (SNDBC), both in Montreal. Initial research was done in 1973 by the group, Les premières féministes canadiennes-françaises, which included Evelyne Bissonnette-Paquette, Johanne Cloutier-Boucher and Rosanne Saint-Jacques, as well as the authors. We wish to thank Paul-André Linteau of the Université du Québec à Montréal for his comments on the text.

1 An example of a church-based association is the Ladies of Sainte-Anne, whose end was 'wholly spiritual' and which, by 1900, claimed a membership

of over 1,500 married women in Montreal alone. See 'Catholic Church Work,' in *Women in Canada, their Life and Work* (Ottawa: Dept. of Agriculture, 1900, 1975), pp.281-99.

2 Justine Lacoste-Beaubien, the sister of Marie Gérin-Lajoie, who was founder of the FNSJB, had to face this situation. As founder of the Sainte-Justine Children's Hospital in 1907, she had to persuade the Quebec government to amend the civil code to allow a married woman (thus legally incapacitated) to make financial transactions in the hospital's name without her husband's authorization. Her request was granted in 1908.

3 Marie Gérin-Lajoie, copy of a manuscript on which she wrote 'published anonymously in several English and French newspapers', m.s. SNDBC archives. Gérin-Lajoie (1867-1945) was the daughter of Sir Alexandre Lacoste, Chief Justice of the Quebec Superior Court. At the age of twenty she married Henri Gérin-Lajoie, lawyer and grandson of the journalist and politician, Etienne Parent. Her mother, Lady Lacoste, was a patroness of charity and a well-known society figure, whose diary recorded the multiple details of raising a family and running a household in nineteenth-century Montreal.

4 Caroline Dessaulles-Béique was the president of the Ladies Auxiliary of the Association Saint-Jean-Baptiste de Montréal and the first president of the Fédération. She was the spouse of Senator F.-L. Béique, Liberal lawyer, financier and president of the Société Saint-Jean-Baptiste from 1899 to 1905. The bourgeois and nationalist orientation of the new Fédération was a reflection of the origins of Béique and Gérin-Lajoie, among others.

5 The first chaplain of the FNSJB was Georges Gauthier, future archbishop of Montreal.

6 See the violently anti-feminist articles of Henri Bourassa in *Le Devoir*, denouncing all forms of feminism, however moderate. Perhaps because of the Catholic nature of its feminism, the Fédération obtained a column in which to publicize its activities. See also S.M. Trofimenkoff, 'Henri Bourassa and the "woman question,"' *Journal of Canadian Studies*, 10, No. 4 (Nov. 1975), pp.3-11.

7 The previous orientation of francophone women's groups can be seen in *Women in Canada, their Life and Work*.

8 See Terry Copp, *The Anatomy of Poverty: The Condition of the Working Class in Montreal 1897-1929* (Toronto: McClelland & Stewart, 1974), Ch. 6 and pp.168-73.

9 Text of Gérin-Lajoie's speech, printed in *Le Devoir*, Jan. 27, 1931.

10 See, for example, the article by Abbé Philippe Perrier, 'Contre le cinéma, tous,' *L'Action Française*, Feb. 1927.

11 *Minutes of the delegates' meeting*, Nov. 6, 1915, FNSJB Archives. For more detail see: C.L. Cleverdon, *The Woman Suffrage Movement in Canada* (Toronto: University of Toronto Press, 1950, 1974) and Micheline Dumont-Johnson, 'History of the Status of Women in the Province of Quebec,' *Cultural Tradition and Political History in Canada: Studies of the Royal Commission on the Status of Women in Canada*, No. 8 (Ottawa: Information Canada, 1975), pp.1-57.

12 M. Gérin-Lajoie, 'La femme peut devenir une aide précieuse dans l'orientation de la politique nationale,' *La Bonne Parole*, Vol. v, No.10 (Dec. 1917), p.1.

13 The anti-suffrage movement manifested itself in various ways: the excited editorials of Henri Bourassa; the opposition of the Jesuits and the Oblates (copy of a letter from M. Gérin-Lajoie to the Vicomtesse de Vélard, Aug. 24, 1922, SNDBC Archives); that of the Action Catholique ('Leur ambition,' *L'Action Catholique*, Apr. 26, 1922); that of women's groups set up to combat the suffrage (*La Presse*, Feb. 3, 1921) and finally, that of most Quebec bishops.

14 The letters of the bishops of Quebec, Chicoutimi, Trois Rivières and Rimouski to M. Gérin-Lajoie, Feb.-Mar., 1922, SNDBC Archives.

15 Françoise to Marie Gérin-Lajoie, July 23, 1909, in the dossier *Congrès 1907-1909*; also Mgr. Bruchési to M. Gérin-Lajoie, July 9 and Aug. 5, 1909, in the dossier *Mgr. Bruchési, Deschamps et autres*, FNSJB Archives. A decade later Marie Gérin-Lajoie signed a petition in favour of compulsory education.

16 Mme F.-L. Béique, *Quatre-vingts ans de souvenirs. Histoire d'une famille* (Montreal: Valiquette, 1939), p.246. It was the only Catholic domestic science school directed by lay persons, until 1919. See Abbé O. Martin, 'Les écoles ménagères. Quelques statistiques,' *Almanach de l'Action sociale catholique, 1917-1922* (Québec: Ateliers typographiques de l'Action sociale Ltée), pp.118-20. For the history of domestic science schools, see the article of Lucien Lemieux, 'La fondation de L'Ecole Ménagère de Saint-Pascal 1905-1909,' *RHAF*, 24, No. 3 (Dec. 1971), pp.552-57.

17 These circles were also formed in schools. The most exclusive was the Notre Dame circle which essentially comprised the graduates of Marguerite-Bourgeoys College. Its program was almost the equivalent of a university course in social science and trained classical college graduates as social workers. Nearly the whole course of study was adopted by the University of Montreal when it opened its school of social work.

18 The FNSJB, together with other feminist organizations, took part in several major legal battles. In 1908, it opposed a project abolishing the *Homestead Act* of 1897 (a law protecting settlers' wives by forbidding husbands to dispose of the family homestead without their wives' consent); in 1915, it supported the Pérodeau Law (which included women in the third degree of successors when a husband died intestate); and finally, in 1923 it successfully obtained a

change in the Bank Law concerning the deposits of married women (this change raised the amount of money a woman married under community of property could deposit, from $500 to $2,000). The latter modification clearly appears to be a reform requested by only a small group of women, since the average earnings of women workers in Montreal according to the 1921 Canadian census were $587.

19 Evangéline Zappa, 'Les associations professionnelles féminines,' *La Bonne Parole*, III, No. 6 (Aug. 1915), pp.4, 6.

20 Marie-Claire Daveluy, 'Caractère des associations professionnelles,' *La Bonne Parole*, v, Nos. 2-3 (Apr. 1917), p.23.

21 Ibid.

22 Marie Gérin-Lajoie (daughter), 'Le syndicalisme féminin,' excerpt from a speech given at the 1921 *Semaine Sociale* and reprinted in Michèle Jean, *Québécoises du vingtième siècle* (Montreal: Editions du Jour, 1974), pp.103-16.

23 *Premier livre des minutes de l'association professionnelle des employées de manufactures, 17 février 1907-13 septembre 1908*, Nov. 21, 1907, FNSJB Archives.

24 *Deuxième livre des minutes de l'association professionnelle des employées de manufactures, 20 septembre 1908-7 mars 1912*, Feb. 20, 1910, FNSJB Archives.

25 Ibid., Sept. 4, 1910. The crowd was estimated at between 12,000 and 20,000 women. See *Le Devoir* and *La Patrie*, Sept. 6, 1910. This holiday was abolished after 1913.

26 *La Gazette du Travail*, 14, No. 4 (Oct. 1913), p.465.

27 See, regarding the problem of the 'domestic crisis', the *Journal-Mémoires de Madame Raoul Dandurand, 1879-1900*, an article of Françoise, 'Le congrès féminin,' *Le Journal de Françoise*, 6, No. 6 (June 15, 1907), pp.89-90 and the *Journal Intime* of Lady Lacoste.

28 The evolution of the National Council of Women of Canada seems to be similar. From 1918 on, the NCWC entered a period of hesitancy which, by the end of the 1920s, indicated its inability to grasp the preoccupations of a younger generation. See Veronica Jane Strong-Boag, *The Parliament of Women: The National Council of Women of Canada, 1893-1929* (Ottawa: The National Museum of Man, 1976).

CHAPTER FOUR

1 For an expansion of these ideas, refer to Carol Bacchi, 'Liberation Deferred: The Ideas of the English-Canadian Suffragists, 1877-1918' (Ph.D. dissertation, McGill University, 1976).

2 For the 16 non-executive male members there was insufficient information on place of birth to include them in this analysis. No birthplace could be found for 55 executive female members.

3 Castell Hopkins, *Canadian Annual Review* (Toronto: University of Toronto Press, 1902), p.87.

4 Martin Robin, *Radical Politics and Canadian Labour, 1880-1930* (Kingston: Industrial Relations Centre, Queen's University, 1968), p.31.

5 *Globe* (Toronto), Sept. 29, 1916. Alice Klein and Wayne Roberts also draw attention to the fact that unions cooperated with middle-class reformers due to their fear of competition from women. 'Besieged Innocence: The "Problem" and the Problems of Working Women – Toronto, 1896-1914,' in *Women at Work: Ontario, 1850-1930,* eds. Janice Acton, Penny Goldsmith and Bonnie Shepard (Toronto: Canadian Women's Educational Press, 1974), p.220.

6 *Winnipeg Voice*, Oct. 1, 1915 and Dec. 20, 1912.

7 Emily Murphy, *Seeds of Pine* (Toronto: Hodder and Sloughton, 1914), p.259.

8 Alice A. Chown, *The Stairway* (Boston: Cornhill Comp., 1921), pp. 146, 153.

9 *Toronto World*, Dec. 7, 1913.

10 *B.C. Federationist*, Oct. 17, 1913 and Jan. 16, 1914; *Winnipeg Voice*, Apr. 3, 1908; *Montreal Gazette*, Mar. 27, 1912.

11 *Winnipeg Voice*, Feb. 18, 1910; Oct. 28, 1910.

12 Ibid., Dec. 20, 1907; July 19, 1907.

13 Ibid., Sept. 18, 1918.

14 *Industrial Banner*, Nov. 26, 1915.

15 *B.C. Federationist*, Feb. 11, 1916.

16 *Industrial Banner*, Aug. 10, 1917; Mar. 15, 1918.

17 Ibid., May 31, 1918.

18 J.M.S. Careless, 'Aspects of Urban Life in the West, 1870-1914,' *Prairie Perspectives,* eds. A.W. Rasporich and H.C. Klassen (Toronto: Holt, Rinehart and Winston, 1970), p.28; W.L. Morton, *The Progressive Party in Canada* (Toronto: University of Toronto Press, 1950), p.5.

19 *Grain Growers' Guide*, Feb. 14, 1914.

20 Ibid., June 26, 1918; Eva Carter, *The History of Organized Farm Women of Alberta* (undated pamphlet), p.19.

21 Manitoba Political Equality League, *Minutes*, Mar. 21, 1914.

22 June Menzies, 'Votes for Saskatchewan's Women,' *Politics in Saskatchewan,* ed. Norman Ward (Don Mills, Ontario: Longmans, 1968), p.84; Archives of Saskatchewan, Zoa Haight Papers, Violet MacNaughton to Zoa Haight, Mar. 30, 1914; Saskatchewan PEFB, *Minutes*, Feb. 13, 1915.

23 Haight Papers, MacNaughton to Haight, Apr. 24, 1916.

24 *Grain Growers' Guide*, Apr. 2, 1913.

25 Ibid., Dec. 11, 1918.

26 Ibid., Dec. 4, 1918.

27 Annie Walker, *Fifty Years of Achievement* (Ontario: Federated Women's Institutes, 1948), p.10; MacNaughton Papers, Irene Parlby to MacNaughton, Mar. 14, 1916; M. Viola Powell, *Forty Years Agrowing: the History of the Ontario Women's Institutes* (Ontario: Port Perry Star, 1941), p.18; National Council of Women of Canada, *Annual Report*, 1903, p.24.

28 *Farm and Ranch Review*, Feb. 21, 1916.

29 Haight Papers, MacNaughton to Haight, July 23, 1914; *Grain Growers' Guide*, Apr. 5, 1911; Dec. 11, 1918.

30 *Grain Growers' Guide*, Oct. 16, 1918; Donald M. Page, 'The Development of a Western Canadian Peace Movement,' *The Twenties in Western Canada*, ed. S. Trofimenkoff (Ottawa: National Museum of Man, 1972), p.90.

31 *Grain Growers' Guide*, Oct. 16, 1918.

32 Ibid., Dec. 4, 1918; Nov. 13, 1914.

33 MacNaughton Papers, Subject File: Woman's Party, 1918-1919, C. Hamilton to MacNaughton, Dec. 16, 1918; *Grain Growers' Guide*, Dec. 11, 1918.

34 *Industrial Banner*, Nov. 22, 1918.

CHAPTER FIVE

1 'Sweet Girl Graduates,' *Queen's College Journal*, Dec. 16, 1876, reprinted in *The Proper Sphere*, eds. W. Mitchinson and R. Cook (Toronto: Oxford University Press, 1976), p.123.

2 See the typically critical assessment of female ability to withstand pressure, 'Higher Education for Women,' *The Canadian Practitioner*, Vol. 17, June 1, 1892, pp.257-60; 'Female Physicians,' *Canada Medical Journal* (Montreal) Vol. VI (June 1870), p.570; 'Co-education,' *Canada Medical Record* (Montreal) Vol. 18 (Feb. 1890), p.119.

3 See Elizabeth MacNab, *A Legal History of Health Professions in Ontario*, A Study for the Committee on the Healing Arts (Toronto: Queen's Printer, 1970), pp.17-41, Ch. 2.

4 Ibid., pp.29-30. For a further discussion of the Patrons of Industry see S. Shortt, 'Social Change and Radical Crisis in Rural Ontario: the Patrons of Industry, 1889-1896,' in *Oliver Mowat's Ontario*, ed. D. Swainson (Toronto: Macmillan, 1972) and M.V. Royce, 'Arguments over the Education of Girls —

Their Admission to Grammar Schools in this Province,' *Ontario History* Vol. LXVII (Dec. 1975), pp.1-13.

5 See, for example, 'Medicus,' 'Over-production of Medical Men,' *Canada Lancet* Vol. XXIV (Dec. 1892) and 'Overcrowded Professions,' *Canada Medical Record* Vol. 23 (1894-95), pp.142-43. See medical suspicion of midwives and their identification with female doctors in Noel and José Parry, *The Rise of the Medical Profession* (London: Croom Helm, 1976), Ch. 8.

6 For a useful survey of such pioneers, see E.P. Lovejoy, *Women Doctors of the World* (New York: Macmillan, 1957). For a more analytical consideration of the situation of females in American medicine, see the important R.H. Shyrock, *Medicine in America* (Baltimore: Johns Hopkins Press, 1966), Ch. IX.

7 See Mrs. J. Harvie, 'The Medical Education of Women,' *Educational Monthly of Canada* Vol. V (Dec. 1883), pp.472-77; Mrs. Ashley Carus-Wilson, *The Medical Education of Women* (Montreal, 1895), p.14; 'Fidelis,' 'Women's Work,' *The Canadian Monthly* Vol. 14 (Aug. 1878), p.30; 'A Woman's Address,' *British Whig* (Kingston, May 4, 1884).

8 *Queen's College Journal* (May 7, 1881), p.147; see Carus-Wilson, *The Medical Education of Women*, pp.19-20. Stephen Leacock, Andrew Macphail, Goldwin Smith and Henri Bourassa were among the most prominent critics of the effects of urban-industrial society on males. This criticism gave added weight to their fears about the influence of feminism; see G. Decarie, 'Something Old, Something New ... "Aspects of Prohibitionism in Ontario in the 1890s,"' *Oliver Mowat's Ontario*, p.169, for one aspect of this antagonism.

9 For a useful survey of their activities, see C. Hacker, *The Indomitable Lady Doctors* (Toronto & Vancouver: Clarke, Irwin & Co., Ltd., 1974), Ch. 2, 3.

10 Elizabeth Smith Shortt Papers, *Diary*, Apr. 22, 1879, University of Waterloo; Adam Shortt Papers, Box 9, Douglas Library, Queen's University. Two of Carson's daughters did in fact complete the program at Toronto Woman's Medical College: Susanna Carson Rijnhart (Trinity, 1888) and Jennie Carson (Trinity, 1889).

11 A. Shortt Papers, Box 9, E. Stowe to E. Smith, July 2, 1879.

12 Smith Shortt Papers, A. McGillivray to Smith, Oct. 24, 1880.

13 Smith Shortt Papers, *Diary*, Oct. 28, 1881.

14 Ibid., Nov. 12, 1882; *British Whig* (Kingston), June 9, 1883.

15 Smith Shortt Papers, M. Oliver to Smith, June 20, 1883.

16 'Medical Aid to Women in India,' *Canada Lancet* XVIII (Oct. 1883), p.51; 'Women's Work in the Church,' *Christian Guardian* (June 25, 1879), p.1; A. Kilborn, 'The Needs and Possibilities of Medical Work for Women in China,' *Missionary Outlook* (May 1899), p. 115; *Sixth General Announcement of the Women's Medical College* (Toronto, 1888-89), p.7.

17 'Miss Oliver's Valedictory,' *Queen's College Journal* (May 14, 1886), p.16; Rev. M.L. Orchard, K.S. McLaurin, *The Enterprise: The Jubilee Story of the Canadian Baptist Mission in India, 1874-1924* (Toronto: Canadian Baptist Foreign Mission Board, c. 1924), Ch. II.

18 Dr. Oliver and Dr. O'Hara, 'Report of the Foreign Missionary Committee,' *Acts and Proceedings of the Presbyterian Church in Canada* 1893-94, p.1xxv; 'Harnessing Power of Chinese Women,' *Globe and Mail*, Apr. 17, 1937.

19 M. O'Hara, *Leaf of the Lotus* (Toronto: John M. Poole, 1931), p.22; S. Carson Rijnhart, *With the Tibetans in Tent and Temple* (1901) and Hacker, *The Indomitable Lady Doctors*, Ch. 6; Wilhelmina Gordon, *Four Servants of God* (n.d.), p.134.

20 See 'Reports of the Foreign Missionary Committee,' *Acts and Proceedings of the Presbyterian Church in Canada, 1888-89*, p.xxxviii.

21 See the ambitions of the valedictorian, A. McGillivray, 'Women's Medical College,' *British Whig*, Oct. 13, 1884.

22 H. MacMurchy, *The Canadian Mother's Book* (Ottawa: Queen's Printer), pp.8-9.

23 See Smith Shortt, 'Women in Municipal Life,' Smith Shortt Papers.

24 H. MacMurchy, *Sterilization? Birth Control?* (Toronto: Macmillan, 1934), p.150; see also MacMurchy, *The Almosts: A Study of the Feeble-Minded* (Boston & New York: Houghton Mifflin Co., 1920).

25 M. Mannington, 'Mental Hygiene,' National Council of Women of Canada *Yearbook* (1930), p.94.

26 Smith Shortt, 'Some Social Aspects of Tuberculosis,' *12th Annual Report of the Canadian Association for the Prevention of Tuberculosis* (1912), p.117.

27 See Brown's appeal to the feminist tradition in 'Bosses Would Sway Women Voters,' *Star Weekly* (Toronto) May 31, 1924.

28 See Appendix, H.E. Macdermott, *One Hundred Years of Medicine in Canada* (Toronto & Montreal: McClelland & Stewart, 1967).

29

	No. of Women Doctors in Canada	Women as a Percentage of All Doctors in Canada
1891	76	1.7
1911	196	2.7
1921	152	1.8
1941	384	3.7

(Canada *Census*, 1891, 1911, 1921, 1941; percentages compiled by the author; no data for 1931). See A. Flexner, *Medical Education in the United States and Canada*, A Report to the Carnegie Foundation for the Advancement of Teaching (New York: 1910, 1950), p.178.

30 See Jill Conway's provocative and enlightening discussion of the failure of professional women in the United States to understand their experience

other than as an expression of 'traditional' maternal femininity: 'Women Reformers and American Culture, 1870-1930,' *Journal of Social History*, Vol. 5, No. 2 (Winter 1971-72), pp.164-77.

CHAPTER SIX

I wish to thank Barbara Roberts, Linda Kealey and Jane Lewis for their useful comments and suggestions. Thanks also to the staff of the Public Archives who, as ever, were exceptionally helpful, and to Margaret Parkins of the Canadian Nurses Association and to Jean McDonald of the Victorian Order of Nurses. A State University of New York research grant helped to finance the research for this article.

1 Dr. Helen MacMurchy, *Infant Mortality* (Toronto: King's Printer, 1911), Conclusion.

2 Ann Oakley, 'Wisewoman and Medicine Man: Changes in the Management of Childbirth,' *The Rights and Wrongs of Women*, eds. Juliet Mitchell and Ann Oakley (Harmondworth, England: Penguin, 1976), pp.39-40; Terry Copp, *The Anatomy of Poverty: The Condition of the Working Class in Montreal 1897-1929* (Toronto: McClelland and Stewart, 1974), pp.95-99.

3 Paul Rutherford, 'Tomorrow's Metropolis: The Urban Reform Movement in Canada 1880-1920,' *The Canadian City*, eds. Gilbert Stelter and Alan Artibise (Toronto: McClelland and Stewart, 1977), pp.368-72.

4 Oakley, 'Wisewoman,' pp.41-42; Veronica Strong-Boag, 'Canada's Women Doctors: Feminism Constrained,' in this volume.

5 Oakley, 'Wisewoman,' pp.49-50; Barbara Ehrenreich and Deirdre English, *Witches, Midwives, and Nurses: A History of Women Healers* (Westbury, New York: The Feminist Press, 1973), pp.33-34.

6 Carol Bacchi, 'Liberation Deferred: The Ideas of the English-Canadian Suffragists, 1887-1918' (Ph.D. dissertation, McGill University, 1976), pp.10-12; T.R. Morrison, '"Their Proper Sphere": Feminism, the Family and Child Centered Social Reform in Ontario 1875-1900,' *Ontario History*, LXVIII, Nos. 1, 2 (Mar., June 1976), pp.45-64, 65-74; Veronica Strong-Boag, *The Parliament of Women: The National Council of Women of Canada, 1893-1929* (Ottawa: National Museum of Man, 1976), pp.6-7; Jill Conway, 'Women Reformers and American Culture 1870-1930,' *Journal of Social History*, Vol. v (Winter 1971-72), pp.164-75; Anne Summers, *Damned Whores and God's Police: The Colonization of Women in Australia* (Ringwood, Victoria: Penguin of Australia, 1975), p.26.

7 Strong-Boag, 'Canada's Women Doctors,' in this volume; Judi Coburn, '"I See and am Silent": A Short History of Nursing in Ontario,' *Women at Work*

Ontario 1850-1930, eds. Janice Acton, Penny Goldsmith, Bonnie Shepard (Toronto: The Canadian Women's Educational Press, 1974), p.139.

8 Brian Mitchell, *European Historical Statistics 1750-1970* (New York: Columbia University Press, 1975), pp.128-31; *Historical Statistics of the United States* (Washington, D.C.: Bureau of Census, 1975), p.57; eds. K. Buckley and M. Urquhart, *Historical Statistics of Canada* (Toronto: Macmillan, 1965), p.40; Dr. Helen MacMurchy, *Infant Mortality: Third Report* (Toronto: King's Printer, 1912), pp.73-73.

9 Bacchi, 'Liberation Deferred,' pp.257-69; Dr. Helen MacMurchy, *Sterilization? Birth Control? A Book for Family Welfare and Safety* (Toronto: Macmillan, 1934).

10 Lady Ishbel Aberdeen, 'We Twa,' quoted in John M. Gibbon, *Victorian Order of Nurses for Canada* (Montreal: Southam Press, 1974), p.4; T.R. Morrison, 'Their Proper Sphere'.

11 Gibbon, *Victorian Order,* pp.6-7.

12 Ibid., p.12; Dr. W.B. Hendry, 'Maternal Welfare,' *Social Welfare* (June 1931), p.182; Coburn, '"I See and am Silent," ' pp.139-40; Canada, Public Archives (hereinafter PAC), MG 28, I, 171, Records of the VON, Vol. 7, Dr. Thomas Gibson to Elizabeth Smellie, the chief superintendent of the VON, Feb. 29, 1936; Strong-Boag, 'Canada's Women Doctors,' in this volume.

13 PAC, MG 28, op. cit.

14 Gibbon, *Victorian Order,* p.25; Dr. Alfred Worcester, 'Nurses and Nursing,' quoted in Gibbon, *Victorian Order,* p.20.

15 Lady Ishbel Aberdeen, 'We Twa,' quoted in Gibbon, *Victorian Order,* p.29; Gibbon, *Victorian Order,* pp.58-60.

16 PAC, MG 30, H, 18, Saskatchewan Homesteaders, Vol. II, pp.401-402. For the urban situation see Copp, *Anatomy of Poverty,* pp.92-99, and Michael Piva, 'The Condition of the Working Class in Toronto 1900-1921' (Ph.D. dissertation, Concordia University, 1975), pp.199-231.

17 PAC, RG 76, Immigration, Vol. 47, file 716, Mrs. Cran's correspondence with the Dominion government; PAC, MG 28, I, 171, Vol. II, Book 3, Minutes of the VON, Nov. 4, 1908; 'A Nursing Problem of the West,' *The Canadian Nurse,* Vol. V, No. 3 (Mar. 1909), pp.117-18.

18 *The Canadian Nurse,* Vol. V, No. 3 (Mar. 1909), pp.118-19.

19 PAC, microfilm reel 15, Toronto Public Library Scrapbooks on Women (hereinafter TPLS), p.127; John Gibbon and Mary Mathewson, *Three Centuries of Canadian Nursing* (Toronto: Macmillan, 1947), pp.323-24; Gibbon, *Victorian Order,* p.64.

20 Ruby Simpson, 'Maternal Welfare and the Maternity Grant,' *The Canadian Nurse,* Vol. XXXVIII, No. 6 (June 1942), pp.400-401.

21 PAC, microfilm reel 16, TPLS, pp.102-103. For additional information about MacMurchy's early reform efforts see Piva, 'The Conditions of the Working Class in Toronto 1900-1921.'

22 Dr. Helen MacMurchy, *Infant Mortality: Reports* (Toronto: King's Printer, 1910, 1911, 1912). These are also available in the Sessional Papers.

23 Ibid. (1910), p.36; PAC, MG 28, I, 32, Ottawa Local Council of Women, Vol. I, 185; Strong-Boag, *The Parliament of Women*, p.265; Mrs. E.M. Paul, 'Home Hygiene-School Nursing,' *Women's Century*, Vol. 3, No. 2 (Aug. 1915), pp.6-7.

24 'The Cradle and the Nation,' *Women's Century*, Vol. 4, No. 5 (Nov. 1916), p.20; PAC, MG 28, I, 25, Vol. 65, resolution of Nov. 16, 1916; PAC, MG 28, I, 161, Vol. 2, correspondence, Montreal branch, 1918-19; Archives of the Canadian Nurses Association, Minutes of the Eighth Annual Meeting of the Canadian Trained Nurses, July 4, 1919, p.68.

25 Archives of the Canadian Nurses Association, Minutes of the Fifth Annual Meeting of the Canadian Trained Nurses, June 15, 1916, p.12.

26 Ibid.

27 Ibid., p.16; p.13.

28 Report of the Nurses Committee of the National Council of Women in Canada, in *The Canadian Nurse*, Vol. XIII, No. 8 (Aug. 1918), p.430-31.

29 Report of the Sixth Annual Meeting of the Canadian Trained Nurses, in *The Canadian Nurse*, Vol. XIII, No. 8 (June 1917), p.429.

30 Ibid., p.435; p.439.

31 Gibbon, *Victorian Order*, pp.67-68; PAC, MG 28, I, 171, Vol. II, Book 4, Minutes of the Executive Council of the VON, Dec. 7, 1916, Jan. 4, 1917, Feb. 1, 1917; PAC, MG 28, I, 171, Vol. 7, Mrs. J.B. Laidlaw to Dr. Gibson, Aug. 15, 1917.

32 PAC, MG 28, I, 171, Vol. 7, Hanington to Hughes, Sept. 27, 1917.

33 Archives of the Canadian Nurses Association, Minutes of the Eighth Annual Meeting of the Canadian Trained Nurses, July 3, 1919, pp.83, 94.

34 PAC, microfilm reel 16, TPLS, p.299.

35 PAC, MG 28, I, 171, Vol. II, Book 5, Minutes of the Executive Council of the VON, Mar. 31, 1920; Ethel Johns, 'The Practice of Midwifery in Canada,' *The Canadian Nurse*, Vol. XXI, No. 1 (Jan. 1925), p.10.

36 Archives of the Canadian Nurses Association, Minutes of the Sixteenth Meeting of the Canadian Association of Nursing Education, June 1923, p.144; Johns, 'The Practice of Midwifery,' p.11.

37 Johns, 'The Practice of Midwifery,' p.13.

38 Ibid.; Kate Brightly, 'Alberta Shows the Way,' *The Canadian Nurse*, Vol. XXXIV, No. 5 (May 1938), p.240.

39 PAC, MG 28, I, 171, Vol. II, Book 6, Minutes of the Executive Council of the VON, Hanington to Charles Morse, Legal Counsel to the VON, Sept. 14, 1923. For an account of the activites of one midwife in the 1920s, see Anne B. Woywitka, 'Homesteader's Woman,' *Alberta History* (Spring 1976), pp.20-24. According to the article, 'Domka Zahara was on call throughout the district as a midwife. She never refused a call, nor lost a mother or child.'

40 PAC, RG 29, Department of Health Records, Vol. 19, 10-3-1, Vol. 2, Report to the vice-chairman of the war committee of the Cabinet on the establishment of a federal department of public health, Oct. 25, 1918; pp.1-2; ibid., Memorandum for Newton Rowell, Jan. 12, 1920; Dr. Helen MacMurchy, *Maternal Mortality in Canada* (Ottawa; King's Printer, 1928).

41 Canada, Department of Pensions and National Health, Annual Report, 1929-30, pp.123-24; ibid., 1930-31, p.144; RG 29, Vol. 992, 499-3-7, part 5, Mrs. R. Payne to the National Council of Family and Child Welfare, Aug. 21, 1931.

CHAPTER SEVEN

1 The following is only a partial list of the women's clubs which were formed in the latter part of the last century: the Woman's Auxiliary to the Board of the Domestic and Foreign Missionary Society of the Church of England in Canada, (1885); The Woman's Baptist Missionary Union of the Maritime Provinces, (1885); The Woman's Foreign Missionary Society of the Presbyterian Church in Canada, Eastern and Western Division, (1876); The Woman's Missionary Society of the Methodist Church, (1881); The Woman's Art Association of Canada, (1890); the National Council of Women, (1893); the Woman's Christian Temperance Union of Canada, (1885); the Young Women's Christian Association, (1893); the Dominion Order of the King's Daughters, (1891); the Victorian Order of Nurses, (1898); the National Home Reading Union, (1895); the Aberdeen Association, (1897); the Girls' Friendly Society of Canada, (1882); the Imperial Order of the Daughters of the Empire, (1900); the Dominion Women's Enfranchisement Association, (1889); plus numerous local musical clubs, historical societies, literary societies, dramatic, athletic and charitable associations.

2 In Ontario and Quebec, the most populated provinces, 22.8 per cent of the population lived in centres classed as urban in 1881. By 1891 this had increased to 33.2 per cent and 29.2 per cent respectively. No province, however, matched British Columbia, whose urban population increased by 30.6 per cent between 1881 and 1891. *Census of Canada 1890-1891*, Vol. 4, p.401; *Sixth Census of Canada*, 1921, Vol. 1, p.346.

3 Barbara Welter, 'The Cult of True Womanhood 1820-1860,' *American Quarterly,* Vol. 18 (Summer 1966), pp.258-71; Jacques Henripin, *Trends and Factors of Fertility in Canada* (Ottawa: Statistics Canada, 1972), pp.39, 36. See Ann D. Gordon and Mari Jo Buhle, 'Sex and Class in Colonial and Nineteenth-Century America,' in ed. Bernice Carroll, *Liberating Women's History* (Chicago: University of Illinois Press, 1976), p.286, for a discussion of the intensification of the mother-child relationship in the American context.

4 The second hypothesis has been suggested by Daniel Scott Smith's concept of domestic feminism. See Daniel Scott Smith, 'Family Limitation, Sexual Control, and Domestic Feminism in Victorian America,' in eds. Mary Hartman, Lois W. Banner, *Clio's Consciousness Raised* (New York: Harper & Row, 1974), pp.119-37.

5 For a discussion of the early temperance movement in Canada and the way in which it was influenced by the American, see J.K. Chapman, 'The Mid-19th Century Temperance Movements in New Brunswick and Maine,' *Canadian Historical Review,* XXXV (1954), pp.43-60. The confrontation with government was experienced by other women's organizations much later since few advocated such controversial reforms. Eventually, however, most women's groups were faced with government reluctance to implement their reforms.

6 Annual Report, Woman's Christian Temperance Union of Ontario, 1898, p.96; ibid., 1899, pp.50-51; Robert Popham, Wolfgang Schmidt, *Statistics of Alcohol Use and Alcoholism in Canada 1871-1956* (Toronto: University of Toronto Press, 1958), pp.15-25.

7 Annual Report, WCTU, Ontario, 1882, pp.5-6; Anne Angus, *Children's Aid Society of Vancouver 1901-1951* (Vancouver: Children's Aid Society, 1951), p.5.

8 The percentage of the WCTU executive who were traceable was small, only 38 per cent.

WCTU *Executive* 1890-1901; *Occupation of Husband:*

	Traceable	%
Business	8	19
Law	6	14
Ministry	9	21
Medicine	4	9.5
Journalism	5	12

(These figures represent only the professions with the largest representations.)

9 State intervention was gradually adopted by most women's reform organiza-

tions. It was the method by which they could cope with an increasingly complex society.

10 The importance of religious faith for the WCTU will be examined later.

11 Annual Report, WCTU, Ontario, Oct. 24, 1878, Resolutions; Annual Report, Woman's Christian Temperance Union of British Columbia, 1889, p.18.

12 Ruth Spence, *Prohibition in Canada* (Toronto: Ontario Branch of the Dominion Alliance, 1919), p.144; Annual Report, WCTU of the Dominion of Canada, 1889, p.3; ibid., p.18; ibid., 1891, p.43.

13 Annual Report, WCTU, Nova Scotia, 1896, p.27.

14 Ibid., 1897, p.3; Rev. W. Peck, *A Short History of the Liquor Traffic* (n.p., 1929), p.14.

15 Annual Report, WCTU N.S., 1897, p.24; Annual Report, WCTU Canada, 1892, p.53.

16 Letitia Youmans, *Campaign Echoes* (Toronto: William Briggs, 1893), pp.206-207.

17 Annual Report, WCTU Ontario, 1880, p.10. For further information on the suffrage movement in Canada and the role the WCTU played, see Catherine Cleverdon, *The Woman Suffrage Movement in Canada*, 2nd ed. (Toronto: University of Toronto Press, 1974).

18 *The Templar Quarterly*, (Aug. 1897), p.28.

19 Annual Report, WCTU New Brunswick, 1899, p.26; Annual Report, WCTU Ontario, 1898, p.66.

20 Annual Report, WCTU Manitoba, 1890-91, pp.43-44; Scott Smith, op.cit., p.125. There is a suggestion in Alison Prentice, 'Education and the Metaphor of the Family: the Upper Canadian Example,' *History of Education Quarterly*, XII, No. 3 (1972), p.286, that the family as a source of identification in mid-nineteenth-century Canadian society was declining, due to the discredit brought upon the concept by the Family Compact.

21 Scrapbook, WCTU, 1898, lent to the author by Mrs. Harris Magog, Quebec. For information on feminine friendships in the United States, see Carroll Smith-Rosenberg, 'The Female World of Love and Ritual: Relations Between Women in Nineteenth-Century America,' *Signs* I (Autumn 1975), pp.1-31.

22 Annual Report, WCTU of the Maritime Provinces, 1890, p.43.

23 Annual Report, WCTU Ontario, 1893, p.117; Annual Report, WCTU B.C., 1899, p.58.

24 Annual Report, WCTU B.C., 1897, p.32; Annual Report, WCTU Ontario, 1894, p.140.

25 Annual Report, WCTU Maritimes, 1890, p.49.

26 Scrapbook, Stanstead County WCTU, 1898.

27 Annual Report, WCTU B.C., 1899, p.60; Annual Report, WCTU Canada, 1892, p.76. This emphasis on heredity was common in the latter nineteenth cen-

tury. See Michael Bliss, 'Pure Books on Avoided Subjects,' Canadian Historical Association, *Historical Papers*, 1970, pp.89-108.

28 WCTU *Executive:*

	Number	%
Presbyterian	7	18
Church of England	4	10
Catholic	—	—
Methodist	17	43-44
Baptist	6	15
Congregational	5	13

29 Annual Report, WCTU Canada, 1891, p.93.

30 Annual Report, WCTU Ontario, Oct. 23, 1878, Resolutions; Annual Report, WCTU Quebec, 1884-85, p.70.

31 Annual Report, WCTU B.C., 1893, p.23.

32 See Jill Conway, 'Women Reformers and American Culture,' *Journal of Social History,* 5, No. 2 (Winter 1971-73), pp.164-77, for an expression of this phenomenon in the American context.

CHAPTER EIGHT

1 Hugh McLeod, *Class and Religion in the Late Victorian City* (London: Croom Helm, 1974), pp.284-86.

2 Richard Allen, *The Social Passion, Religion and Social Reform in Canada, 1914-28* (Toronto: University of Toronto Press, 1973), p.4; Ramsay Cook, 'Francis Marion Benyon and the Crisis of Christian Reformism,' in eds. Carl Berger and Ramsay Cook, *The West and the Nation* (Toronto: McClelland and Stewart, 1976), pp.192, 203; Benjamin B. Smillie, 'The Social Gospel in Canada: A Theological Critique,' in Richard Allen, *The Social Gospel in Canada* (Ottawa: National Museum of Man, 1975), pp.330-33.

3 Goldwin French, 'The Evangelical Creed in Canada,' in ed. W.L. Morton, *The Shield of Achilles* (Toronto: McClelland and Stewart, 1968), p.17; K.S. Inglis, *Churches and the Working Classes in Victorian England* (Toronto: University of Toronto Press, 1963), pp.304-306; Cook, 'Benyon,' pp.202-203; Allen, *Social Passion*, pp.5-7.

4 Allen, *Social Passion*, p.17; David O. Moberg, *The Great Reversal: Evangelism Versus Social Concern* (Philadelphia and New York: J.B. Lippincott and Company, 1972); Norris Alden Magnuson, 'Salvation in the Slums: Evangelical Social Work, 1865-1920' (Doctoral dissertation, University of Minnesota, 1968), pp.104-11.

5 Owen Chadwick, *The Victorian Church* I (London: Adam and Charles Black, 1966), p.351; Inglis, *Churches and the Working Classes*, Ch. 7.

6 Kathleen Heasman, *Evangelicals in Action: An Appraisal of Their Social Work in the Victorian Era* (London: Geoffrey Bles, 1962), pp.48-68; David Owen, *English Philanthropy* (Cambridge, Mass.: Harvard University Press, 1964), pp.211-14; Kathleen Woodroofe, *From Charity to Social Work in England and the United States* (Toronto: University of Toronto Press, 1962); Maurice Bruce, *The Coming of the Welfare State* (London: B.T. Batsford Ltd., 1966), Ch. 5.

7 Heasman, *Evangelicals*, pp. 88-106; J. Neil Sutherland, *Children in English-Canadian Society* (Toronto: University of Toronto Press, 1976), Part One; G.J. Parr, 'The Home Children: British Juvenile Immigrants to Canada, 1868-1924' (Doctoral dissertation, Yale University, 1976), Ch. 1 and 3; Ivy Pinchbeck and Margaret Hewitt, *Children in English Society* II (London: Routledge and Kegan Paul, 1973), pp.562-63, 575-78.

8 Public Archives of Canada (PAC), Immigration Branch Records, RG 76 3115 7, 'Statement showing the annual and total immigration by individuals and societies of juveniles (Boys and Girls, British), December 22, 1917'; Sutherland, *Children*, Part One; Parr, 'Home Children,' Ch. 1, 3 and 10; Lee Holcombe, *Victorian Ladies at Work* (London: David and Charles, 1973), pp.5-6, 16; W.A. Carrothers, *Emigration from the British Isles* (London: P.S. King and Son, 1929), p. 257; G.F. Plant, *Oversea Settlement* (London: Oxford University Press, 1951), pp.61-64.

9 *Christian*, Oct. 27, 1881, p.10; Heasman, *Evangelicals*, p.23; George C. Needham, *Street Arabs* (Philadelphia: Hubbard Bros., 1888), p.153; Chadwick, *Victorian Church*, I, p.423.

10 K.S. Inglis has also found that policy commitments were more important than denominational affiliation in bringing British evangelicals together. See his *Churches and the Working Classes*, p.305.

11 Note the discussion of the influence of Arminianism upon Canadian reformers in Alison Prentice, 'The School Promoters: Education and Social Class in Mid-Nineteenth Century Upper Canada' (Doctoral dissertation, University of Toronto, 1974), pp.25-26.

12 Timothy L. Smith, *Revivalism and Social Reform in Mid-Nineteenth Century America* (New York and Nashville: Abingdon Press, 1957), pp.152, 157, 176.

13 Annie Macpherson, 'Winter Labour for Spring Transplanting,' *Occasional Emigration Papers* XII (November 1872), p.1; 'Fruits of Revival,' *Christian*, Mar. 16, 1911, p.16; French, 'Evangelical Creed,' p.20; Magnuson, 'Salvation,' pp.104, 106, 111; Moberg, *Reversal*, pp.15, 30.

14 See Sarah Geldard, 'A Home and a Hearty Welcome,' in Needham, *Street Arabs*, p.288. *Children's Advocate*, February 1883, pp.28-29; John Herridge

Notes

Batt, *Dr. Barnardo* (London: S.W. Partidge & Co., 1904), p.4; Southwark Rescue Society, *Boys and Girls*, July 1896, p.2; Alan Trachtenberg, 'The Camera and Dr. Barnardo,' *Aperture*, XIX, No. 4, p.72.

15 *Times* (London), Mar. 31, 1869; Needham, *Street Arabs*, p.22; *Rescue*, January 1893, p.1; Charles Dickens, *Oliver Twist* (London: Clapham and Hall), pp.272, 274; J.J. Tobias, *Urban Crime in Victorian England* (New York: Schoeken Books, 1967), pp.85-87. For queries (as yet without satisfactory response) concerning street children, see Thomas Bender, 'Studying Nineteenth Century Cities,' *History of Education Quarterly*, XII (1972), p.94.

16 James F. Findlay, *Dwight L. Moody* (Chicago: University of Chicago Press, 1969), pp.294, 361-62; Heasman, *Evangelicals*, p.18; Prentice, 'School Promoters,' pp.34-36; Susan E. Houston, 'The Impetus to Reform: Urban Crime, Poverty and Ignorance in Ontario, 1850-1875' (Doctoral dissertation, University of Toronto, 1974), pp.169, 171, 173; *Night and Day*, II (1878), p.75 and V (1881), p.120; National Children's Home, *Report* (1889-90), p.5; *Children's Advocate* (May 1871), pp.1-2; Thomas John Barnardo, *A City Waif: How I Fished for and Caught Her* and *The Story of a Young Thief* (London: J.F. Shaw & Co., 1885), *Preventive Homes and the Work Done in Them* (London: Haughton & Co., 1878), p.17; 'Report of the Departmental Committee on the Education and Maintenance of Pauper Children in the Metropolis,' *British Parliamentary Papers* XLIII (1896), I, p.670.

17 George E. Morgan, *A Veteran in Revival, R.R. Morgan: His Life and Times* (London: Morgan & Scott, 1909), p.150; Harriet Warm Schupf, 'The Perishing and Dangerous Classes: Efforts to Deal with the Neglected Vagrant and Delinquent Juvenile in England, 1840-1875' (Doctoral dissertation, Columbia University, 1971), pp.73-74; Liverpool Sheltering Homes, *Report* (1882), p.3; 'Balance Sheet,' *Occasional Emigration Papers*, XIV (Mar. 1873), p.1.

18 Annie Macpherson, *The Little London Arabs* (London: privately printed, 1870), pp.62-64; 'Industrial Education vs. Crime,' Howard Association, *Report* (1877), p.11; *Times* (London), Apr. 5, 1887; *Night and Day*, XVI, (1892), p.110; S.L. Barnardo and James Marchant, *Memoirs of the Late Dr. Barnardo* (London, 1907), p.184; Samuel Smith, 'Social Reform,' *Nineteenth Century* (May 1883), p.909.

19 Ellen Logan and Annie Macpherson, *Emigration: The Only Remedy for Chronic Pauperism in East London* (London: privately printed, 1869); Lillian M. Birt, *The Children's Homefinder* (London: J. Nisbet and Company, 1913), pp.59-61; Needham, *Street Arabs,* p.165; Birt, *Children's Homefinder*, p.14; *Christian*, Jan. 1, 1904.

20 Ernest R. Sandeen, *The Roots of Fundamentalism: British and American Millenarianism, 1800-1930* (Chicago: University of Chicago Press, 1970), p.146;

CAMROSE LUTHERAN COLLEGE
LIBRARY

HQ
1453
.N45
38176

Timothy L. Smith, *Revivalism and Social Reform*, pp.152-57; David O. Moberg, *Reversal*, pp.30-33.

21 *Christian*, May 16, 1872, p.5 and Jan. 18, 1883, p.31; Morgan, *Veteran*, p.151; PAC, Lowe Papers, MG 29 B 13 Vol. 1, Dixon, General Correspondence, Annie Macpherson to William Dixon, Mar. 1, 1872; 'Report to President of the Local Government Board by Andrew Doyle, Local Government Board Inspector,' *British Parliamentary Papers*, LXIII (1875), p.23; Barnardo and Marchant, *Memoirs*, p.230.

22 *Christian*, July 30, 1874, p.11 and Aug. 29, 1878, p.8; 'Report of the Departmental Committee on the Education and Maintenance of Pauper Children in the Metropolis,' op. cit., pp.668-70; Barnardo and Marchant, *Memoirs*, pp.164-65; Annie Macpherson, *Summer in Canada* (London: privately printed, 1872), p.25; William Bradfield, *Life of Thomas Bowman Stephenson* (London: C.H. Kelly, 1913), pp.135-36; *Night and Day*, XI (1887), p.84; Annie Macpherson, *Canadian Homes for London Wanderers* (London: privately printed, 1870), p.34; *Christian*, July 25, 1878, p.8; Liverpool Sheltering Homes, *Report* (1882), p.9.

23 *Children's Advocate* (Oct. 1881), p.151; Annie Macpherson, *Little Matchbox-Makers* (London: privately printed, 1870), pp.57-58; Macpherson, *Little London Arabs*, p.69; Macpherson, *Winter in London* (London: privately printed, 1872), p.48; 'Our Gutter Children,' broadsheet by George Cruickshank, London, 1869, Print Room, Victoria and Albert Museum; Needham, *Street Arabs*, p.169.

24 *Night and Day*, XXV (1902), p.62; Macpherson, *Matchbox-Makers*, p.42; *Night and Day*, I (1877), p.24; William Edmondson, *Making Rough Places Plain* (Manchester: Sherratt and Hugh, 1921), p.91; *Christian*, Sept. 26, 1878, p.11; Ian Bradley, *The Call to Seriousness: The Evangelical Impact on the Victorians* (New York: MacMillan, 1976), p.6.

CHAPTER NINE

1 Third Annual Meeting and Conference of the National Council of Women of Canada, *Women Workers of Canada* (Montreal, May 1896), p.202, Mrs. Archibald of Halifax; p.197, Mrs. John Cox of Montreal.

2 See Bernard Semmel, *Imperialism and Social Reform* (Cambridge: Harvard University Press, 1960).

3 Veronica Strong-Boag, *Parliament of Women: The National Council of Women of Canada 1893-1929* (Ottawa: National Museum of Man, 1976), p.194, p.182.

4 Ibid., p.194.

5 Ibid., p.145, p.193. This idea is partly based on a discussion with Carman Miller of McGill University about the transition from 'hard', culturally 'masculine' imperialism to 'soft', culturally 'feminine' imperialism after the Boer War horrors.

6 Strong-Boag, p.167; Carol Bacchi, *Liberation Deferred: The Ideas of the English-Canadian Suffragists 1877-1918*, (Ph.D. thesis, McGill University, 1976), pp.257-80. Most reformers were euthenists who believed the human race could be biologically improved by controlling the environment, or they adhered to a kind of hybrid eugenics doctrine that saw euthenics and eugenics as complementary rather than mutually exclusive.

7 Ellen Layton, 'On the superintendence of female emigrants,' *Transactions* (London: National Association for the Promotion of Social Sciences, 1863), p.616.

8 Testimony of Lady Knightsley, *Royal Commission on Natural Resources, Trade, and Legislation of Certain Parts of His Majesty's Dominions. Minutes of Evidence. Part I. Migration* (London: Fisher Unwin, 1912).

9 Ibid.

10 *Report on agricultural settlements in British colonies, 1906, Minutes of evidence*, 2979, LXXXI, p.597.

11 *Royal Commission on Natural Resources*, op.cit., p.93.

12 Ibid., p.57. My discussions with Deborah Gorham of Carleton University about moral and social purity and British and Canadian reformers were helpful in the writing of this section.

13 Ibid.

14 Report of the Immigration Committee, YWCA, June 11, 1914. MG 281, 198, Vol. 13.

15 World's YWCA Conference, Stockholm, 1914; report of Mrs. Falconer, 'On Immigration to Canada,' p.137.

16 Report of the Immigration Committee, ibid., 1915; letter from G.H. Webster, Secretary to the Eastern Canadian Passenger Association, to Ida Fairbairn, Sept. 13, 1917; letter from Fairbairn to Mrs. Hamilton, Aug. 15, 1917; letter to Mrs. Hamilton, Sept. 10, 1917.

17 World's YWCA Conference, p.138.

18 *Royal Commission on Natural Resources*, ibid., p.57.

19 NCWC Report, 1900, p.110.

20 Una Monk, *New horizons: A hundred years of women's migration* (London: Women's Migration and Overseas Appointments Society, HMSO, 1963), p.17; NCWC Report, op.cit.; Girls' Home of Welcome Association Report, 1898-99.

21 'A Sketch of Miss FitzGibbon's Life,' Women's Canadian Historical Society of Toronto, *Transaction* No. 14 (1914-15), pp.15-16.

22 RG 76, Vol. 338, file 356358.

23 Ibid., letter from FitzGibbon to Scott, Mar. 24, 1911 and Nov. 18, 1914.

24 *Annual Report of the Toronto Women's Welcome Hostel,* 1914-15; ibid., 1916.

25 RG 76, ibid.

26 Suzann Buckley, 'British Female Emigration and Imperial Development' (Paper presented to the Canadian Historical Association, Quebec, 1976).

27 Carl Berger, *A Sense of Power, Studies in the Ideas of Canadian Imperialism* (Toronto: University of Toronto Press, 1970), pp.179-80; Richard Faber, *The Vision and the Need: Late Victorian Imperialist Aims* (London: Faber and Faber, 1966), p.122. For social imperialism, see Bernard Semmel, *Imperialism and Social Reform*, op.cit.; James Morris, *Heaven's Command: An Imperial Progress* (New York: Harcourt Brace Jovanovich, 1973), p.338; see Violet Markham, *May Tennant: A Portrait* (London: Falcon, 1949), pp.36-38. See also Markham's autobiography, *Return Passage* (London: Oxford, 1953), p.48.

28 Michael Katz, *The People of Hamilton, Canada West: Family and Class in a Mid-19 Century City* (Cambridge: Harvard University Press, 1975), p.306.